Test Cricket Lists 1877-2022

Second Edition (2022)

Matthew Geddes

First published in Australia in 2022 by
Parallel Partners
PO Box 190
Crookwell NSW 2583

Geddes, Matthew
Test Cricket Lists (1877-2022)
ISBN 978-1645-70243-6

Produced by Parallel Partners

Index

Introduction

Even as the shortened version of cricket, known as T20 grows in popularity; test cricket remains the pinnacle for those wishing to represent their country. Considered the highest standard of the game, test status is the goal for emerging nations who are playing other versions of cricket, including one day international matches.

By the mid-1800s, England had formed a team of professional cricketers that played amateur teams around the country. They toured Canada and the United States for exhibition matches, which were popular and financially successful.

In 1861, with the Civil War raging in the USA, England opted to instead tour Australia. The time involved in travel saw a weakened England win just half of its matches; but they saw fit to again tour Australia in 1863, with a stop over in New Zealand.

In 1868, an Aboriginal Australian team was the first squad from the nation to tour England. After further visits to North America and Australia, an English squad led by James Lillywhite toured Australia in 1876-77, and played two matches against a national team that have since been recognised as the first test matches.

Test matches were exclusive to England and Australia until England toured South Africa in 1889, playing two test matches. Australia toured South Africa in 1902-03; and the three nationas played a tournament in England in 1912.

Like most sports, especially international ones, test cricket was suspended during the First World War. Australia toured South Africa in 1921-22 to resume test cricket, and England returned a year later.

The West Indies had been a collective of English speaking nations in the Caribbean since the 1890s, but had to wait until 1928 to become a test playing nation. Their match against England that year was awarded full test status by the International Cricket Board, making West Indies the fourth official test playing team.

At the end of the decade, England opted to visit New Zealand after an Australian tour. The test between England and New Zealand in 1930 saw the hosts become the fifth nation to play test cricket.

India joined the test cricket club in 1932 when they played a one-off test in England. They hosted England for two tests the following year.

Test cricket was again suspended during the Second World War. After the war, the nation of Pakistan was established. Already well versed in cricket as part of the Indian scene, Pakistan played their first tests in 1952 while visiting India. They quickly became competitive against the other test playing nations.

South Africa was suspended from international competition in 1970 due to the political situation in the country. They were re-admitted to the test playing community in 1991.

Cricket had been played in Sri Lanka for over 150 years before the nation made its international debut at the 1975 World Cup. They played their first test against England in 1982.

When known as Rhodesia, Zimbabwe had a national cricket team which participated in African competitions. The country achieved independence in 1980, and joined the International Cricket Council in 1981. They participated in the World Cup tournaments of 1983, 1987 and 1992. They played their first test match against India in 1992.

Prior to Bangladesh's independence in 1971, several teams from what was then known as East Pakistan played in Pakistani leagues. Bangladesh became a member of the ICC in 1986, and played their first test match against India in 2000.

In 2018, Afghanistan and Ireland were awarded test status, but have played few matches as of 2022.

Explanatory Notes

For newer fans of cricket, it is important to highlight how certain lists of records are interpreted. While most tests, runs, wickets and catches as a fielder are self explanatory, other categories may require some clarity.

Firstly, all years in brackets in all lists indicate the timeframe of a player's test career. Those marked with an asterisk (*) indicate that the player's test career is still active as at time of writing.

An asterisk (*) against the run total in the highest score total indicates the batsman was not out.

For dismissals as a wicket keeper, the abbreviations in brackets (ct, st) refer to catches and stumpings.

The figure in brackets in the lists for batting averages indicate the number of innings played. The figures in brackets for bowling averages (followed by a W) indicates the number of test wickets taken by a bowler during their test career.

In the world records section, the nations' abbreviations are as follows: (ENG) England, (AUS) Australia, (SAF) South Africa, (WI) West Indies, (NZ) New Zealand, (IND) India, (PAK) Pakistan, (SL) Sri Lanka, (ZIM) Zimbabwe.

AUSTRALIA

Cricket was established in Australia shortly after the arrival of the British at the end of the eighteenth century. A team from England toured Australia in 1861; and in 1868, and Aboriginal Australian team toured England.

In the summer of 1876-77, an England team toured Australia and played a combined New South Wales and Victorian side. This has since been recognised as the first official test match between England and Australia. In 1880, Australia toured England and played their first away test matches. The rivalry between Australia and England grew into the Ashes series which began in 1882.

In 1902, Australia toured South Africa for the first time. The teams joined England for a three-way tournament in 1912; but test cricket was suspended shortly afterwards due to the outbreak of war in Europe in 1914.

Australia resumed tours to England in 1921, and that year visited South Africa for a second time. In the summer of 1930-31, they hosted West Indies.

Shortly after the end of the Second World War, Australia toured New Zealand to play the first tests between the nations. Australia hosted India for the first time in the summer of 1947-48.

In 1955, Australia toured West Indies for the first time, winning the five test series 3-0. The following year, they played Pakistan for the first time in a losing effort in Karachi.

In 1960, the prize for the winner of the series between Australia and West Indies was the Frank Worrall Trophy. This was the series of the famous tied test. The trophy is still the spoils for the victor of each series between the teams.

Australia toured South Africa in 1969-70, just before the host nation was banned from international cricket due to the political fallout of apartheid in the country.

New Zealand toured Australia for the first time in the summer of 1973-74. In 1977, Australia and England played the Centenary Test in Melbourne, just as international cricket was being torn apart by the birth of the rival World Series Cricket.

Australia battled on through the next three years without many of their star players; but benefited from bringing back veteran captain Bob Simpson for a home series against India, which Australia won 3-2 in an epic five test series.

Cricket's civil war ended in time for the 1979-80 Frank Worrall Trophy, won by the West Indies. In

MOST TESTS

Ricky Ponting	168 (1995-2012)
Steve Waugh	168 (1985-2004)
Allan Border	156 (1978-1994)
Shane Warne	145 (1992-2007)
Mark Waugh	128 (1991-2002)
Glenn McGrath	124 (1993-2007)
Ian Healy	119 (1988-1999)
Michael Clarke	115 (2004-2015)
Nathan Lyon	110 (2011-2022)*
David Boon	107 (1984-1996)
Justin Langer	105 (1993-2007)
Mark Taylor	104 (1989-1999)
Matthew Hayden	103 (1994-2009)
Adam Gilchrist	96 (1999-2008)
Rod Marsh	96 (1970-1984)
David Warner	96 (2011-2022)*
Greg Chappell	87 (1970-1984)
Steve Smith	87 (2010-2022)*

Neil Harvey	79 (1948-1963)
Mike Hussey	79 (2005-2013)
Brett Lee	76 (1999-2008)
Ian Chappell	75 (1964-1980)
Michael Slater	74 (1993-2001)
Doug Walters	74 (1965-1981)
Mitchell Johnson	73 (2007-2015)
Jason Gillespie	71 (1996-2006)
Craig McDermott	71 (1984-1996)
Mitchell Starc	71 (2011-2022)*
Kim Hughes	70 (1977-1984)
Dennis Lillee	70 (1971-1984)
Bill Lawry	67 (1961-1971)
Damien Martyn	67 (1992-2006)
Peter Siddle	67 (2008-2019)
Brad Haddin	66 (2008-2015)
Ian Redpath	66 (1964-1976)
Richie Benaud	63 (1952-1964)
Bob Simpson	62 (1957-1978)

MOST RUNS

Ricky Ponting	13378 (1995-2012)
Allan Border	11174 (1978-1994)
Steve Waugh	10927 (1985-2004)
Michael Clarke	8643 (2004-2015)
Matthew Hayden	8625 (1994-2009)
Steve Smith	8161 (2010-2022)*
Mark Waugh	8029 (1991-2002)
David Warner	7817 (2011-2022)*
Justin Langer	7696 (1993-2007)
Mark Taylor	7525 (1989-1999)
David Boon	7422 (1984-1996)
Greg Chappell	7110 (1970-1984)
Don Bradman	6996 (1928-1948)
Mike Hussey	6235 (2005-2013)
Neil Harvey	6149 (1948-1963)
Adam Gilchrist	5570 (1999-2008)
Doug Walters	5357 (1965-1981)
Ian Chappell	5345 (1964-1980)

Michael Slater	5312 (1993-2001)
Bill Lawry	5234 (1961-1971)
Bob Simpson	4869 (1957-1978)
Ian Redpath	4737 (1964-1976)
Kim Hughes	4415 (1977-1984)
Damien Martyn	4406 (1992-2006)
Ian Healy	4356 (1988-1999)
Simon Katich	4188 (2001-2010)
Usman Khawaja	3775 (2011-2022)*
Shane Watson	3731 (2005-2015)
Rod Marsh	3633 (1970-1984)
Dean Jones	3631 (1984-1992)
Arthur Morris	3533 (1946-1955)
Clem Hill	3412 (1896-1912)
Graeme Wood	3374 (1978-1988)
Brad Haddin	3266 (2008-2015)
Victor Trumper	3163 (1899-1912)
Shane Warne	3154 (1992-2007)
Colin McDonald	3107 (1952-1961)

MOST WICKETS

Shane Warne	708 (1992-2007)
Glenn McGrath	563 (1993-2007)
Nathan Lyon	438 (2011-2022)*
Dennis Lillee	355 (1971-1984)
Mitchell Johnson	313 (2007-2015)
Brett Lee	310 (1999-2008)
Craig McDermott	291 (1984-1996)
Mitchell Starc	287 (2011-2022)*
Jason Gillespie	259 (1996-2006)
Richie Benaud	248 (1952-1964)
Graham McKenzie	246 (1961-1971)
Ray Lindwall	228 (1946-1960)
Peter Siddle	221 (2008-2019)
Clarrie Grimmett	216 (1925-1936)
Josh Hazlewood	215 (2014-2022)*
Merv Hughes	212 (1985-1994)
Stuart MacGill	208 (1998-2008)
Jeff Thomson	200 (1972-1985)

Pat Cummins	199 (2011-2022)*
Alan Davidson	186 (1953-1963)
Geoff Lawson	180 (1980-1989)
Keith Miller	170 (1946-1956)
Terry Alderman	170 (1981-1991)
Bill Johnston	160 (1947-1955)
Bill O'Reilly	144 (1932-1946)
Hugh Trumble	141 (1890-1904)
Max Walker	138 (1972-1977)
Ashley Mallett	132 (1968-1980)
Bruce Yardley	126 (1978-1983)
Rodney Hogg	123 (1978-1984)
Monty Noble	121 (1898-1909)
Ryan Harris	113 (2010-2015)
Bruce Reid	113 (1985-1992)
Michael Kasprowicz	113 (1996-2006)
Ian Johnson	109 (1946-1956)
Paul Reiffel	104 (1992-1998)
George Giffen	103 (1881-1896)

1982, Australia toured Sri Lanka and won the first test match between the two nations.

In 1985-86, Australia and New Zealand began to play for the Trans-Tasman Trophy. New Zealand won the inaugural contest, played in Australia.

Australia hosted Sri Lanka for the first time in the summer of 1987-88, winning the sole test match. After a decade of struggle, Australia became of the top test playing nations in the world during the 1990s. They won the Ashes in England in 1993, the Trans-Transman Trophy in 1993-94, and the Frank Worrall Trophy in 1994-95.

South Africa returned to test cricket in 1991, and toured Australia in 1993. It would take fifteen years for South Africa to leave Australia victorious.

From 1996, Australia and India have competed for the Border-Gavaskar Trophy. India won the trophy at home in a one-off test, and Australia had to wait until the summer of 1999-2000 to claim the prize.

Australia played Zimbabwe for the first time in 1999-2000, and Bangladesh in 2003. They continued to dominate test cricket in the new century, although the Ashes have changed hands on occasion. In 2018-19, India defeated Australia in a test series in Australia for the first time. They repeated the effort in the summer of 2020-21.

HIGHEST SCORES

Matthew Hayden	380 V Zimbabwe, 2003
David Warner	335* V Pakistan, 2019
Mark Taylor	334* V Pakistan, 1998
Don Bradman	334 V England, 1930
Michael Clarke	329* V India, 2012
Bob Simpson	311 V England, 1964
Bob Cowper	307 V England, 1966
Don Bradman	304 V England, 1934
Don Bradman	299* V South Africa, 1932
Don Bradman	270 V England, 1937
Adam Voges	269* V West Indies, 2015
Graham Yallop	268 V Pakistan, 1983
Bill Ponsford	266 V England, 1934
Michael Clarke	259* V South Africa, 2012
Ricky Ponting	257 V India, 2003
Don Bradman	254 V England, 1930
David Warner	253 V New Zealand, 2015
Doug Walters	250 V New Zealand, 1977

Justin Langer	250 V England, 2002
Greg Chappell	247* V New Zealand, 1974
Don Bradman	244 V England, 1934
Doug Walters	242 V West Indies, 1969
Ricky Ponting	242 V India, 2003
Adam Voges	239 V New Zealand, 2016
Steve Smith	239 V England, 2017
Greg Chappell	235 V Pakistan, 1980
Sid Barnes	234 V England, 1946
Don Bradman	234 V England, 1946
Don Bradman	232 V England, 1930
Stan McCabe	232 V England, 1938
Michael Clarke	230 V South Africa, 2012
Don Bradman	226 V South Africa, 1931
Bob Simpson	225 V England, 1966
Don Bradman	223 V West Indies, 1931
Justin Langer	223 V India, 2000
Ricky Ponting	221 V India, 2012
Mark Taylor	219 V England, 1989

MOST CENTURIES

Ricky Ponting	41 (1995-2012)
Steve Waugh	32 (1985-2004)
Matthew Hayden	30 (1994-2009)
Don Bradman	29 (1928-1948)
Michael Clarke	28 (2004-2015)
Steve Smith	28 (2010-2022)*
Allan Border	27 (1978-1984)
Greg Chappell	24 (1970-1984)
David Warner	24 (2011-2022)*
Justin Langer	23 (1993-2007)
Neil Harvey	21 (1948-1963)
David Boon	21 (1984-1996)
Mark Waugh	20 (1991-2002)
Mike Hussey	19 (2005-2013)
Mark Taylor	19 (1989-1999)
Adam Gilchrist	17 (1999-2008)
Doug Walters	15 (1965-1981)

MOST 50s (50-99)

Allan Border	63 (1978-1994)
Ricky Ponting	62 (1995-2012)
Steve Waugh	50 (1985-2004)
Mark Waugh	47 (1991-2002)
Mark Taylor	40 (1989-1999)
Steve Smith	36 (2010-2022)*
David Warner	34 (2011-2022)*
Doug Walters	33 (1965-1981)
David Boon	32 (1984-1996)
Greg Chappell	31 (1970-1984)
Ian Redpath	31 (1964-1976)
Justin Langer	30 (1993-2007)
Matthew Hayden	29 (1994-2009)
Mike Hussey	29 (2005-2013)
Michael Clarke	27 (2004-2015)
Bill Lawry	27 (1961-1971)
Bob Simpson	27 (1957-1978)

MOST DISMISSALS AS WICKET KEEPER

Adam Gilchrist	416 (379ct, 37st) (1999-2008)
Ian Healy	395 (366ct, 29st) (1988-1999)
Rod Marsh	355 (343ct, 12st) (1970-1984)
Brad Haddin	270 (262ct, 8st) (2008-2015)
Wally Grout	187 (163ct, 24st) (1957-1966)
Tim Paine	157 (150ct, 7st) (2010-2021)*
Bert Oldfield	130 (78ct, 52st) (1920-1937)
Gil Langley	98 (83ct, 15st) (1951-56)
Matthew Wade	74 (63ct, 11st) (2012-2021)*
Sammy Carter	65 (44ct, 21st) (1907-1921)
Peter Nevill	63 (61ct, 2st) (2015-2016)
James Kelly	63 (43ct, 20st) (1896-1905)
Brian Taber	60 (56ct, 4st) (1966-1970)
Jack Blackham	59 (35ct, 24st) (1877-1894)
Don Tallon	58 (50ct, 8st) (1946-1953)
Barry Jarman	54 (50ct, 4st) (1959-1969)
Steve Rixon	47 (42ct, 5st) (1977-1985)
Wayne Phillips	43 (43ct) (1983-1986)

MOST CATCHES (FIELDER)

Ricky Ponting	196 (1995-2012)
Mark Waugh	181 (1991-2002)
Mark Taylor	157 (1989-1999)
Allan Border	156 (1978-1994)
Steve Smith	141 (2010-2022)*
Michael Clarke	134 (2004-2015)
Matthew Hayden	128 (1994-2009)
Shane Warne	125 (1992-2007)
Greg Chappell	122 (1970-1984)
Steve Waugh	112 (1985-2004)
Bob Simpson	110 (1957-1978)
Ian Chappell	105 (1964-1980)
David Boon	99 (1984-1996)
Mike Hussey	85 (2005-2013)
Ian Redpath	83 (1964-1976)
David Warner	76 (2011-2022)*
Justin Langer	73 (1993-2007)
Richie Benaud	65 (1952-1964)

BEST BATTING AVERAGES (MINIMUM 20 INNINGS)

Don Bradman	99.94 (80) (1928-1948)
Adam Voges	61.87 (31) (2015-2016)
Steve Smith	60.00 (154) (2010-2022)*
Marnus Labuschagne	54.02 (48) (2018-2022)*
Greg Chappell	53.86 (151) (1970-1984)
Ricky Ponting	51.85 (287) (1995-2012)
Jack Ryder	51.62 (32) (1920-1929)
Mike Hussey	51.52 (137) (2005-2013)
Steve Waugh	51.06 (260) (1985-2004)
Matthew Hayden	50.73 (184) (1994-2009)
Allan Border	50.56 (265) (1978-1994)
Michael Clarke	49.10 (198) (2004-2015)
Neil Harvey	48.41 (137) (1948-1963)
Doug Walters	48.26 (125) (1965-1981)
Bill Ponsford	48.22 (48) (1924-1934)
Stan McCabe	48.21 (62) (1930-1938)
Adam Gilchrist	47.60 (137) (1999-2008)
Usman Khawaja	47.18 (90) (2011-2022)*

Bill Lawry	47.15 (123) (1961-1971)
Bob Cowper	46.81 (46) (1964-1968)
Bill Brown	46.82 (35) (1934-1948)
Bob Simpson	46.81 (111) (1957-1978)
Lindsay Hassett	46.56 (69) (1938-1953)
Dean Jones	46.55 (89) (1984-1992)
David Warner	46.52 (176) (2011-2022)*
Arthur Morris	46.48 (79) (1946-1955)
Damien Martyn	46.37 (109) (1992-2006)
Bill Woodfull	46.00 (54) (1926-1934)
Norm O'Neill	45.55 (69) (1958-1965)
Justin Langer	45.27 (182) (1993-2007)
Herbie Collins	45.06 (31) (1920-1926)
Simon Katich	45.03 (99) (2001-2010)
Darren Lehmann	44.95 (42) (1998-2004)
David Boon	43.65 (190) (1984-1996)
Mark Taylor	43.49 (186) (1989-1999)
Ian Redpath	43.45 (120) (1964-1976)
Kepler Wessels	42.95 (42) (1982-1985)

BEST BOWLING AVERAGES (2000+ BALLS)

John Ferris	14.25 (48W) (1887-1890)
Charlie Turner	16.53 (101W) (1887-1895)
Bert Ironmonger	17.97 (74W) (1928-1933)
Fred Spofforth	18.41 (94W) (1877-1887)
Alan Davidson	20.53 (186W) (1953-1963)
Ernie Toshack	21.04 (47W) (1946-1948)
Bill Whitty	21.12 (65W) (1909-1912)
Joey Palmer	21.51 (78W) (1880-1886)
Glenn McGrath	21.64 (563W) (1993-2007)
Pat Cummins	21.66 (199W) (2011-2022)*
Hugh Trumble	21.78 (141W) (1890-1904)
Bill O'Reilly	22.59 (144W) (1932-1946)
Jack Saunders	22.73 (79W) (1902-1908)
Lindsay Kline	22.82 (34W) (1957-1961)
Keith Miller	22.97 (170W) (1946-1956)
Ray Lindwall	23.03 (228W) (1946-1960)
Herbert Hordern	23.36 (46W) (1911-1912)
Ryan Harris	23.52 (113W) (2010-2015)

Stuart Clark	23.86 (94W) (2006-2009)
Bill Johnston	23.91 (160W) (1947-1955)
Dennis Lillee	23.92 (355W) (1971-1984)
Clarrie Grimmett	24.21 (216W) (1925-1936)
Bruce Reid	24.63 (113W) (1985-1992)
Monty Noble	25.00 (121W) (1898-1909)
Shane Warne	25.41 (708W) (1992-2007)
Damien Fleming	25.89 (75W) (1994-2001)
Josh Hazlewood	25.92 (215W) (2014-2022)*
Doug Bollinger	25.92 (50W) (2009-2010)
Gary Gilmour	26.03 (54W) (1973-1977)
Frank Laver	26.05 (37W) (1899-1909)
Len Pascoe	26.06 (64W) (1977-1982)
Jason Gillespie	26.13 (259W) (1996-2006)
Colin Miller	26.15 (69W) (1998-2001)
James Pattinson	26.33 (81W) (2011-2020)
Colin McCool	26.61 (36W) (1946-1950)
Tom Garrett	26.94 (36W) (1877-1888)
Paul Reiffel	26.96 (104W) (1992-1998)

BEST BOWLING FIGURES IN AN INNINGS

Arthur Mailey	9/121 V England, 1921
Glenn McGrath	8/24 V Pakistan, 2004
Frank Laver	8/31 V England, 1909
Glenn McGrath	8/38 V England, 1997
Albert Trott	8/43 V England, 1895
Nathan Lyon	8/50 V India, 2017
Bob Massie	8/53 V England, 1972
Ashley Mallett	8/59 V Pakistan, 1972
Mitchell Johnson	8/61 V Sth Africa, 2008
Hugh Trumble	8/65 V England, 1902
Graham McKenzie	8/71 V West Indies, 1968
Shane Warne	8/71 V England, 1994
Bob Massie	8/84 V England, 1972
Merv Hughes	8/87 V West Indies, 1988
Craig McDermott	8/97 V England, 1991
Stuart MacGill	8/108 V Bangladesh, 2006
Geoff Lawson	8/112 V West Indies, 1984
Craig McDermott	8/141 V England, 1985

BEST BOWLING FIGURES IN A MATCH

Bob Massie	16/137 V England, 1972
Fred Spofforth	14/90 V England, 1882
Clarrie Grimmett	14/199 V Sth Africa, 1932
Monty Noble	13/77 V England, 1902
Fred Spofforth	13/110 V England, 1879
Bruce Reid	13/148 V England, 1990
Nathan Lyon	13/154 V Bangladesh, 2017
Clarrie Grimmett	13/173 V Sth Africa, 1936
Merv Hughes	13/217 V West Indies, 1988
Arthur Mailey	13/236 V England, 1921
Steve O'Keefe	12/70 V India, 2017
Charlie Turner	12/87 V England, 1888
Hugh Trumble	12/89 V England, 1896
Stuart MacGill	12/107 V England, 1999
Alan Davidson	12/124 V India, 1959
Bruce Reid	12/126 V India, 1991
Mitchell Johnson	12/127 V Sth Africa, 2014
Shane Warne	12/128 V Sth Africa, 1994

MOST FIVE WICKETS IN AN INNINGS

Shane Warne	37 (1992-2007)
Glenn McGrath	29 (1993-2007)
Dennis Lillee	23 (1971-1984)
Clarrie Grimmett	21 (1925-1936)
Nathan Lyon	20 (2011-2022)*
Graham McKenzie	16 (1961-1971)
Richie Benaud	16 (1952-1964)
Terry Alderman	14 (1981-1991)
Alan Davidson	14 (1953-1963)
Craig McDermott	14 (1984-1996)
Mitchell Starc	13 (2011-2022)*
Stuart MacGill	12 (1998-2008)
Ray Lindwall	12 (1946-1960)
Mitchell Johnson	12 (2007-2015)
Charlie Turner	11 (1887-1895)
Bill O'Reilly	11 (1932-1946)
Geoff Lawson	11 (1980-1989)
Brett Lee	10 (1999-2008)

AUSTRALIA TEST SERIES RESULTS

DATE OPPONENT	RESULT (W-L-D)
1876-77 V England	1-1-0
1878-79 v England	1-0-0
1880 in England	0-1-0
1881-82 V England	2-0-2
1882 in England	1-0-0
1882-83 V England	1-2-0
1882-83 V England	1-0-0
1884 in England	0-1-2
1884-85 V England	2-3-0
1886 in England	0-3-0
1886-87 V England	0-2-0
1887-88 V England	0-1-0
1888 in England	1-2-0
1890 in England	0-2-0
1891-92 V England	2-1-0
1893 in England	0-1-2
1894-95 V England	2-3-0

1896 in England	1-2-0
1897-98 V England	4-1-0
1899 in England	1-0-4
1901-02 V England	4-1-0
1902 in England	2-1-2
1902-03 in South Africa	2-0-1
1903-04 V England	3-2-0
1905 in England	0-2-3
1907-08 V England	4-1-0
1909 in England	2-1-2
1910-11 V South Africa	4-1-0
1911-12 V England	1-4-0
1912 V South Africa[1]	2-0-1
1912 in England	0-1-2
1920-21 V England	5-0-0
1921 in England	3-0-2
1921-22 in South Africa	1-0-2

[1] Series was played in England

1924-25 V England	4-1-0
1926 in England	0-1-4
1928-29 V England	1-4-0
1930 in England	2-1-2
1930-31 V West Indies	4-1-0
1931-32 V South Africa	5-0-0
1932-33 V England	1-4-0
1934 in England	2-1-2
1935-36 in South Africa	4-0-1
1936-37 V England	3-2-0
1938 in England	1-1-2
1945-46 in New Zealand	1-0-0
1946-47 V England	3-0-2
1947-48 V India	4-0-1
1948 in England	4-0-1
1949-50 in South Africa	4-0-1
1950-51 in England	4-1-0
1951-52 V West Indies	4-1-0
1952-53 V South Africa	2-2-1

1953 in England	0-1-4
1954-55 V England	1-3-1
1955 in West Indies	3-0-2
1956 in England	1-2-2
1956-57 in Pakistan	0-1-0
1956-57 in India	2-0-1
1957-58 in South Africa	3-0-2
1958-59 V England	4-0-1
1959-60 in Pakistan	2-0-1
1959-60 in India	2-1-2
1960-61 V West Indies	2-1-2[2]
1961 in England	2-1-2
1962-63 V England	1-1-3
1963-64 V South Africa	1-1-3
1964 in England	1-0-4
1964-65 in India	1-1-1
1964-65 in Pakistan	0-0-1

[2] Includes one tied test

1964-65 V Pakistan	0-0-1
1964-65 in West Indies	1-2-2
1965-66 V England	1-1-3
1966-67 in South Africa	1-3-1
1967-68 V India	4-0-0
1968 in England	1-1-3
1968-69 V West Indies	3-1-1
1969-70 in India	3-1-1
1969-70 in South Africa	0-4-0
1970-71 V England	0-2-5
1972 in England	2-2-1
1972-73 V Pakistan	3-0-0
1972-73 in West Indies	2-0-3
1973-74 V New Zealand	2-0-1
1973-74 in New Zealand	1-1-1
1974-75 V England	4-1-1
1975 in England	1-0-3
1975-76 V West Indies	5-1-0
1976-77 V Pakistan	1-1-1

1976-77 in New Zealand	1-0-1
1976-77 V England	1-0-0
1977 in England	0-3-2
1977-78 V India	3-2-0
1977-78 in West Indies	1-3-1
1978-79 V England	1-5-0
1978-79 V Pakistan	1-1-0
1979-80 in India	0-2-4
1979-80 V West Indies	0-2-1
1979-80 V England	3-0-0
1979-80 in Pakistan	0-1-2
1980 in England	0-0-1
1980-81 V New Zealand	2-0-1
1980-81 V India	1-1-1
1981 in England	1-3-2
1981-82 V Pakistan	2-1-0
1981-82 V West Indies	1-1-1
1981-82 in New Zealand	1-1-1
1982-83 in Pakistan	0-3-0

1982-83 V England	2-1-2
1982-83 in Sri Lanka	1-0-0
1983-84 V Pakistan	2-0-3
1983-84 in West Indies	0-3-2
1984-85 V West Indies	1-3-1
1985 in England	1-3-2
1985-86 V New Zealand	1-2-0
1985-86 V India	0-0-3
1985-86 in New Zealand	0-1-2
1986-87 in India	0-0-3[3]
1986-87 V England	1-2-2
1987-88 V New Zealand	1-0-2
1987-88 V England	0-0-1
1987-88 V Sri Lanka	1-0-0
1988-89 in Pakistan	0-1-2
1988-89 V West Indies	1-3-1
1989 in England	4-0-2

[3] Includes one tied test

1989-90 V New Zealand	0-0-1
1989-90 V Sri Lanka	1-0-1
1989-90 V Pakistan	1-0-2
1989-90 in New Zealand	0-1-0
1990-91 V England	3-0-2
1990-91 in West Indies	1-2-2
1991-92 V India	4-0-1
1992 in Sri Lanka	1-0-2
1992-93 V West Indies	1-2-2
1992-93 in New Zealand	1-1-1
1993 in England	4-1-1
1993-94 V New Zealand	2-0-1
1993-94 V South Africa	1-1-1
1993-94 in South Africa	1-1-1
1994-95 in Pakistan	0-1-2
1994-95 V England	3-1-1
1994-95 in West Indies	2-1-1
1995-96 V Pakistan	2-1-0
1995-96 V Sri Lanka	3-0-0

1996-97 in India	0-1-0
1996-97 V West Indies	3-2-0
1996-97 in South Africa	2-1-0
1997 in England	3-2-1
1997-98 V New Zealand	2-0-1
1997-98 V South Africa	1-0-2
1997-98 in India	1-2-0
1998-99 in Pakistan	1-0-2
1998-99 V England	3-1-1
1998-99 in West Indies	2-2-0
1999 in Sri Lanka	0-1-2
1999-2000 in Zimbabwe	1-0-0
1999-2000 V Pakistan	3-0-0
1999-2000 V India	3-0-0
1999-2000 in New Zealand	3-0-0
2000-01 V West Indies	5-0-0
2000-01 in India	1-2-0
2001 in England	4-1-0
2001-02 V New Zealand	0-0-3

2001-02 V South Africa	3-0-0
2001-02 in South Africa	2-1-0
2002-03 V Pakistan[4]	3-0-0
2002-03 V England	4-1-0
2003 in West Indies	3-1-0
2003 V Bangladesh	2-0-0
2003-04 V Zimbabwe	2-0-0
2003-04 V India	1-1-2
2003-04 in Sri Lanka	3-0-0
2004 V Sri Lanka	1-0-1
2004-05 in India	2-1-1
2004-05 V New Zealand	2-0-0
2004-05 V Pakistan	3-0-0
2004-05 in New Zealand	2-0-1
2005 in England	1-2-2
2005-06 V ICC World XI	1-0-0
2005-06 V South Africa	2-0-1

[4] Series played in Sri Lanka and United Arab Emirates

2005-06 in South Africa	3-0-0
2005-06 in Bangladesh	2-0-0
2006-07 V England	5-0-0
2007-08 V Sri Lanka	2-0-0
2007-08 V India	2-1-1
2008 in West Indies	2-0-1
2008-09 in India	0-2-2
2008-09 V New Zealand	2-0-0
2008-09 V South Africa	1-2-0
2008-09 in South Africa	2-1-0
2009 in England	1-2-2
2009-10 V West Indies	2-0-1
2009-10 V Pakistan	3-0-0
2009-10 in New Zealand	2-0-0
2010 V Pakistan[5]	1-1-0
2010-11 in India	0-2-2
2010-11 V England	1-3-1

[5] Series played in England

2011 in Sri Lanka	1-0-2
2011-12 in South Africa	1-1-0
2011-12 V New Zealand	1-1-0
2011-12 V India	4-0-0
2011-12 in West Indies	2-0-1
2012-13 V South Africa	0-1-2
2012-13 V Sri Lanka	3-0-0
2012-13 in India	0-4-0
2013 in England	0-3-2
2013-14 V England	5-0-0
2013-14 in South Africa	2-1-0
2014-15 V Pakistan[6]	0-2-0
2014-15 V India	2-0-2
2015 in West Indies	2-0-0
2015 in England	2-3-0
2015-16 V New Zealand	2-0-1
2015-16 V West Indies	2-0-1

[6] Series played in United Arab Emirates

2015-16 in New Zealand	2-0-0
2016 in Sri Lanka	0-3-0
2016-17 V South Africa	1-2-0
2016-17 V Pakistan	3-0-0
2016-17 in India	1-2-1
2017 in Bangladesh	1-1-0
2017-18 V England	4-0-1
2017-18 in South Africa	1-3-0
2018-19 V Pakistan[7]	0-1-1
2018-19 V India	1-2-1
2018-19 V Sri Lanka	2-0-0
2019 in England	2-2-1
2019-20 V Pakistan	2-0-0
2019-20 V New Zealand	3-0-0
2020-21 V India	1-2-1
2021-22 V England	4-0-1
2021-22 in Pakistan	1-0-2
2022 in Sri Lanka	1-1-0

[7] Series played in United Arab Emirates

ENGLAND

Cricket teams claiming to represent England have been around since an "All-England" team played Kent in 1739. By 1846, a semi-professional England team toured the nation playing mostly amateur county club teams.

In 1859, an England team toured Canada and the United States. The tour was a popular and financial success, but the outbreak of the Civial War in the USA saw England look to Australia in the 1860s.

In 1877, England played a combined New South Wales and Victoria side, which has since been recognised as the first official test match between England and Australia.

England hosted Australia for the first time in 1880, and the Ashes was born in 1882 which is still contested between the two nations.

In 1888 England toured South Africa for the first time. After a number of tours, South Africa returned the favour in 1907.

England resumed their rivalries with Australia and South Africa after the First World War, and hosted a team from West Indies for the first time in 1928.

England easily won all three tests. England toured West Indies for the first time the following year.

England hosted India for a sole test in 1932. They toured India the following year and won the three test series 2-0. In 1937, a team from New Zealand toured England for the first time, but lost the three test series 1-0 after two tight draws.

Test cricket resumed after the Second World War, with England struggling against the new power house teams Australia and West Indies. In 1954, they hosted Pakistan, and tied their four test series.

England regained the Ashes in 1954-55, and went undefeated in test series for the next four years. In 1961, England played their first tests in Pakistan.

Since 1963, England and West Indies have played for the Wisden Trophy. West Indies won the trophy in 1963, winning the five test series 3-1.

England were undefeated in test series between 1967 and 1971. After struggling against India, they lost the Ashes in Australia in 1974-75.

After losing the Centenary Test to Australia in Melbourne in 1977, England, like most test playing nations, were impacted by the introduction of World Series Cricket. They remained a force at test level during cricket's Civil War, but began to fade in the 1980s, losing to New Zealand and Pakistan.

England hosted Sri Lanka for the first time in 1984, playing a draw in their sole test. They toured Sri Lanka for the first time in 1992-93, but lost the only test match played between the two nations.

In 1996-97, England played its first test matches against Zimbabwe while in Africa. Both tests finished in a draw.

England played its first test matches against Bangladesh while on tour in South Asia in 2003-04. England won both matches against the test minnows, and again won both tests when Bangladesh toured in England in 2005.

In 2005, England regained the Ashes on home soil. A year later, they toured Australia, and were crushed 5-0 in the Ashes test series.

England play for several other trophies. Winners of the series between England and South Africa are awarded the Basil D'Oliveria Trophy; while England and India compete for the Pataudi Trophy.

In 2019, England defeated Ireland in the first test match between the nations.

MOST TESTS

James Anderson	175 (2003-2022)*
Alastair Cook	161 (2006-2018)
Stuart Broad	159 (2007-2022)*
Alec Stewart	133 (1990-2003)
Joe Root	124 (2012-2022)*
Ian Bell	118 (2004-2015)
Graham Gooch	118 (1975-1995)
David Gower	117 (1978-1992)
Mike Atherton	115 (1989-2001)
Colin Cowdrey	114 (1954-1975)
Geoff Boycott	108 (1964-1982)
Kevin Pitersen	104 (2005-2014)
Ian Botham	102 (1977-1992)
Andrew Strauss	100 (2004-2012)
Graham Thorpe	100 (1993-2005)
Nasser Hussain	96 (1990-2004)
Alan Knott	95 (1967-1981)
Godfrey Evans	91 (1946-1959)

Bob Willis	90 (1971-1984)
Jonny Bairstow	89 (2012-2022)*
Ben Stokes	86 (2013-2022)*
Derek Underwood	86 (1966-1982)
Wally Hammond	85 (1927-1947)
Ken Barrington	82 (1955-1968)
Michael Vaughan	82 (1999-2008)
Mike Gatting	79 (1978-1995)
Tom Graveney	79 (1951-1969)
Len Hutton	79 (1937-1955)
Allan Lamb	79 (1982-1992)
Matt Prior	79 (2007-2014)
Denis Compton	78 (1937-1957)
Andrew Flintoff	78 (1998-2009)
John Edrich	77 (1963-1976)
Marcus Trescothick	76 (2000-2006)
Mark Butcher	71 (1997-2004)
Brian Statham	70 (1951-1965)
Paul Collingwood	68 (2003-2011)

MOST RUNS

Alastair Cook	12472 (2006-2018)
Joe Root	10504 (2012-2022)*
Graham Gooch	8900 (1975-1995)
Alec Stewart	8463 (1990-2003)
David Gower	8231 (1978-1992)
Kevin Pietersen	8181 (2005-2014)
Geoff Boycott	8114 (1964-1982)
Mike Atherton	7728 (1989-2001)
Ian Bell	7727 (2004-2015)
Colin Cowdrey	7624 (1954-1975)
Wally Hammond	7249 (1927-1947)
Andrew Strauss	7037 (2004-2012)
Len Hutton	6971 (1937-1955)
Ken Barrington	6806 (1955-1968)
Graham Thorpe	6744 (1993-2005)
Marcus Trescothick	5825 (2000-2006)
Denis Compton	5807 (1937-1957)
Nasser Hussain	5764 (1990-2004)

Michael Vaughan	5719 (1999-2008)
Johnny Bairstow	5482 (2012-2022)*
Ben Stokes	5429 (2013-2022)*
Jack Hobbs	5410 (1908-1930)
Ian Botham	5200 (1977-1992)
John Edrich	5138 (1963-1976)
Tom Graveney	4882 (1951-1969)
Allan Lamb	4656 (1982-1992)
Herbert Sutcliffe	4555 (1924-1935)
Peter May	4537 (1951-1961)
Ted Dexter	4502 (1958-1968)
Mike Gatting	4409 (1978-1995)
Alan Knott	4389 (1967-1981)
Mark Butcher	4288 (1997-2004)
Paul Collingwood	4259 (2003-2011)
Robin Smith	4236 (1988-1996)
Matt Prior	4099 (2007-2014)
Jonathan Trott	3835 (2009-2015)
Andrew Flintoff	3795 (1998-2009)

MOST WICKETS

James Anderson	667 (2003-2022)*
Stuart Broad	566 (2007-2022)*
Ian Botham	383 (1977-1992)
Bob Willis	325 (1971-1984)
Fred Trueman	307 (1952-1965)
Derek Underwood	297 (1966-1982)
Graeme Swann	255 (2008-2013)
Brian Statham	252 (1951-1965)
Matthew Hoggard	248 (2000-2008)
Alec Bedser	236 (1946-1955)
Andy Caddick	234 (1993-2003)
Darren Gough	229 (1994-3003)
Steve Harmison	222 (2002-2009)
Andrew Flintoff	219 (1998-2009)
John Snow	202 (1965-1976)
Moeen Ali	194 (2014-2021)
Jim Laker	193 (1948-1959)
Ben Stokes	192 (2013-2022)*

Sydney Barnes	189 (1901-1914)
Angus Fraser	177 (1989-1998)
Tony Lock	174 (1952-1968)
Monty Panesar	167 (2006-2013)
Maurice Tate	155 (1924-1935)
Fred Titmus	153 (1955-1975)
John Emburey	147 (1978-1995)
Hedley Verity	144 (1931-1939)
Chris Old	143 (1972-1981)
Ashley Giles	143 (1998-2006)
Tony Greig	141 (1972-1977)
Phil DeFreitas	140 (1986-1995)
Graham Dilley	138 (1979-1989)
Trevor Bailey	132 (1949-1959)
Dominic Cork	131 (1995-2002)
Chris Woakes	130 (2013-2022)*
Devon Malcolm	128 (1989-1997)
Wilfred Rhodes	127 (1899-1930)

HIGHEST SCORES

Len Hutton	364 V Australia, 1938
Wally Hammond	336* V New Zealand, 1933
Graham Gooch	333 V India, 1990
Andy Sandham	325 V West Indies, 1930
John Edrich	310* V New Zealand, 1965
Alastair Cook	294 V India, 2011
Tip Foster	287 V Australia, 1903
Peter May	285* V West Indies, 1957
Denis Compton	278 V Pakistan, 1954
Zak Crawley	267 V Pakistan, 2020
Alastair Cook	263 V Pakistan, 2015
Dennis Amiss	262* V West Indies, 1974
Tom Graveney	258 V West Indies, 1957
Ben Stokes	258 V South Africa, 2016
Ken Barrington	256 V Australia, 1964
Joe Root	254 V Pakistan, 2016
Wally Hammond	251 V Australia, 1928
Geoff Boycott	246* V India, 1967

Alastair Cook	244* V Australia, 2017
Eddie Paynter	243 V South Africa, 1939
Alastair Cook	243 V West Indies, 2017
Wally Hammond	240 V Australia, 1938
Alastair Cook	235* V Australia, 2010
Ian Bell	235 V India, 2011
Wally Hammond	231* V Australia, 1936
Joe Root	228 V Sri Lanka, 2021
Wally Hammond	227 V New Zealand, 1933
Kevin Pietersen	227 V Australia, 2010
Kevin Pietersen	226 V West Indies, 2007
Jonathan Trott	226 V Bangladesh, 2010
Joe Root	226 V New Zealand, 2019
Rob Key	221 V West Indies, 2004
Bill Edrich	219 V South Africa, 1939
Marcus Trescothick	219 V South Africa, 2003
Joe Root	218 V India, 2021
Wally Hammond	217 V India, 1936
Eddie Paynter	216* V Australia, 1938

MOST CENTURIES

Alastair Cook	33 (2006-2018)
Joe Root	28 (2012-2022)*
Kevin Pietersen	23 (2005-2014)
Wally Hammond	22 (1927-1947)
Colin Cowdrey	22 (1954-1975)
Geoff Boycott	22 (1964-1982)
Ian Bell	22 (2004-2015)
Andrew Strauss	21 (2004-2012)
Ken Barrington	20 (1955-1968)
Graham Gooch	20 (1975-1995)
Len Hutton	19 (1937-1955)
Michael Vaughan	18 (1999-2008)
David Gower	18 (1978-1992)
Denis Compton	17 (1937-1957)
Herbert Sutcliffe	16 (1924-1935)
Graham Thorpe	16 (1993-2005)
Mike Atherton	16 (1989-2001)

MOST 50S (50-99)

Alastair Cook	57 (2006-2018)
Joe Root	54 (2012-2022)*
Ian Bell	46 (2004-2015)
Graham Gooch	46 (1975-1995)
Mike Atherton	46 (1989-2001)
Alec Stewart	45 (1990-2003)
Geoff Boycott	42 (1964-1982)
David Gower	39 (1978-1992)
Graham Thorpe	39 (1993-2005)
Colin Cowdrey	38 (1954-1975)
Kevin Pietersen	35 (2005-2014)
Ken Barrington	35 (1955-1968)
Len Hutton	33 (1937-1955)
Nasser Hussain	33 (1990-2004)
Alan Knott	30 (1967-1981)
Marcus Trescothick	29 (2000-2006)
Denis Compton	28 (1937-1957)
Jack Hobbs	28 (1908-1930)

MOST DISMISSALS AS WICKET KEEPER

Alan Knott	269 (250ct, 19st) (1967-1981)
Matt Prior	256 (243ct, 13st) (2007-2014)
Alec Stewart	241 (227ct, 14st) (1990-2003)
Godfrey Evans	219 (173ct, 46st) (1946-1959)
Johnny Bairstow	193 (180ct, 13st) (2012-2022)*
Bob Taylor	174 (167ct, 7st) (1971-1984)
Jack Russell	165 (153ct, 12st) (1988-1998)
Geraint Jones	133 (128ct, 5st) (2004-2006)
Jos Buttler	131 (130ct, 1St) (2014-2022)*
Jim Parks	112 (101ct, 11st) (1954-1968)
Les Ames	95 (72ct, 23st) (1929-1939)
Dick Lilley	92 (70ct, 22st) (1896-1909)
Paul Downton	75 (70ct, 5st) (1981-1988)
Bert Strudwick	73 (61ct, 12st) (1910-1926)
George Duckworth	60 (45ct, 15st) (1924-1936)
John Murray	55 (52ct, 3st) (1961-1967)
Chris Read	54 (48ct, 6st) (1999-2007)
Ben Foakes	53 (48ct, 5st) (2018-2022)*

MOST CATCHES (FIELDER)

Alastair Cook	175 (2006-2018)
Joe Root	163 (2012-2022)*
Andrew Strauss	121 (2004-2012)
Ian Botham	120 (1977-1992)
Colin Cowdrey	120 (1954-1975)
Wally Hammond	110 (1927-1947)
Graham Thorpe	105 (1993-2005)
Graham Gooch	103 (1975-1995)
James Anderson	101 (2003-2022)*
Ian Bell	100 (2004-2015)
Paul Collingwood	95 (2003-2011)
Marcus Trescothick	95 (2000-2006)
Graeme Hick	90 (1991-2001)
Ben Stokes	90 (2013-2022)*
Tony Greig	87 (1972-1977)
Mike Atherton	83 (1989-2001)
Tom Graveney	78 (1951-1969)
Allan Lamb	75 (1982-1992)

BEST BATTING AVERAGES (MINIMUM 20 INNINGS)

Herbet Sutcliffe	60.73 (84) (1924-1935)
Eddie Paynter	59.23 (31) (1931-1939)
Ken Barrington	58.67 (131) (1955-1968)
Wally Hammond	58.45 (140) (1927-1947)
Jack Hobbs	56.94 (102) (1908-1930)
Len Hutton	56.67 (138) (1937-1955)
Ernest Tyldesley	55.00 (20) (1921-1929)
Denis Compton	50.06 (131) (1937-1957)
Joe Root	50.01 (228) (2012-2022)*
Phil Mead	49.37 (26) (1911-1928)
Stanley Jackson	48.79 (33) (1893-1905)
Douglas Jardine	48.00 (33) (1928-1934)
Ted Dexter	47.89 (102) (1958-1968)
Geoff Boycott	47.72 (193) (1964-1982)
Patsy Hendren	47.63 (83) (1920-1935)
Kevin Pietersen	47.28 (181) (2005-2014)
Raman Subba Row	46.85 (22) (1958-1961)
Peter May	46.77 (106) (1951-1961)

Joe Hardstaff	46.74 (38) (1935-1948)
Jack Robertson	46.36 (21) (1947-1952)
Dennis Amiss	46.30 (88) (1966-1977)
Phil Sharpe	46.23 (21) (1963-1969)
Maurice Leyland	46.06 (65) (1928-1938)
Alastair Cook	45.35 (291) (2006-2018)
Kumar Ranjitsinhji	44.95 (26) (1896-1902)
Graham Thorpe	44.66 (179) (1993-2005)
Tom Graveney	44.38 (123) (1951-1969)
David Gower	44.25 (204) (1978-1992)
Jonathan Trott	44.08 (93) (2009-2015)
Colin Cowdrey	44.06 (188) (1954-1975)
Geoff Pullar	43.86 (49) (1959-1963)
Marcus Trescothick	43.79 (143) (2000-2006)
Robin Smith	43.67 (112) (1988-1996)
John Edrich	43.54 (127) (1963-1976)
Cyril Washbrook	42.81 (66) (1937-1956)
Ian Bell	42.69 (205) (2004-2015)
Graham Gooch	42.58 (215) (1975-1995)

BEST BOWLING AVERAGES (2000+ BALLS)

George Lohmann	10.75 (112W) (1886-1896)
Billy Barnes	15.54 (51W) (1880-1890)
Billy Bates	16.42 (50W) (1881-1887)
Sydney Barnes	16.43 (189W) (1901-1914)
Bobby Peel	16.98 (101W) (1884-1896)
Johnny Briggs	17.75 (118W) (1884-1899)
Frank Tyson	18.56 (76W) (1954-1959)
Colin Blythe	18.63 (100W) (1901-1910)
Ollie Robinson	19.80 (51W) (2021-2022)*
Johnny Wardle	20.39 (102W) (1948-1957)
George Ulyett	20.40 (50W) (1877-1890)
Frank Foster	20.57 (45W) (1911-1912)
Ken Higgs	20.74 (71W) (1965-1968)
Jim Laker	21.24 (193W) (1948-1959)
Fred Trueman	21.57 (307W) (1952-1965)
Ted Peate	22.03 (31W) (1881-1886)
Jack Hearne	22.08 (49W) (1892-1899)
Bill Bowes	22.33 (68W) (1932-1946)

William Atewell	22.35 (28W) (1884-1892)
Peter Loader	22.51 (39W) (1954-1959)
Dick Barlow	22.55 (34W) (1881-1887)
Hedley Verity	24.37 (144W) (1931-1939)
Brian Statham	24.82 (252W) (1951-1965)
Alec Bedser	24.89 (236W) (1946-1955)
Bob Willis	25.20 (325W) (1971-1984)
Tom Richardson	25.22 (88W) (1893-1898)
David Larter	25.43 (37W) (1962-1965)
Tony Lock	25.58 (174W) (1952-1968)
Derek Underwood	25.83 (297W) (1966-1982)
Mike Hendrick	25.83 (87W) (1974-1981)
Tich Freeman	25.86 (66W) (1924-1929)
Roy Tattersall	26.08 (58W) (1951-1954)
Maurice Tate	26.16 (155W) (1924-1925)
James Anderson	26.22 (667W) (2003-2022)*
John Snow	26.66 (202W) (1965-1976)
John Lever	26.72 (73W) (1976-1986)
Wilfred Rhodes	26.96 (127W) (1899-1930)

BEST BOWLING FIGURES IN AN INNINGS

Jim Laker	10/53 V Australia, 1956
George Lohmann	9/28 V South Africa, 1896
Jim Laker	9/37 V Australia, 1956
Devon Malcolm	9/57 V South Africa, 1994
Sydney Barnes	9/103 V South Africa, 1913
George Lohmann	8/7 V South Africa, 1896
Johnny Briggs	8/11 V South Africa, 1889
Stuart Broad	8/15 V Australia, 2015
Sydney Barnes	8/29 V South Africa, 1912
Fred Trueman	8/31 V India, 1952
Ian Botham	8/34 V Pakistan, 1978
George Lohmann	8/35 V Australia, 1887
Hedley Verity	8/43 V Australia, 1934
Bob Willis	8/43 V Australia, 1981
Derek Underwood	8/51 V Pakistan, 1974
Angus Fraser	8/53 V West Indies, 1998
Sydney Barnes	8/56 V South Africa, 1913
George Lohmann	8/58 V Australia, 1892

BEST BOWLING FIGURES IN A MATCH

Jim Laker	19/90 V Australia, 1956
Sydney Barnes	17/159 V South Africa, 1913
Johnny Briggs	15/28 V South Africa, 1889
George Lohmann	15/45 V South Africa, 1896
Colin Blythe	15/99 V South Africa, 1907
Hedley Verity	15/104 V Australia, 1934
Wilfred Rhodes	15/124 V Australia, 1904
Alex Bedser	14/99 V Australia, 1953
Billy Bates	14/102 V Australia, 1883
Sydney Barnes	14/144 V South Africa, 1914
Sydney Barnes	13/57 V South Africa, 1912
Derek Underwood	13/71 V Pakistan, 1974
John Ferris	13/91 V South Africa, 1892
Ian Botham	13/106 V India, 1980
Tony Greig	13/156 V West Indies, 1974
Sydney Barnes	13/163 V Australia, 1902
Tom Richardson	13/244 V Australia, 1896
Jack White	13/256 V Australia, 1929

MOST FIVE WICKETS IN AN INNINGS

James Anderson	32 (2003-2021)*
Ian Botham	27 (1977-1992)
Sydney Barnes	24 (1901-1914)
Stuart Broad	19 (2007-2021)*
Fred Trueman	17 (1952-1965)
Graeme Swann	17 (2008-2013)
Derek Underwood	17 (1966-1982)
Bob Willis	16 (1971-1984)
Alec Bedser	15 (1946-1955)
Angus Fraser	13 (1989-1998)
Andy Caddick	13 (1993-2003)
Monty Panesar	12 (2006-2013)
Tom Richardson	11 (1893-1898)
George Lohmann	9 (1886-1896)
Colin Blythe	9 (1901-1910)
Johnny Briggs	9 (1884-1899)
Darren Gough	9 (1994-2003)
Jim Laker	9 (19481959)

ENGLAND TEST SERIES RESULTS

DATE OPPONENT	RESULT (W-L-D)
1876-77 in Australia	1-1-0
1878-79 in Australia	0-1-0
1880 V Australia	1-0-0
1881-82 in Australia	0-2-2
1882 V Australia	0-1-0
1882-83 in Australia	2-1-0
1882-83 in Australia	1-0-0
1884 V Australia	1-0-2
1884-85 in Australia	3-2-0
1886 V Australia	3-0-0
1886-87 in Australia	2-0-0
1887-88 in Australia	1-0-0
1888 V Australia	2-1-0
1888-89 in South Africa	2-0-0
1890 V Australia	2-0-0
1891-92 in South Africa	1-0-0
1891-92 in Australia	1-2-0

1893 V Australia	1-0-2
1894-95 in Australia	3-2-0
1895-96 in South Africa	3-0-0
1896 V Australia	2-1-0
1897-98 in Australia	1-4-0
1898-99 in South Africa	2-0-0
1899 V England	0-1-4
1901-02 in Australia	1-4-0
1902 V Australia	1-2-2
1903-04 in Australia	3-2-0
1905 V Australia	2-0-3
1905-06 in South Africa	1-4-0
1907 V South Africa	1-0-2
1907-08 in Australia	1-4-0
1909 V Australia	1-2-2
1909-10 in South Africa	2-3-0
1911-12 in Australia	4-1-0
1912 V South Africa	3-0-0
1912 V Australia	1-0-2

1913-14 in South Africa	4-0-1
1920-21 in Australia	0-5-0
1921 V Australia	0-3-2
1922-23 in South Africa	2-1-2
1924 V South Africa	3-0-2
1924-25 in Australia	1-4-0
1926 V Australia	1-0-4
1927-28 in South Africa	2-2-1
1928 V West Indies	3-0-0
1928-29 in Australia	4-1-0
1929 V South Africa	2-0-3
1929-30 in New Zealand	1-0-3
1929-30 in West Indies	1-1-2
1930 V Australia	1-2-2
1930-31 in South Africa	0-1-4
1931 V New Zealand	1-0-2
1932 V India	1-0-0
1932-33 in Australia	4-1-0
1932-33 in New Zealand	0-0-2

1933 V West Indies	2-0-1
1933-34 in India	2-0-1
1934 V Australia	1-2-2
1934-35 in West Indies	1-2-1
1935 V South Africa	0-1-4
1936 V India	2-0-1
1936-37 in Australia	2-3-0
1937 V New Zealand	1-0-2
1938 V Australia	1-1-2
1938-39 in South Africa	1-0-4
1939 V West Indies	1-0-2
1946 V India	1-0-2
1946-47 in Australia	0-3-2
1946-47 V New Zealand	0-0-1
1947 V South Africa	3-0-2
1947-48 in West Indies	0-2-2
1948 V Australia	0-4-1
1948-49 in South Africa	2-0-3
1949 V New Zealand	0-0-4

1950 V West Indies	1-3-0
1950-51 in Australia	1-4-0
1950-51 in New Zealand	1-0-1
1951 V South Africa	3-1-1
1951-52 in India	1-1-3
1952 V India	3-0-1
1953 V Australia	1-0-4
1953-54 in West Indies	2-2-1
1954 V Pakistan	1-1-2
1954-55 in Australia	3-1-1
1954-55 in New Zealand	2-0-0
1955 V South Africa	3-2-0
1956 V Australia	2-1-2
1956-57 in South Africa	2-2-1
1957 V West Indies	3-0-2
1958 V New Zealand	4-0-1
1958-59 in Australia	0-4-1
1958-59 in New Zealand	1-0-1
1959 V India	5-0-0

1959-60 in West Indies	1-0-4
1960 V South Africa	3-0-2
1961 V Australia	1-2-2
1961-62 in India	0-2-3
1961-62 in Pakistan	1-0-2
1962 V Pakistan	4-0-1
1962-63 in Australia	1-1-3
1962-63 in New Zealand	3-0-0
1963 V West Indies	1-3-1
1963-64 in India	0-0-5
1964 V Australia	0-1-4
1964-65 in South Africa	1-0-4
1965 V New Zealand	3-0-0
1965 V South Africa	1-0-2
1965-66 in Australia	1-1-3
1965-66 in New Zealand	0-0-3
1966 V West Indies	1-3-1
1967 V India	3-0-0
1967 V Pakistan	2-0-1

1967-68 in West Indies	1-0-4
1968 V Australia	1-1-3
1968-69 in Pakistan	0-0-3
1969 V West Indies	2-0-1
1969 V New Zealand	2-0-1
1970-71 in Australia	2-0-5
1970-71 in New Zealand	1-0-1
1971 V Pakistan	1-0-2
1971 V India	0-1-2
1972 V Australia	2-2-1
1972-73 in India	1-2-2
1972-73 in Pakistan	0-0-3
1973 V New Zealand	2-0-1
1973 V West Indies	0-2-1
1973-74 in West Indies	1-1-3
1974 V India	3-0-0
1974 V Pakistan	0-0-3
1974-75 in Australia	1-4-1
1974-75 in New Zealand	1-0-1

1975 V Australia	0-1-3
1976 V West Indies	0-3-2
1976-77 in India	3-1-1
1976-77 in Australia	0-1-0
1977 V Australia	3-0-2
1977-78 in Pakistan	0-0-3
1977-78 in New Zealand	1-1-1
1978 V Pakistan	2-0-1
1978 V New Zealand	3-0-0
1978-79 in Australia	5-1-0
1979 V India	1-0-3
1979-80 in Australia	0-3-0
1979-80 in India	1-0-0
1980 V West Indies	1-0-4
1980 V Australia	0-0-1
1980-81 in West Indies	0-2-2
1981 V Australia	3-1-2
1981-82 in India	0-1-5
1981-82 in Sri Lanka	1-0-0

1982 V India	1-0-2
1982 V Pakistan	2-1-0
1982-83 in Australia	1-2-2
1983 V New Zealand	3-1-0
1983-84 in New Zealand	0-1-2
1983-84 in Pakistan	0-1-2
1984 V West Indies	0-5-0
1984 V Sri Lanka	0-0-1
1984-85 in India	2-1-2
1985 V Australia	3-1-2
1985-86 in West Indies	0-5-0
1986 V India	0-2-1
1986 V New Zealand	0-1-2
1986-87 in Australia	2-1-2
1987 V Pakistan	0-1-4
1987-88 in Pakistan	0-1-2
1987-88 in Australia	0-0-1
1987-88 in New Zealand	0-0-3
1988 V West Indies	0-4-1

1988 V Sri Lanka	1-0-0
1989 V Australia	0-4-2
1989-90 in West Indies	1-2-1
1990 V New Zealand	1-0-2
1990 V India	1-0-2
1990-91 in Australia	0-3-2
1991 V West Indies	2-2-1
1991 V Sri Lanka	1-0-0
1991-92 in New Zealand	2-0-1
1992 V Pakistan	1-2-2
1992-93 in India	0-3-0
1992-93 in Sri Lanka	0-1-0
1993 V Australia	1-4-1
1993-94 in West Indies	1-3-1
1994 V New Zealand	1-0-2
1994 V South Africa	1-1-1
1994-95 in Australia	1-3-1
1995 V West Indies	2-2-2
1995-96 in South Africa	0-1-4

1996 V India	1-0-2
1996 V Pakistan	0-2-1
1996-97 in Zimbabwe	0-0-2
1996-97 in New Zealand	2-0-1
1997 V Australia	2-3-1
1997-98 in West Indies	1-3-2
1998 V South Africa	2-1-2
1998 V Sri Lanka	0-1-0
1998-99 in Australia	1-3-1
1999 V New Zealand	1-2-1
1999-2000 in South Africa	1-2-2
2000 V Zimbabwe	1-0-1
2000 V West Indies	3-1-1
2000-01 in Pakistan	1-0-2
2000-01 in Sri Lanka	2-1-0
2001 V Pakistan	1-1-0
2001 V Australia	1-4-0
2001-02 in India	0-1-2
2001-02 in New Zealand	1-1-1

2002 V Sri Lanka	2-0-1
2002 V India	1-1-2
2002-03 in Australia	1-4-0
2003 V Zimbabwe	2-0-0
2003 V South Africa	2-2-1
2003-04 in Bangladesh	2-0-0
2003-04 in Sri Lanka	0-1-2
2003-04 in West Indies	3-0-1
2004 V New Zealand	3-0-0
2004 V West Indies	4-0-0
2004-05 in South Africa	2-1-2
2005 V Bangladesh	2-0-0
2005 V Australia	2-1-2
2005-06 in Pakistan	0-2-1
2005-06 in India	1-1-1
2006 V Sri Lanka	1-1-1
2006 V Pakistan	3-0-1
2006-07 in Australia	0-5-0
2007 V West Indies	3-0-1

2007 V India	0-1-2
2007-08 in Sri Lanka	0-1-2
2007-08 in New Zealand	2-1-0
2008 V New Zealand	2-0-1
2008 V South Africa	1-2-1
2008-09 in India	0-1-1
2008-09 in West Indies	0-1-4
2009 V West Indies	2-0-0
2009 V Australia	2-1-2
2009-10 in South Africa	1-1-2
2009-10 in Bangladesh	2-0-0
2010 V Bangladesh	2-0-0
2010 V Pakistan	3-1-0
2010-11 in Australia	3-1-1
2011 V Sri Lanka	1-0-2
2011 V India	4-0-0
2011-12 V Pakistan[8]	0-3-0

[8] Series played in United Arab Emirates

2011-12 in Sri Lanka	1-0-2
2012 V West Indies	2-0-1
2012 V South Africa	0-2-1
2012-13 in India	2-1-1
2012-13 in New Zealand	0-0-3
2013 V New Zealand	2-0-0
2013 V Australia	3-0-2
2013-14 in Australia	0-5-0
2014 V Sri Lanka	0-1-1
2014 V India	3-1-1
2015 in West Indies	1-1-1
2015 V New Zealand	1-1-0
2015 V Australia	3-2-0
2015-16 V Pakistan[9]	0-2-1
2015-16 in South Africa	2-1-1
2016 V Sri Lanka	2-0-1
2016 V Pakistan	2-2-0

[9] Series played in United Arab Emirates

2016-17 in Bangladesh	1-1-0
2016-17 in India	0-4-1
2017 V South Africa	3-1-0
2017 V West Indies	2-1-0
2017-18 in Australia	0-4-1
2017-18 in New Zealand	0-1-1
2018 V Pakistan	1-1-0
2018 V India	4-1-0
2018-19 in Sri Lanka	3-0-0
2018-19 in West Indies	1-2-0
2019 V Ireland	1-0-0
2019 V Australia	2-2-1
2019-20 in New Zealand	0-1-1
2019-20 in South Africa	3-1-0
2020 V West Indies	1-0-0
2020 V Pakistan	1-0-2
2020-21 in Sri Lanka	2-0-0
2020-21 in India	1-3-0
2021 V New Zealand	0-1-1
2021-22 in Australia	0-4-1

2021-22 in West Indies	0-1-2
2022 V New Zealand	3-0-0
2022 V India	2-2-1
2022 V South Africa	2-1-0

SOUTH AFRICA

Cricket came to South Africa in 1808, shortly after British forces established a colony at the Cape of Good Hope during the Napoleonic Wars.

By the 1840s, the game had spread to other provinces, such as Transvaal and Orange Free State. By the 1870s, South Africa had a thriving local provinicial competition.

England first toured South Africa in 1888, and won two matches which are now considered the first test matches played between the nations.

South Africa hosted Australia in 1902-03, and made their first trip to England in 1907. Australia played South Africa in England in 1912, and later that year all three test playing nations featured in a tournament in England.

After the First World War, it wasn't until 1921 that South Africa played test cricket. That year they hosted Australia. The following year, England toured; but it took until 1930-31 for South Africa to again win a series; at home against England.

In 1931-32, South Africa toured New Zealand for the first time, and won both tests. They defeated England 1-0 in a five test series in England in 1935, their last series win before World War II.

South Africa resumed test cricket with a tour of England in 1947, but would have to wait until 1952-53 for another series win, when they defeated New Zealand while on tour.

South Africa did not play tests against West Indies, India or Pakistan due to the apartheid policies of their nation's government. In 1970, these polices saw South Africa ostracised by the international community, and they were suspended from competing in test cricket.

Regime change finally came to South Africa in the early 1990s, and they were re-admitted to the ICC in 1991. Their first test in the new era was an away loss to West Indies in 1991.

South Africa hosted India, and toured Sri Lanka in 1993. In 1994-95 they played their first test matches against Pakistan.

South Africa became one of the top test cricket playing nations in the world in the 1990s. They played Zimbabwe for the first time in 1995-96.

Since 2000, the prize for the winner of test series between South Africa and West Indies was the Sir Vivian Richards Trophy.

MOST TESTS

Jacques Kallis	165 (1995-2013)
Mark Boucher	146 (1997-2012)
Hashim Amla	124 (2004-2019)
Graeme Smith	116 (2002-2014)
AB de Villiers	114 (2004-2018)
Shaun Pollock	108 (1995-2008)
Gary Kirsten	101 (1993-2004)
Makhaya Ntini	101 (1998-2009)
Dale Steyn	93 (2004-2019)
Herschelle Gibbs	90 (1996-2008)
Morne Morkel	86 (1008-2016)
Dean Elgar	79 (2012-2022)*
Allan Donald	72 (1992-2002)
Daryll Cullinan	70 (1993-2001)
Faf du Plessis	69 (2012-2021)
Hansie Cronje	68 (1992-2000)
Ashwell Prince	66 (2002-2011)
Vernon Philander	64 (2011-2020)

Neil McKenzie	58 (2000-2009)
Kagiso Rabada	55 (2015-2022)*
Quinton de Kock	54 (2014-2021)
Jonty Rhodes	52 (1992-2000)
John Waite	50 (1951-1965)
Lance Klusener	49 (1996-2004)
Temba Bavuma	49 (2014-2022)*
Jacques Rudolph	49 (2003-2012)
Jean-Paul Duminy	46 (2008-2017)
Keshav Maharaj	45 (2016-2022)*
Paul Adams	45 (1995-2004)
Dave Nourse	45 (1902-1924)
Nicky Boje	43 (2000-2006)
Bruce Mitchell	42 (1929-1949)
David Richardson	42 (1992-1998)
Herbie Taylor	42 (1912-1932)
Trevor Goddard	41 (1955-1970)
Roy McLean	40 (1951-1964)

MOST RUNS

Jacques Kallis	13206 (1995-2013)
Hashim Amla	9282 (2004-2019)
Graeme Smith	9253 (2002-2014)
AB de Villiers	8765 (2004-2018)
Gary Kirsten	7289 (1993-2004)
Herschelle Gibbs	6167 (1996-2008)
Mark Boucher	5498 (1997-2012)
Dean Elgar	4971 (2012-2022)*
Daryll Cullinan	4554 (1993-2001)
Faf du Plessis	4163 (2012-2021)
Shaun Pollock	3781 (1995-2008)
Hansie Cronje	3714 (1992-2000)
Ashwell Prince	3665 (2002-2011)
Bruce Mitchell	3471 (1929-1949)
Quinton de Kock	3300 (2014-2021)
Neil McKenzie	3253 (2000-2009)
Dudley Nourse	2960 (1935-1951)
Herbie Taylor	2936 (1912-1932)

Jacques Rudolph	2622 (2003-2012)
Temba Bavuma	2612 (2014-2022)*
Jonty Rhodes	2532 (1992-2000)
Eddie Barlow	2516 (1961-1970)
Trevor Goddard	2516 (1955-1970)
Jackie McGlew	2440 (1951-1962)
John Waite	2405 (1951-1965)
Graeme Pollock	2256 (1963-1970)
Dave Nourse	2234 (1902-1924)
Roy McLean	2120 (1951-1964)
Jean-Paul Duminy	2103 (2008-2017)
Alviro Petersen	2093 (2010-2015)
Aiden Markram	2009 (2017-2022)*
Andrew Hudson	2007 (1992-1998)
Brian McMillan	1968 (1992-1998)
Eric Rowan	1965 (1935-1951)
Lance Klusener	1906 (1996-2004)
Vernon Philander	1779 (2011-2020)
Aubrey Faulkner	1754 (1906-1924)

MOST WICKETS

Dale Steyn	439 (2004-2019)
Shaun Pollock	421 (1995-2008)
Makhaya Ntini	390 (1998-2009)
Alan Donald	330 (1992-2002)
Morne Morkel	309 (2006-2018)
Jacques Kallis	291 (1995-2013)
Kagiso Rabada	257 (2015-2022)*
Vernon Philander	224 (2011-2020)
Hugh Tayfield	170 (1949-1960)
Keshav Maharah	154 (2016-2022)*
Paul Adams	134 (1995-2004)
Trevor Goddard	123 (1955-1970)
Andre Nel	123 (2001-2008)
Peter Pollock	116 (1961-1970)
Neil Adcock	104 (1953-1962)
Paul Harris	103 (2007-2011)
Nicky Boje	100 (2000-2006)
Fanie de Villiers	85 (1993-1998)

Cyril Vincent	84 (1927-1935)
Aubrey Faulkner	82 (1906-1924)
Lance Klusener	80 (1996-2004)
Brian McMillan	75 (1992-1998)
Bert Vogler	64 (1906-1911)
Jimmy Sinclair	63 (1896-1911(
Jimmy Blanckenberg	60 (1913-1924)
Duanne Olivier	59 (2017-2022)*
Peter Heine	58 (1955-1962)
Norman Mann	58 (1947-1951)
Anrich Nortje	57 (2019-2022)*
Imran Tahir	57 (2011-2015)
Reggie Schwarz	55 (1906-1912)
Nantie Hayward	54 (1999-2004)
Athol Rowan	54 (1947-1951)
Craig Matthews	52 (1992-1995(
"Buster" Nupen	50 (1921-1936)
Lungi Ngidi	49 (2018-2022)*

HIGHEST SCORES

Hashim Amla	311* V England, 2012
AB de Villiers	278* V Pakistan, 2010
Graeme Smith	277 V England, 2003
Daryll Cullinan	275* V New Zealand, 1999
Gary Kirsten	275 V England, 1999
Graeme Pollock	274 V Australia, 1970
Graeme Smith	259 V England, 2003
Jackie McGlew	255* V New Zealand, 1953
Hashim Amla	253* V India, 2012
Eric Rowan	236 V England, 1951
Graeme Smith	234 V Pakistan, 2013
Graeme Smith	232 V Bangladesh, 2008
Dudley Nourse	231 V Australia, 1935
Herschelle Gibbs	228 V Pakistan, 2003
Neil McKenzie	226 V Bangladesh, 2008
Jacques Kallis	224 V Sri Lanka, 2012
Jacques Rudolph	222* V Bangladesh, 2003
Gary Kirsten	220 V Zimbabwe, 2001

AB de Villiers	217* V India, 2008
Herschelle Gibbs	211* V New Zealand, 1999
Gary Kirsten	210 V England, 1998
Graeme Pollock	209 V Australia, 1966
Dudley Nourse	208 V England, 1951
Hashim Amla	208 V West Indies, 2014
Aubrey Faulkner	204 V Australia, 1910
Jacques Kallis	201* V India, 2010
Eddie Barlow	201 V Australia, 1964
Hashim Amla	201 V England, 2016
Graeme Smith	200 V Bangladesh, 2002
Dean Elgar	199 V Bangladesh, 2017
Faf du Plessis	199 V Sri Lanka, 2020
Herschelle Gibbs	196 V India, 2001
Hashim Amla	196 V Australia, 2012
Herschelle Gibbs	192 V West Indies, 2004
Bruce Mitchell	189* V England, 1947
Jacques Kallis	189* V Zimbabwe, 2001
Alan Melville	189 V England, 1947

MOST CENTURIES

Jacques Kallis	45 (1995-2013)
Hashim Amla	28 (2014-2019)
Graeme Smith	27 (2002-2014)
AB de Villiers	22 (2004-2018)
Gary Kirsten	21 (1993-2004)
Daryll Cullinan	14 (1993-2001)
Herschelle Gibbs	14 (1996-2008)
Dean Elgar	13 (2012-2022)*
Ashwell Prince	11 (2002-2011)
Faf du Plessis	10 (2012-2021)
Dudley Nourse	9 (1935-1951)
Bruce Mitchell	8 (1929-1949)
Graeme Pollock	7 (1963-1970)
Jackie McGlew	7 (1951-1962)
Herbie Taylor	7 (1912-1932)
Eddie Barlow	6 (1961-1970)
Jean-Paul Duminy	6 (2008-2017)
Jacques Rudolph	6 (2003-2012)

MOST 50S (50-99)

Jacques Kallis	58 (1995-2013)
AB de Villiers	46 (2004-2018)
Hashim Amla	41 (2004-2019)
Graeme Smith	38 (2002-2014)
Mark Boucher	35 (1997-2012)
Gary Kirtsen	34 (1993-2004)
Herschelle Gibbs	26 (1996-2008)
Hanse Cronje	23 (1992-2000)
Dean Elgar	22 (2012-2022)*
Quinton de Kock	22 (2014-2021)
Faf du Plessis	21 (2012-2021)
Bruce Mitchell	21 (1929-1949)
Daryll Cullinan	20 (1993-2001)
Temba Bavuma	19 (2014-2022)*
Trevor Goddard	18 (1955-1970)
Herbie Taylor	17 (1912-1932)
Jonty Rhodes	17 (1992-2000)

MOST DISMISSALS AS WICKET KEEPER

Mark Boucher	553 (530ct, 23st) (1997-2012)
Quinton de Kock	232 (221ct, 11st) (2014-2021)
David Richardson	152 (150ct, 2st) (1992-1998)
John Waite	141 (124ct, 17st) (1951-1965)
AB de Villiers	106 (101ct, 5st) (2004-2018)
Denis Lindsay	56 (54ct, 2st) (1963-1970)
Jock Cameron	51 (39ct, 12st) (1927-1935)
Percy Sherwell	36 (20ct, 16st) (1906-1911)
Kyle Verreynne	33 (30ct, 3st) (2021-2022)*
Tommy Ward	32 (19ct, 13st) (1912-1924)
Billy Wade	17 (15ct, 2st) (1938-1950)
Dane Vilas	13 (13ct) (2015-2016)
Ernest Halliwell	12 (10ct, 2st) (1892-1902)
Ronnie Grieveson	10 (7ct, 3st) (1939)

MOST CATCHES (FIELDER)

Jacques Kallis	196 (1995-2013)
Graeme Smith	166 (2002-2014)
AB de Villiers	121 (2004-2018)
Hashim Amla	108 (2004-2019)
Herschelle Gibbs	94 (1996-2008)
Dean Elgar	84 (2012-2022)*
Gary Kirsten	83 (1993-2004)
Shaun Pollock	72 (1995-2008)
Daryll Cullinan	67 (1993-2001)
Faf du Plessis	63 (2012-2021)
Bruce Mitchell	56 (1929-1949)
Neil McKenzie	54 (2000-2009)
Brian McMillan	49 (1992-1998)
Trevor Goddard	48 (1955-1970)
Ashwell Prince	47 (2002-2011)
Dave Nourse	43 (1902-1924)
Russell Endean	38 (1951-1958)
Jean-Paul Duminy	38 (2008-2017)

BEST BATTING AVERAGE (MINIMUM 20 INNINGS)

Graeme Pollock	60.97 (41) (1963-1970)
Jacques Kallis	55.25 (278) (1995-2013)
Dudley Nourse	53.81 (62) (1935-1951)
AB de Villiers	50.66 (191) (2004-2018)
Colin Bland	49.08 (39) (1961-1966)
Bruce Mitchell	48.88 (80) (1929-1949)
Graeme Smith	48.70 (203) (2002-2014)
Hashim Amla	46.64 (215) (2004-2019)
Eddie Barlow	45.74 (57) (1961-1970)
Gary Kirsten	45.27 (176) (1993-2004)
Daryll Cullinan	44.21 (115) (1993-2001)
Eric Rowan	43.66 (50) (1935-1951)
Jackie McGlew	42.06 (64) (1951-1962)
Herschelle Gibbs	41.95 (154) (1996-2008)
Ashwell Prince	41.64 (104) (2002-2011)
Aubrey Faulkner	40.79 (47) (1906-1924)
Herbie Taylor	40.77 (76) (1912-1932)
Faf du Plessis	40.02 (118) (2012-2021)

Brian McMillan	39.36 (62) (1992-1998)
Dean Elgar	38.83 (139) (2012-2022)*
Quinton de Kock	38.82 (91) (2014-2021)
Kepler Wessels	38.03 (29) (1992-1994)
Bob Catterall	37.92 (43) (1922-1931)
Denis Lindsay	37.66 (31) (1963-1970)
Neil McKenzie	37.39 (94) (2000-2009)
Hansie Cronje	36.41 (111) (1992-2000)
Jonty Rhodes	35.66 (80) (1992-2000)
Jacques Rudolph	35.43 (83) (2003-2012)
Alviro Petersen	34.88 (64) (2010-2015)
Trevor Goddard	34.46 (78) (1955-1970)
Temba Bavuma	34.36 (87) (2014-2022)*
Aiden Markram	34.05 (60) (2017-2022)*
Russell Endean	33.95 (52) (1951-1958)
Andrew Hudson	33.45 (63) (1992-1998)
Lance Klusener	32.86 (69) (1996-2004)
Jean-Paul Duminy	32.85 (74) (2008-2017)

BEST BOWLING AVERAGES (2000+ BALLS)

Neil Adcock	21.10 (104W) (1953-1962)
Lungi Ngidi	21.61 (49W) (2018-2022)*
Alf Hall	22.15 (40W) (1923-1931)
Alan Donald	22.25 (330W) (1992-2002)
Vernon Philander	22.32 (224W) (2011-2020)
Kagiso Rabada	22.46 (257) (2015-2022)*
Kyle Abbott	22.71 (39W) (2013-2017)
Bert Vogler	22.73 (64W) (1906-1911)
Dale Steyn	22.95 (439W) (2004-2019)
Shaun Pollock	23.11 (421W) (1995-2008)
Peter Pollock	24.18 (116W) (1961-1970)
Fanie de Villiers	24.27 (85W) (1993-1998)
Peter Heine	25.08 (58W) (1955-1962)
Reggie Schwarz	25.76 (55W) (1906-1912)
Hugh Tayfield	25.91 (170W) (1949-1960)
Trevor Goddard	26.22 (123W) (1955-1970)
Aubrey Faulkner	26.58 (82W) (1906-1924)
Anrich Nortje	27.52 (57W) (2019-2022)*

Morne Morkel	27.66 (309W) (2006-2018)
John Watkins	28.13 (29W) (1949-1957)
Makhaya Ntini	28.82 (390W) (1998-2009)
Craig Matthews	28.88 (52W) (1992-1995)
Charlie Llewellyn	29.60 (48W) (1896-1912)
Nantie Hayward	29.75 (54W) (1999-2004)
Hansie Cronje	29.95 (43W) (1992-2000)
Jimmy Blanckenberg	30.28 (60W) (1913-1924)
Keshav Maharaj	30.61 (154W) (2016-2022)*
Joe Partridge	31.20 (44W) (1963-1965)
Cyril Vincent	31.32 (84W) (1927-1935)
Jimmy Sinclair	31.68 (63W) (1896-1911)
Andre Nel	31.86 (123W) (2001-2008)
Jacques Kallis	32.62 (291W) (1995-2013)
Sandy Bell	32.64 (48W) (1929-1935)
Neville Quinn	32.71 (35W) (1929-1932)
Paul Adams	32.87 (134W) (1995-2004)
Norman Mann	33.10 (58W) (1947-1951)
Sid Pegler	33.44 (47W) (1910-1924)

BEST BOWLING FIGURES IN AN INNINGS

Hugh Tayfield	9/113 V England, 1957
Keshav Maharaj	9/129 V Sri Lanka, 2018
Godfrey Lawrence	8/53 V New Zealand, 1961
Lance Klusener	8/64 V India, 1996
Hugh Tayfield	8/69 V England, 1957
Tip Snooke	8/70 V England, 1906
Alan Donald	8/71 V Zimbabwe, 1995
Hugh Tayfield	7/23 V Australia, 1950
George Bissett	7/29 V England, 1928
Kyle Abbott	7/29 V Pakistan, 2013
Makhaya Ntini	7/37 V West Indies, 2005
Keshav Maharaj	7/40 V Bangladesh, 2022
Dale Steyn	7/51 V India, 2010
Alf Hall	7/63 V England, 1923
Sid Pegler	7/65 V England, 1912
Hugh Tayfield	7/81 V Australia, 1952
Marchant de Lange	7/81 V Sri Lanka, 2011

BEST BOWLING FIGURES IN A MATCH

Makhaya Ntini	13/132 V West Indies, 2005
Kagiso Rabada	13/144 V England, 2016
Hugh Tayfield	13/165 V Australia, 1952
Hugh Tayfield	13/192 V England, 1957
Tip Snooke	12/127 V England, 1906
Alan Donald	12/139 V India, 1992
Bert Vogler	12/181 V England, 1910
Keshav Maharaj	12/283 V Sri Lanka, 2018
Dale Steyn	11/60 V Pakistan, 2013
Duanne Olivier	11/96 V Pakistan, 2018
Alf Hall	11/112 V England, 1923
Alan Donald	11/113 V Zimbabwe, 1995
Alan Donald	11/127 V England, 1999
"Buster" Nupen	11/150 V England, 1930
Kagiso Rabada	11/150 V Australia, 2018
Sydney Burke	11/196 V New Zealand, 1962
Kagiso Rabada	10/63 V Bangladesh, 2017
Peter Pollock	10/87 V England, 1965

MOST FIVE WICKETS IN AN INNINGS

Dale Steyn	26 (2004-2019)
Alan Donald	20 (1992-2002)
Makhaya Ntini	18 (1998-2009)
Shaun Pollock	16 (1995-2008)
Hugh Tayfield	14 (1949-1960)
Vernon Philander	13 (2011-2020)
Kagiso Rabada	12 (2015-2022)*
Peter Pollock	9 (1961-1970)
Keshav Maharaj	9 (2016-2022)*
Morne Morkel	8 (2006-2018)
Bert Volger	5 (1906-1911)
"Buster" Nupen	5 (1921-1936)
Fanie de Villiers	5 (1993-1998)
Neil Adcock	5 (1953-1962)
Trevor Goddard	5 (1955-1970)
Jacques Kallis	5 (1995-2013)

SOUTH AFRICA TEST SERIES RESULTS

DATE OPPONENT	RESULT (W-L-D)
1888-89 V England	0-2-0
1891-92 V England	0-1-0
1895-96 V England	0-3-0
1898-99 V England	0-2-0
1902-03 V Australia	0-2-1
1905-06 V England	4-1-0
1907 in England	0-1-2
1909-10 V England	3-2-0
1910-11 in Australia	1-4-0
1912 V Australia[10]	0-2-1
1912 in England	0-3-0
1913-14 V England	0-1-2
1922-23 V England	1-2-2
1924 in England	0-3-2
1927-28 V England	2-2-1

[10] Series played in England

1929 in England	0-2-3
1930-31 V England	1-0-4
1931-32 in Australia	0-5-0
1931-32 in New Zealand	2-0-0
1935 in England	1-0-4
1935-36 V Australia	0-4-1
1938-39 V England	0-1-4
1947 in England	0-3-2
1948-49 V England	0-2-3
1949-50 V Australia	0-4-1
1951 in England	1-3-1
1952-53 in Australia	2-2-1
1952-53 in New Zealand	1-0-1
1953-54 V New Zealand	4-0-1
1955 in England	2-3-0
1956-57 V England	2-2-1
1957-58 V Australia	0-3-2
1960 in England	0-3-2
1961-62 V New Zealand	2-2-1

1963-64 in Australia	1-1-3
1963-64 in New Zealand	0-0-3
1964-65 V England	0-1-4
1965 in England	1-0-2
1966-67 V Australia	3-1-1
1969-70 V Australia	4-0-0
1991-92 in West Indies	0-1-0
1992-93 V India	1-0-3
1993 in Sri Lanka	1-0-2
1993-94 in Australia	1-1-1
1993-94 V Australia	1-1-1
1994 in England	1-1-1
1994-95 V New Zealand	2-1-0
1994-95 V Pakistan	1-0-0
1994-95 in New Zealand	1-0-0
1995-96 in Zimbabwe	1-0-0
1995-96 V England	1-0-4
1996-97 in India	1-2-0
1996-97 V India	2-0-1

1996-97 V Australia	1-2-0
1997-98 in Pakistan	1-0-2
1997-98 in Australia	1-2-0
1997-98 V Pakistan	1-1-1
1997-98 V Sri Lanka	0-2-0
1998 in England	1-2-2
1998-99 V West Indies	5-0-0
1998-99 in New Zealand	1-0-2
1999-2000 V Zimbabwe[11]	2-0-0
1999-2000 V England	2-1-2
1999-2000 in India	2-0-0
2000 in Sri Lanka	1-1-1
2000-01 V New Zealand	2-0-1
2000-01 V Sri Lanka	2-0-1
2000-01 in West Indies	2-1-2
2001-02 in Zimbabwe	1-0-1
2001-02 V India	1-0-1

[11] Series was played in both nations

2001-02 in Australia	0-3-0
2001-02 V Australia	1-2-0
2002-03 V Bangladesh	2-0-0
2002-03 V Sri Lanka	2-0-0
2002-03 V Pakistan	2-0-0
2003 in Bangladesh	2-0-0
2003 in England	2-2-1
2003-04 in Pakistan	0-1-1
2003-04 V West Indies	3-0-1
2003-04 in New Zealand	1-1-1
2004 in Sri Lanka	0-1-1
2004-05 in India	0-1-1
2004-05 V England	1-2-2
2004-05 V Zimbabwe	2-0-0
2005 in West Indies	2-0-2
2005-06 in Australia	0-2-1
2005-06 V Australia	0-3-0
2005-06 V New Zealand	2-0-1
2006 in Sri Lanka	0-2-0

2006-07 V India	2-1-0
2006-07 V Pakistan	2-1-0
2007-08 in Pakistan	1-0-1
2007-08 V New Zealand	2-0-0
2007-08 V West Indies	2-1-0
2007-08 in Bangladesh	2-0-0
2007-08 in India	1-1-1
2008 in England	2-1-1
2008-09 V Bangladesh	2-0-0
2008-09 in Australia	2-1-0
2008-09 V Australia	1-2-0
2009-10 V England	1-1-2
2009-10 in India	1-1-0
2010 in West Indies	2-0-1
2010-11 V Pakistan[12]	0-0-2
2010-11 V India	1-1-1
2011-12 V Australia	1-1-0

[12] Series played in United Arab Emirates

2011-12 V Sri Lanka	2-1-0
2011-12 in New Zealand	1-0-2
2012 in England	2-0-1
2012-13 in Australia	1-0-2
2012-13 V New Zealand	2-0-0
2012-13 V Pakistan	3-0-0
2013-14 V Pakistan[13]	1-1-0
2013-14 V India	1-0-1
2013-14 V Australia	1-2-0
2014 in Sri Lanka	1-0-1
2014 in Zimbabwe	1-0-0
2014-15 V West Indies	2-0-1
2015 in Bangladesh	0-0-2
2015-16 in India	0-3-1
2015-16 V England	1-2-1
2016 V New Zealand	1-0-1
2016-17 in Australia	2-1-0

[13] Series played in United Arab Emirates

2016-17 V Sri Lanka	3-0-0
2016-17 in New Zealand	1-0-2
2017 in England	1-3-0
2017-18 V Bangladesh	2-0-0
2017-18 V Zimbabwe	1-0-0
2017-18 V India	2-1-0
2017-18 V Australia	3-1-0
2018 in Sri Lanka	0-2-0
2018-19 V Pakistan	3-0-0
2018-19 V Sri Lanka	0-2-0
2019-20 in India	0-3-0
2019-20 V England	1-3-0
2020-21 V Sri Lanka	2-0-0
2020-21 V Pakistan	0-2-0
2021 in West Indies	2-0-0
2021-22 in New Zealand	1-1-0
2021-22 V Bangladesh	2-0-0
2022 in England	1-2-0

WEST INDIES

The West Indies member associations are Barbados, Trinidad and Tobago, Jamaica, Guyana, and representatives of the Leeward Islands and the Windward Islands.

Colonised English speaking nations of the Caribbean formed a team known as the West Indies as early as the 1880s to tour the United States and Canada. They also received visits from touring England teams in the 1890s.

Teams were selected to play visiting English teams, and in 1928 a squad was selected to tour England to play their first test matches. England won all three tests.

England toured West Indies for the first time in 1929, and a year later West Indies made their first visit to Australia. In 1934-35, West Indies won their first test series, beating England 2-1.

When test cricket resumed after World War II, West Indies toured India in 1948-49, New Zealand in 1951-52, and Pakistan in 1958-59.

In 1960-61, West Indies toured Australia to compete for the Frank Worrall Trophy for the first time. The series saw the dramatic first tied test played in Brisbane.

West Indies became one of the dominant test nations in the first half of the 1960s. They won the first Wisden Trophy in 1963 by defeating England. The two nations still compete for the prize.

In the mid-1970s, West Indies again rose to prominence as a new batch of players found their way into the test team. They were beaten in India in 1979, but didn't lose another test series until defeated by Australia in 1994-95.

West Indies played Sri Lanka for the first time in 1993-94, and Zimbabwe in 1999-2000. Since 2000, the Sir Vivian Richards Trophy has been the prize for the winner of test series between West Indies and South Africa.

In 2001, the trophy for the winner of test series between West Indies and Zimbabwe has been named after former West Indies captain and star batsman, Clive Lloyd.

West Indies won their first test series against Bangladesh in 2004, but wins have been few and far between since. They defeated Afghanistan in the first test between the nations in 2019.

MOST TESTS

Shivnarine Chanderpaul	164 (1994-2015)
Courtney Walsh	132 (1984-2001)
Brian Lara	130 (1990-2006)
Viv Richards	121 (1974-1991)
Desmond Haynes	116 (1978-1994)
Clive Lloyd	110 (1966-1985)
Gordon Greenidge	108 (1974-1991)
Chris Gayle	103 (2000-2014)
Carl Hooper	102 (1987-2002)
Curtly Ambrose	98 (1988-2000)
Garfield Sobers	93 (1954-1974)
Ramnaresh Sarwan	87 (2000-2011)
Richie Richardson	86 (1983-1995)
Jeff Dujon	81 (1981-1991)
Malcolm Marshall	81 (1978-1991)
Lance Gibbs	79 (1958-1976)
Rohan Kanhai	79 (1957-1974)
Kraigg Braithwaite	79 (2011-2022)*

Denesh Ramdin	74 (2005-2016)
Kemar Roach	73 (2009-2022)*
Marlon Samuels	71 (2000-2016)
Alvin Kallicharran	66 (1972-1981)
Ridley Jacobs	65 (1998-2004)
Deryck Murray	62 (1963-1980)
Larry Gomes	60 (1976-1987)
Michael Holding	60 (1975-1987)
Roy Fredericks	59 (1968-1977)
Joel Garner	58 (1977-1987)
Darren Bravo	56 (2010-2020)
Shannon Gabriel	56 (2012-2021)
Jason Holder	56 (2014-2022)*
Fidel Edwards	55 (2003-2012)
Jimmy Adams	54 (1992-2001)
Sherwin Campbell	52 (1995-2002)
Gus Logie	52 (1983-1991)
Frank Worrell	51 (1948-1963)

MOST RUNS

Brian Lara	11912 (1990-2006)
Shivnarine Chanderpaul	11867 (1994-2015)
Viv Richards	8540 (1974-1991)
Garfield Sobers	8032 (1954-1974)
Gordon Greenidge	7558 (1974-1991)
Clive Lloyd	7515 (1966-1985)
Desmond Haynes	7487 (1978-1994)
Chris Gayle	7214 (2000-2014)
Rohan Kanhai	6227 (1957-1974)
Richie Richardson	5949 (1983-1995)
Ramnaresh Sarwan	5842 (2000-2011)
Carl Hooper	5762 (1987-2002)
Kraigg Braithwaite	4893 (2011-2022)*
Everton Weekes	4455 (1948-1958)
Alvin Kallicharran	4399 (1972-1981)
Roy Fredericks	4344 (1968-1977)
Marlon Samuels	3917 (2000-2016)
Frank Worrell	3860 (1948-1963)

Clyde Walcott	3798 (1948-1960)
Darren Bravo	3538 (2010-2020)
Jeff Dujon	3322 (1981-1991)
Conrad Hunte	3245 (1958-1967)
Larry Gomes	3171 (1976-1987)
Basil Butcher	3104 (1958-1969)
Jimmy Adams	3012 (1992-2001)
Denesh Ramdin	2898 (2005-2016)
Sherwin Campbell	2882 (1995-2002)
Wavell Hinds	2608 (2000-2005)
Ridley Jacobs	2577 (1998-2004)
Jason Holder	2571 (2014-2022)*
Jermaine Blackwood	2566 (2014-2022)*
Seymour Nurse	2523 (1960-1969)
Gus Logie	2470 (1983-1991)
Dwayne Bravo	2200 (2004-2010)
George Headley	2190 (1930-1954)
Daren Ganga	2160 (1998-2008)
Jeffrey Stollmeyer	2159 (1939-1955)

MOST WICKETS

Courtney Walsh	519 (1984-2001)
Curtly Ambrose	405 (1988-2000)
Malcolm Marshall	376 (1978-1991)
Lance Gibbs	309 (1958-1976)
Joel Garner	259 (1977-1987)
Kemar Roach	252 (2009-2022)*
Michael Holding	249 (1975-1987)
Garfield Sobers	235 (1954-1974)
Andy Roberts	202 (1974-1983)
Wes Hall	192 (1958-1969)
Fidel Edwards	165 (2003-2012)
Ian Bishop	161 (1989-1998)
Shannon Gabriel	161 (2012-2021)
Sonny Ramadhin	158 (1950-1961)
Jason Holder	142 (2014-2022)*
Alf Valentine	139 (1950-1962)
Mervyn Dillon	131 (1997-2004)
Jerome Taylor	130 (2003-2016)

Colin Croft	125 (1977-1982)
Devendra Bishoo	117 (2011-2018)
Carl Hooper	114 (1987-2002)
Vanburn Holder	109 (1969-1979)
Pedro Collins	106 (1999-2006)
Charlie Griffith	94 (1960-1969)
Patrick Patterson	93 (1986-1992)
Corey Collymore	93 (1999-2007)
Kenny Benjamin	92 (1992-1998)
Sulieman Benn	87 (2008-2015)
Dwayne Bravo	86 (2004-2010)
Daren Powell	85 (2002-2009)
Daren Sammy	84 (2007-2013)
Roston Chase	79 (2016-2021)
Chris Gayle	73 (2000-2014)
Shane Shillingford	70 (2010-2014)
Frank Worrell	69 (1948-1963)
Alzarri Joseph	62 (2016-2022)*
Winston Benjamin	61 (1987-1995)

HIGHEST SCORES

Brian Lara	400* V England, 2004
Brian Lara	375 V England, 1994
Garfield Sobers	365* V Pakistan, 1958
Chris Gayle	333 V Sri Lanka, 2010
Chris Gayle	317 V Sth Africa, 2005
Lawrence Rowe	302 V England, 1974
Viv Richards	291 V England, 1976
Ramnaresh Sarwan	291 V England, 2009
Brian Lara	277 V Australia, 1993
George Headley	270* V England, 1935
Ramnaresh Sarwan	261* V Bangladesh, 2004
Frank Worrell	261 V England, 1950
Conrad Hunte	260 V Pakistan, 1958
Marlon Samuels	260 V Bangladesh, 2012
Seymour Nurse	258 V New Zealand, 1969
Rohan Kanhai	256 V India, 1958
Faoud Bacchus	250 V India, 1979
Clive Lloyd	242* V India, 1975

Frank Worrell	237 V India, 1953
Carl Hooper	233 V India, 2002
Viv Richards	232 V England, 1976
Garfield Sobers	226 V England, 1960
Gordon Greenidge	226 V Australia, 1991
Brian Lara	226 V Australia, 2005
George Headley	223 V England, 1930
Gordon Greenidge	223 V England, 1984
Brian Lara	221 V Sri Lanka, 2001
Clyde Walcott	220 V England, 1954
Denis Atkinson	219 V Australia, 1955
Darren Bravo	218 V New Zealand, 2013
Rohan Kanhai	217 V Pakistan, 1959
Brian Lara	216 V Pakistan, 2006
Gordon Greenidge	214* V England, 1984
Lawrence Rowe	214 V New Zealand, 1972
Gordon Greenidge	213 V New Zealand, 1987
Brian Lara	213 V Australia, 1999
Wavell Hinds	213 V Sth Africa, 2005

MOST CENTURIES

Brian Lara	34 (1990-2006)
Shivnarine Chanderpaul	30 (1994-2015)
Garfield Sobers	26 (1954-1974)
Viv Richards	24 (1974-1991)
Clive Lloyd	19 (1966-1985)
Gordon Greenidge	19 (1974-1991)
Desmond Haynes	18 (1978-1994)
Richie Richardson	16 (1983-1995)
Clyde Walcott	15 (1948-1960)
Everton Weekes	15 (1948-1958)
Rohan Kanhai	15 (1957-1974)
Ramnaresh Sarwan	15 (2000-2011)
Chris Gayle	15 (2000-2014)
Carl Hooper	13 (1987-2002)
Alvin Kallicharran	12 (1972-1981)
George Headley	10 (1930-1954)
Kraigg Braithwaite	10 (2011-2022)*

MOST 50S (50-99)

Shivnarine Chanderpaul	66 (1994-2015)
Brian Lara	48 (1990-2006)
Viv Richards	45 (1974-1991)
Clive Lloyd	39 (1966-1985)
Desmond Haynes	39 (1978-1994)
Chris Gayle	37 (2000-2014)
Gordon Greenidge	34 (1974-1991)
Ramnaresh Sarwan	31 (2000-2011)
Garfield Sobers	30 (1954-1974)
Rohan Kanhai	28 (1957-1974)
Kraigg Braithwaite	27 (2011-2022)*
Richie Richardson	27 (1983-1995)
Carl Hooper	27 (1987-2002)
Roy Fredericks	26 (1968-1977)
Marlon Samuels	24 (2000-2016)
Frank Worrell	22 (1948-1963)
Alvin Kallicharran	21 (1972-1981)
Everton Weekes	19 (1948-1958)

MOST DISMISSALS AS WICKET KEEPER

Jeff Dujon	270 (265ct, 5st) (1981-1991)
Ridley Jacobs	219 (207ct, 12st) (1998-2004)
Denesh Ramdin	217 (205ct, 12st) (2005-2016)
Deryck Murray	189 (181ct, 8st) (1963-1980)
Junior Murray	101 (98ct, 3st) (1993-2002)
Gerry Alexander	90 (85ct, 5st) (1957-1961)
Shane Dowrich	90 (85ct, 5st) (2015-2020)
Courtney Browne	81 (79ct, 2st) (1995-2005)
David Murray	62 (57ct, 5st) (1978-1982)
Joshua Da Silva	61 (57ct, 4st) (2020-2022)*
Carlton Baugh	48 (43ct, 5st) (2003-2012)
Jackie Hendriks	47 (42ct, 5st) (1962-1969)
David Williams	42 (40ct, 2st) (1992-1998)
Clyde Walcott	38 (27ct, 11st) (1948-1960)
Ivan Barrow	21 (16ct, 5st) (1930-1939)
Mike Findlay	21 (19ct, 2st) (1969-1973)
David Allan	18 (15ct, 3st) (1962-1966)
Alfie Binns	17 (14ct, 3st) (1953-1956)

MOST CATCHES (FIELDER)

Brian Lara	164 (1990-2006)
Viv Richards	122 (1974-1991)
Carl Hooper	115 (1987-2002)
Garfield Sobers	109 (1954-1974)
Chris Gayle	96 (2000-2014)
Gordon Greenidge	96 (1974-1991)
Richie Richardson	90 (1983-1995)
Clive Lloyd	90 (1966-1985)
Shivnarine Chanderpaul	66 (1994-2015)
Daren Sammy	65 (2007-2013)
Desmond Haynes	65 (1978-1994)
Roy Fredericks	62 (1968-1977)
Jason Holder	59 (2014-2022)*
Gus Logie	57 (1983-1991)
Ramnaresh Sarwan	53 (2000-2011)
Lance Gibbs	52 (1958-1976)
Darren Bravo	51 (2010-2020)
Alvin Kallicharran	51 (1972-1981)

BEST BATTING AVERAGES (MINIMUM 20 INNINGS)

George Headley	60.83 (40) (1930-1954)
Everton Weekes	58.61 (81) (1948-1958)
Garfield Sobers	57.78 (160) (1954-1974)
Clyde Walcott	56.68 (74) (1948-1960)
Charlie Davis	54.20 (29) (1968-1973)
Brian Lara	53.17 (230) (1990-2006)
Shivnarine Chanderpaul	51.37 (280) (1994-2015)
Viv Richards	50.23 (182) (1974-1991)
Frank Worrell	49.48 (87) (1948-1963)
Seymour Nurse	47.60 (54) (1960-1969)
Rohan Kanhai	47.53 (137) (1957-1974)
Clive Lloyd	46.67 (175) (1966-1985)
Allan Rae	46.18 (24) (1948-1953)
Conrad Hunte	45.06 (78) (1958-1967)
Gordon Greenidge	44.72 (185) (1974-1991)
Alvin Kallicharran	44.43 (109) (1972-1981)
Richie Richardson	44.39 (146) (1983-1995)
Lawrence Rowe	43.55 (49) (1972-1980)

Basil Butcher	43.11 (78) (1958-1969)
Roy Fredericks	42.49 (109) (1968-1977)
Jeffrey Stollmeyer	42.33 (56) (1939-1955)
Desmond Haynes	42.29 (202) (1978-1994)
Chris Gayle	42.18 (182) (2000-2014)
Jimmy Adams	41.26 (90) (1992-2001)
Ramnaresh Sarwan	40.01 (154) (2000-2011)
Larry Gomes	39.63 (91) (1976-1987)
Kyle Mayers	38.90 (23) (2021-2022)*
Nkrumah Bonner	37.47 (24) (2021-2022)*
John Holt	36.75 (31) (1954-1959)
Darren Bravo	36.47 (102) (2010-2020)
Carl Hooper	36.46 (173) (1987-2002)
Gus Logie	35.79 (78) (1983-1991)
Kraigg Braithwaite	34.45 (152) (2011-2022)*
Joey Carew	34.15 (36) (1963-1972)
Joe Solomon	34.00 (46) (1958-1965)
Brendan Nash	33.42 (33) (2008-2011)
Wavell Hinds	33.01 (80) (2000-2005)

BEST BOWLING AVERAGES (2000+ BALLS)

Malcolm Marshall	20.04 (376W) (1978-1991)
Joel Garner	20.97 (259W) (1977-1987)
Curtly Ambrose	20.99 (405W) (1988-2000)
Colin Croft	23.30 (125W) (1977-1982)
Michael Holding	23.68 (249W) (1975-1987)
Ian Bishop	24.27 (161W) (1989-1998)
Courtney Walsh	24.44 (519W) (1984-2001)
Andy Roberts	25.61 (202W) (1974-1983)
Wes Hall	26.38 (192W) (1958-1969)
Roy Gilchrist	26.69 (57W) (1957-1959)
Kemar Roach	26.83 (252W) (2009-2022)*
Winston Benjamin	27.01 (61W) (1987-1995)
Gerry Gomez	27.41 (58W) (1939-1954)
Sylvester Clarke	27.85 (42W) (1978-1982)
Jason Holder	28.03 (142W) (2014-2022)*
Roger Harper	28.06 (46W) (1983-1993)
Herman Griffith	28.25 (44W) (1928-1933)
Charlie Griffith	28.54 (94W) (1960-1969)

Sonny Ramadhin	28.98 (158W) (1950-1961)
Lance Gibbs	29.09 (309W) (1958-1976)
Jermaine Lawson	29.64 (51W) (2002-2005)
Keith Boyce	30.01 (60W) (1971-1976)
Baron Constantine	30.10 (58W) (1928-1939)
Kenny Benjamin	30.27 (92W) (1992-1998)
Alf Valentine	30.32 (139W) (1950-1962)
Dinanath Ramnarine	30.73 (45W) (1998-2002)
Franklyn Rose	30.88 (53W) (1997-2000)
Patrick Patterson	30.90 (93W) (1986-1992)
John Goddard	31.81 (33W) (1948-1957)
Shannon Gabriel	31.84 (161W) (2012-2021)
Corey Collymore	32.30 (93W) (1999-2007)
Reon King	32.69 (53W) (1999-2005)
Winston Davis	32.71 (45W) (1983-1988)
Vanburn Holder	33.27 (109W) (1969-1979)
Mervyn Dillon	33.57 (131W) (1997-2004)
Cameron Cuffy	33.83 (43W) (1994-2002)
Collie Smith	33.85 (48W) (1955-1959)

BEST FIGURES IN AN INNINGS

Jack Noreiga	9/95 V India, 1971
Colin Croft	8/29 V Pakistan, 1977
Lance Gibbs	8/38 V India, 1962
Curtly Ambrose	8/45 V England, 1990
Devendra Bishoo	8/49 V Pakistan, 2016
Roston Chase	8/60 V England, 2019
Shannon Gabriel	8/62 V Sri Lanka, 2018
Michael Holding	8/92 V England, 1976
Alf Valentine	8/104 V England, 1950
Malcolm Marshall	7/22 V England, 1988
Curtly Ambrose	7/25 V Australia, 1993
Courtney Walsh	7/37 V New Zealand, 1995
Sonny Ramadhin	7/49 V England, 1957
Denis Atkinson	7/53 V New Zealand, 1956
Malcolm Marshall	7/53 V England, 1984
Andy Roberts	7/54 V Australia, 1975
Gerry Gomez	7/55 V Australia, 1952
Corey Collymore	7/57 V Sri Lanka, 2003

BEST FIGURES IN A MATCH

Michael Holding	14/149 V England, 1976
Courtney Walsh	13/55 V New Zealand, 1995
Shannon Gabriel	13/121 V Sri Lanka, 2018
Andy Roberts	12/121 V India, 1975
Curtly Ambrose	11/84 V England, 1994
Malcolm Marshall	11/89 V India, 1989
Jason Holder	11/103 V Bangladesh, 2018
Michael Holding	11/107 V Australia, 1981
Malcolm Marshall	11/120 V New Zealand, 1985
Wes Hall	11/126 V India, 1958
Corey Collymore	11/134 V Pakistan, 2005
Keith Boyce	11/147 V England, 1973
Sonny Ramadhin	11/152 V England, 1950
Lance Gibbs	11/157 V England, 1963
Alf Valentine	11/204 V England, 1950
Wilfred Ferguson	11/229 V England, 1948
Malcolm Marshall	10/92 V England, 1988
Shane Shillingford	10/93 V Zimbabwe, 2013

MOST FIVE WICKETS IN AN INNINGS

Malcolm Marshall	22 (1978-1991)
Curtly Ambrose	22 (1988-2000)
Courtney Walsh	22 (1984-2001)
Lance Gibbs	18 (1958-1976)
Michael Holding	13 (1975-1987)
Fidel Edwards	12 (2003-2012)
Andy Roberts	11 (1974-1983)
Sonny Ramadhin	10 (1950-1961)
Kemar Roach	10 (2009-2022)*
Wes Hall	9 (1958-1969)
Jason Holder	8 (2014-2022)*
Alf Valentine	8 (1950-1962)
Joel Garner	7 (1977-1987)
Shane Shillingford	6 (2010-2014)
Sulieman Benn	6 (2008-2015)
Shannon Gabriel	6 (2012-2021)
Ian Bishop	6 (1989-1998)
Garfield Sobers	6 (1954-1974)

WEST INDIES TEST SERIES RESULTS

DATE OPPONENT	RESULT (W-L-D)
1928 in England	0-3-0
1929-30 V England	1-1-2
1930-31 in Australia	1-4-0
1933 in England	0-2-1
1934-35 v England	2-1-1
1939 in England	0-1-2
1947-48 V England	2-0-2
1948-49 in India	1-0-4
1950 in England	3-1-0
1951-52 in Australia	1-4-0
1951-52 in New Zealand	1-0-1
1952-53 V India	1-0-4
1953-54 V England	2-2-1
1955 V Australia	0-3-2
1955-56 in New Zealand	3-1-0
1957 in England	0-3-2
1957-58 V Pakistan	3-1-1

1958-59 in India	3-0-2
1958-59 in Pakistan	1-2-0
1959-60 V England	0-1-4
1960-61 in Australia	1-2-2[14]
1961-62 V India	5-0-0
1963 in England	3-1-1
1964-65 V Australia	2-1-2
1966 in England	3-1-1
1966-67 in India	2-0-1
1967-68 V England	0-1-4
1968-69 in Australia	1-3-1
1968-69 in New Zealand	1-1-1
1969 in England	0-2-1
1970-71 V India	0-1-4
1971-72 V New Zealand	0-0-5
1972-73 V Australia	0-2-3
1973 in England	2-0-1

[14] Includes one tied test

1973-74 V England	1-1-3
1974-75 in India	3-2-0
1974-75 in Pakistan	0-0-2
1975-76 in Australia	1-5-0
1975-76 V India	2-1-1
1976 in England	3-0-2
1976-77 V Pakistan	2-1-2
1977-78 V Australia	3-1-1
1978-79 in India	0-1-5
1979-80 in Australia	2-0-1
1979-80 in New Zealand	0-1-2
1980 in England	1-0-4
1980-81 in Pakistan	1-0-3
1980-81 V England	2-0-2
1981-82 in Australia	1-1-1
1982-83 V India	2-0-3
1983-84 in India	3-0-3
1983-84 V Australia	3-0-2
1984 in England	5-0-0

1984-85 in Australia	3-1-1
1984-85 V New Zealand	2-0-2
1985-86 V England	5-0-0
1986-87 in Pakistan	1-1-1
1986-87 in New Zealand	1-1-1
1987-88 in India	1-1-2
1987-88 V Pakistan	1-1-1
1988 in England	4-0-1
1988-89 in Australia	3-1-1
1988-89 V India	3-0-1
1989-90 V England	2-1-1
1990-91 in Pakistan	1-1-1
1990-91 V Australia	2-1-2
1991 in England	2-2-1
1991-92 V South Africa	1-0-0
1992-93 in Australia	2-1-2
1992-93 V Pakistan	2-0-1
1993-94 in Sri Lanka	0-0-1
1993-94 V England	3-1-1

1994-95 in India	1-1-1
1994-95 in New Zealand	1-0-1
1994-95 V Australia	1-2-1
1995 in England	2-2-2
1995-96 V New Zealand	1-0-1
1996-97 in Australia	2-3-0
1996-97 V India	1-0-4
1997 V Sri Lanka	1-0-1
1997-98 in Pakistan	0-3-0
1997-98 V England	3-1-2
1998-99 in South Africa	0-5-0
1998-99 V Australia	2-2-0
1999-2000 in New Zealand	0-2-0
1999-2000 V Zimbabwe	2-0-0
2000 V Pakistan	1-0-2
2000 in England	1-3-1
2000-01 in Australia	0-5-0
2000-01 V South Africa	1-2-2
2001 in Zimbabwe	1-0-1

2001-02 in Sri Lanka	0-3-0
2001-02 V Pakistan[15]	0-2-0
2002 V India	2-1-2
2002 V New Zealand	0-1-1
2002-03 in India	0-2-1
2002-03 in Bangladesh	2-0-0
2003 V Australia	1-3-0
2003 V Sri Lanka	1-0-1
2003-04 in Zimbabwe	1-0-1
2003-04 in South Africa	0-3-1
2003-04 V England	0-3-1
2004 V Bangladesh	1-0-1
2004 in England	0-4-0
2005 V South Africa	0-2-2
2005 V Pakistan	1-1-0
2005 in Sri Lanka	0-2-0
2005-06 in Australia	0-3-0

[15] Series played in United Arab Emirates

2005-06 in New Zealand	0-2-1
2006 V India	0-1-3
2006-07 in Pakistan	0-2-1
2007 in England	0-3-1
2007-08 in South Africa	1-2-0
2007-08 V Sri Lanka	1-1-0
2008 V Australia	0-2-1
2008-09 in New Zealand	0-0-2
2008-09 V England	1-0-4
2009 in England	0-2-0
2009 V Bangladesh	0-2-0
2009-10 in Australia	0-2-1
2010 V South Africa	0-2-1
2010-11 in Sri Lanka	0-0-3
2011 V Pakistan	1-1-0
2011 V India	0-1-2
2011-12 in Bangladesh	1-0-1
2011-12 in India	0-2-1
2011-12 V Australia	0-2-1

2012 in England	0-2-1
2012 V New Zealand	2-0-0
2012-13 in Bangladesh	2-0-0
2012-13 V Zimbabwe	2-0-0
2013-14 in India	0-2-0
2013-14 in New Zealand	0-2-1
2014 V New Zealand	1-2-0
2014 V Bangladesh	2-0-0
2014-15 V South Africa	0-2-1
2015 V England	1-1-1
2015 V Australia	0-2-0
2015-16 in Sri Lanka	0-2-0
2015-16 in Australia	0-2-1
2016 V India	0-2-2
2016-17 V Pakistan[16]	1-2-0
2017 V Pakistan	1-2-0
2017 in England	1-0-1

[16] Series played in United Arab Emirates

2017-18 in Zimbabwe	1-0-1
2017-18 in New Zealand	0-2-0
2018 V Sri Lanka	1-1-1
2018 V Bangladesh	2-0-0
2018-19 in India	0-2-0
2018-19 in Bangladesh	0-2-0
2018-19 V England	2-1-0
2019 V India	0-2-0
2019-20 V Afghanistan[17]	1-0-0
2020 in England	1-2-0
2020-21 in New Zealand	0-2-0
2020-21 in Bangladesh	2-0-0
2020-21 V Sri Lanka	0-0-2
2021 V South Africa	0-2-0
2021 V Pakistan	1-1-0
2021-22 in Sri Lanka	0-2-0
2022 V England	1-0-2
2022 V Bangladesh	2-0-0

[17] Series played in India

NEW ZEALAND

Cricket has been played in New Zealand since the 1830s. An informal competition was established in Wellington in the 1840s, but the game became established when a team from England toured in 1864. Several further English teams visited New Zealand in the following decades, as did teams from Australia.

1894 saw the first team claiming to represent New Zealand play an official match. They lost to a visiting team from New South Wales. New Zealand played two non-test matches against Australia in 1904-05; and made a tour of England in 1927. Their performances in England were strong enough for the International Cricket Board to grant the nation test status.

England toured New Zealand in the summer of 1929-30 and the first test matches against the newest member of the ICB. England won a dour four test series 1-0.

New Zealand visited England in 1931, and hosted South Africa later that year. They played their first tests against Australia in 1945-46, and hosted West Indies in 1951-52.

New Zealand toured South Africa for the first time in 1953-54; and followed up with a tour of Pakistan and India in 1955-56.

In 1969-70, New Zealand toured Pakistan and won a test series for the first time. They won of the three tests, while the other two were drawn.

New Zealand had to wait another decade to win a test series. In 1979-80 they upset West Indies 1-0 in a three test series at home.

New Zealand improved in the 1980s, and recorded wins against every test playing nation, including Sri Lanka, who they first played in 1982-83.

Since 1985-86, New Zealand and Australia have battled for the Trans-Tasman Trophy. New Zealand won the trophy in their first two seris.

New Zealand faced Zimbabwe for the first time in 1992-93; and Bangldesh in 2001-02. The Trans-Tasman Trophy continues to be the greatest prize for New Zealand cricket, but in 2019-20 they were beaten in all three matches in Australia.

MOST TESTS

Daniel Vettori	112 (1997-2014)
Ross Taylor	112 (2007-2022)
Stephen Fleming	111 (1994-2008)
Brendon McCullum	101 (2004-2016)
Kane Williamson	88 (2010-2022)*
Tim Southee	88 (2008-2022)*
Richard Hadlee	86 (1973-1990)
John Wright	82 (1978-1993)
Nathan Astle	81 (1996-2006)
Trent Boult	78 (2011-2022)*
Adam Parore	78 (1990-2002)
Martin Crowe	77 (1982-1995)
BJ Watling	75 (2009-2021)*
Chris Martin	71 (2000-2013)
Tom Latham	68 (2014-2022)*
Ian Smith	63 (1980-1992)
Chris Cairns	62 (1989-2004)
Bevan Congdon	61 (1965-1978)

Neil Wagner	59 (2012-2022)*
John Reid	58 (1949-1965)
Ken Rutherford	56 (1985-1995)
Craig McMillan	55 (1997-2005)
Jeremy Coney	52 (1974-1987)
Mark Burgess	50 (1968-1980)
Henry Nicholls	48 (2016-2022)*
Danny Morrison	48 (1987-1997)
Martin Guptill	47 (2009-2016)
Geoff Howarth	47 (1975-1985)
Lance Cairns	43 (1974-1985)
Ewen Chatfield	43 (1975-1989)
Bert Sutcliffe	42 (1947-1965)
John Bracewell	41 (1980-1990)
Mark Greatbatch	41 (1988-1996)
Glenn Turner	41 (1969-1983)
Jeff Crowe	39 (1983-1990)
Graham Dowling	39 (1961-1972)
Bruce Edgar	39 (1978-1986)

MOST RUNS

Ross Taylor	7683 (2007-2022)
Kane Williamson	7368 (2010-2022)*
Stephen Fleming	7172 (1994-2008)
Brendon McCullum	6453 (2004-2016)
Martin Crowe	5444 (1982-1995)
John Wright	5334 (1978-1993)
Nathan Astle	4702 (1996-2006)
Tom Latham	4623 (2014-2022)*
Daniel Vettori	4523 (1997-2014)
BJ Watling	3790 (2009-2021)
Bevan Congdon	3448 (1965-1978)
John Reid	3428 (1949-1965)
Chris Cairns	3320 (1989-2004)
Richard Hadlee	3124 (1973-1990)
Craig McMillan	3116 (1997-2005)
Glenn Turner	2991 (1969-1983)
Andrew Jones	2922 (1987-1995)
Adam Parore	2865 (1990-2002)

Mark Richardson	2776 (2000-2004)
Bert Sutcliffe	2727 (1947-1965)
Mark Burgess	2684 (1968-1980)
Jeremy Coney	2668 (1974-1987)
Henry Nicholls	2603 (2016-2022)*
Martin Guptill	2586 (2009-2016)
Geoff Howarth	2531 (1975-1985)
Ken Rutherford	2465 (1985-1995)
Graham Dowling	2306 (1961-1972)
Bryan Young	2034 (1993-1999)
Mark Greatbatch	2021 (1988-1996)
Bruce Edgar	1958 (1978-1986)
Tim Southee	1855 (2008-2022)*
Ian Smith	1815 (1980-1992)
Matt Horne	1788 (1997-2003)
Jacob Oram	1780 (2002-2009)
Mathew Sinclair	1635 (1999-2010)
Jeff Crowe	1601 (1983-1990)
Scott Styris	1586 (2002-2007)

MOST WICKETS

Richard Hadlee	431 (1973-1990)
Daniel Vettori	361 (1997-2014)
Tim Southee	347 (2008-2022)*
Trent Boult	317 (2011-2022)*
Neil Wagner	246 (2012-2022)*
Chris Martin	233 (2000-2013)
Chris Cairns	218 (1989-2004)
Danny Morrison	160 (1987-1997)
Lance Cairns	130 (1974-1985)
Ewen Chatfield	123 (1975-1989)
Richard Collinge	116 (1965-1978)
Bruce Taylor	111 (1965-1973)
John Bracewell	102 (1980-1990)
Dick Motz	100 (1961-1969)
Simon Doull	98 (1992-2000)
Dion Nash	93 (1992-2001)
Shane Bond	87 (2001-2009)
Hedley Howarth	86 (1969-1977)

John Reid	85 (1949-1965)
James Franklin	82 (2001-2013)
Daryl Tuffey	77 (2000-2010)
Dipak Patel	75 (1987-1997)
Stephen Boock	74 (1978-1989)
Iain O'Brien	73 (2005-2009)
Kyle Jamieson	72 (2020-2022)*
Doug Bracewell	72 (2011-2016)
Dayle Hadlee	71 (1969-1978)
Tony MacGibbon	70 (1951-1958)
Jeetan Patel	65 (2006-2017)
Frank Cameron	62 (1961-1965)
Paul Wiseman	61 (1998-2005)
Jacob Oram	60 (2002-2009)
Bevan Congdon	59 (1965-1978)
Martin Snedden	58 (1981-1990)
Shayne O'Connor	53 (1997-2001)
Matt Henry	53 (2015-2022)*

HIGHEST SCORES

Brendon McCullum	302 V India, 2014
Martin Crowe	299 V Sri Lanka, 1991
Ross Taylor	290 V Australia, 2015
Stephen Fleming	274* V Sri Lanka, 2003
Bryan Young	267* V Sri Lanka, 1997
Tom Latham	264* V Sri Lanka, 2018
Stephen Fleming	262 V South Africa, 2006
Glenn Turner	259 V West Indies, 1972
Tom Latham	252 V Bangladesh, 2022
Kane Williamson	251 V West Indies, 2020
Kane Williamson	242* V Sri Lanka, 2015
Graham Dowling	239 V India, 1968
Kane Williamson	238 V Pakistan, 2021
Bert Sutcliffe	230* V India, 1955
Brendon McCullum	225 V India, 2010
Lou Vincent	224 V Sri Lanka, 2005
Brendon McCullum	224 V India, 2014
Glenn Turner	223* V West Indies, 1972

Nathan Astle	222 V England, 2002
Ross Taylor	217* V West Indies, 2013
Mathew Sinclair	214 V West Indies, 1999
Martin Donnelly	206 V England, 1949
BJ Watling	205 V England, 2019
Mathew Sinclair	204* V Pakistan, 2001
Stephen Fleming	202 V Bangladesh, 2004
Brendon McCullum	202 V Pakistan, 2014
Jesse Ryder	201 V India, 2009
Kane Williamson	200* V Bangladesh, 2019
Ross Taylor	200 V Bangladesh, 2019
Devon Conway	200 V England, 2021
Brendon McCullum	195 V Sri Lanka, 2014
Stephen Fleming	192 V Pakistan, 2003
Kane Williamson	192 V Pakistan, 2014
Daryl Mitchell	190 V England, 2022
Martin Guptill	189 V Bangladesh, 2010
Martin Crowe	188 V West Indies, 1985
Martin Crowe	188 V Australia, 1985

MOST CENTURIES

Kane Williamson	24 (2010-2021)*
Ross Taylor	19 (2007-2022)
Martin Crowe	17 (1982-1995)
John Wright	12 (1978-1993)
Brendon McCullum	12 (2004-2016)
Tom Latham	12 (2014-2022)*
Nathan Astle	11 (1996-2006)
Stephen Fleming	9 (1994-2008)
BJ Watling	8 (2009-2022)*
Henry Nicholls	8 (2016-2022)*
Glenn Turner	7 (1969-1983)
Andrew Jones	7 (1987-1995)
Bevan Congdon	7 (1965-1978)
John Reid	6 (1979-1986)
Geoff Howarth	6 (1975-1985)
Craig McMillan	6 (1997-2005)
John Reid	6 (1949-1965)
Daniel Vettori	6 (1997-2014)

MOST 50S (50-99)

Stephen Fleming	46 (1994-2008)
Ross Taylor	35 (2007-2022)
Kane Williamson	33 (2010-2021)*
Brendon McCullum	31 (2004-2016)
Nathan Astle	24 (1996-2006)
Tom Latham	23 (2014-2022)*
John Wright	23 (1978-1993)
Daniel Vettori	23 (1997-2014)
John Reid	22 (1949-1965)
Chris Cairns	22 (1989-2004)
BJ Watling	19 (2009-2021)
Bevan Congdon	19 (1965-1978)
Craig McMillan	19 (1997-2005)
Mark Richardson	19 (2000-2004)
Martin Crowe	18 (1982-1995)
Ken Rutherford	18 (1985-1995)
Martin Guptill	17 (2009-2016)

MOST DISMISSALS AS WICKET KEEPER

BJ Watling	265 (257ct, 8st) (2009-2021)
Adam Parore	201 (194ct, 7st) (1990-2002)
Brendon McCullum	179 (168ct, 11st) (2004-2016)
Ian Smith	176 (168ct, 8st) (1980-1992)
Ken Wadsworth	96 (92ct, 4st) (1969-1976)
Warren Lees	59 (52ct, 7st) (1976-1983)
Artie Dick	51 (47ct, 4st) (1961-1965)
Tom Blundell	48 (46ct, 2 st) (2017-2022)*
Robbie Hart	30 (29ct, 1st) (2002-2003)
Frank Mooney	30 (22ct, 8st) (1949-1954)
Lee Germon	29 (27ct, 2st) (1995-1997)
Eric Petrie	25 (25ct) (1955-1966)
Kruger van Wyk	24 (23ct, 1st) (2012)
Tony Blain	20 (18ct, 2st) (1986-1994)
John Ward	17 (16ct, 1st) (1964-1968)
Ken James	16 (11ct, 5st) (1930-1933)
Roy Harford	11 (11ct) (1968)

MOST CATCHES (FIELDER)

Stephen Fleming	171 (1994-2008)
Ross Taylor	163 (2007-2022)
Kane Williamson	74 (2010-2021)*
Martin Crowe	71 (1982-1995)
Nathan Astle	70 (1996-2006)
Tom Latham	69 (2014-2022)*
Tim Southee	69 (2008-2022)*
Jeremy Coney	64 (1974-1987)
Daniel Vettori	58 (1997-2014)
Bryan Young	54 (1993-1999)
Martin Guptill	50 (2009-2016)
Trent Boult	43 (2011-2022)*
Bevan Congdon	43 (1965-1978)
Glenn Turner	42 (1969-1983)
Jeff Crowe	41 (1983-1990)
John Reid	39 (1949-1965)
Richard Hadlee	39 (1973-1990)
John Wright	38 (1978-1993)

BEST BATTING AVERAGES (MINIMUM 20 INNINGS)

Kane Williamson	52.62 (154) (2010-2022)*
John Reid	46.28 (31) (1979-1986)
Martin Crowe	45.36 (131) (1982-1995)
Mark Richardson	44.77 (65) (2000-2004)
Ross Taylor	44.66 (196) (2007-2022)
Glenn Turner	44.64 (73) (1969-1983)
Andrew Jones	44.27 (74) (1987-1995)
Tom Blundell	41.10 (33) (2017-2022)*
Jesse Ryder	40.93 (33) (2008-2011)
Tom Latham	40.55 (119) (2014-2022)*
Bert Sutcliffe	40.10 (76) (1947-1965)
Stephen Fleming	40.06 (189) (1994-2008)
Henry Nicholls	38.85 (73) (2016-2022)*
Colin de Grandhomme	38.70 (44) (2016-2022)*
Brendon McCullum	38.64 (176) (2004-2016)
Craig McMillan	38.46 (91) (1997-2005)
John Wright	37.82 (148) (1978-1993)
Jeremy Coney	37.57 (85) (1974-1987)

BJ Watling	37.52 (117) (2009-2021)
Nathan Astle	37.02 (137) (1996-2006)
Mark Craig	36.81 (25) (2014-2016)
Jacob Oram	36.32 (59) (2002-2009)
Scott Styris	36.04 (48) (2002-2007)
Lou Vincent	34.15 (40) (2001-2007)
James Neesham	33.76 (22) (2014-2017)
Chris Cairns	33.53 (104) (1989-2004)
John Reid	33.28 (108) (1949-1965)
Corey Anderson	32.52 (22) (2013-2016)
Geoff Howarth	32.44 (83) (1975-1985)
Bevan Congdon	32.22 (114) (1965-1978)
Mathew Sinclair	32.05 (56) (1999-2010)
Bryan Young	31.78 (68) (1993-1999)
George Rabone	31.22 (20) (1949-1955)
Mark Burgess	31.20 (92) (1968-1980)
Graham Dowling	31.16 (77) (1961-1972)
Shane Thomson	30.90 (35) (1990-1995)
Mark Greatbatch	30.62 (71) (1988-1996)

BEST BOWLING AVERAGES (2000+ BALLS)

Kyle Jamieson	19.45 (72W) (2020-2022)*
Jack Cowie	21.53 (45W) (1937-1949)
Shane Bond	22.09 (87W) (2001-2009)
Richard Hadlee	22.29 (431W) (1973-1990)
Bruce Taylor	26.60 (111W) (1965-1973)
Neil Wagner	26.71 (246W) (2012-2022)*
Trent Boult	27.49 (317W) (2011-2022)*
Ajaz Patel	27.65 (43W) (2018-2022)*
Dion Nash	28.48 (93W) (1992-2001)
Tim Southee	28.99 (347W) (2008-2022)*
Richard Collinge	29.25 (116W) (1965-1978)
Simon Doull	29.30 (98W) (1992-2000)
Chris Cairns	29.40 (218W) (1989-2004)
Frank Cameron	29.82 (62W) (1961-1965)
Tony MacGibbon	30.85 (70W) (1951-1958)
Dick Motz	31.48 (100W) (1961-1969)
Daryl Tuffey	31.75 (77W) (2000-2010)
Ewen Chatfield	32.17 (123W) (1975-1989)

Shayne O'Connor	32.52 (53W) (1997-2001)
Lance Cairns	32.92 (130W) (1974-1985)
Colin de Grandhomme	32.95 (49W) (2016-2022)*
Kyle Mills	33.02 (44W) (2004-2009)
Jacon Oram	33.05 (60W) (2002-2009)
Iain O'Brien	33.27 (73W) (2005-2009)
John Reid	33.35 (85W) (1949-1965)
Dayle Hadlee	33.64 (71W) (1969-1978)
Chris Martin	33.81 (233W) (2000-2013)
James Franklin	33.97 (82W) (2001-2013)
Daniel Vettori	34.15 (361W) (1997-2014)
Stephen Boock	34.64 (74W) (1978-1989)
Willie Watson	34.67 (40W) (1986-1993)
Danny Morrison	34.68 (160W) (1987-1997)
Bob Blair	35.23 (43W) (1953-1964)
Tom Burtt	35.45 (33W) (1947-1953)
Bryan Yuile	35.67 (34W) (1963-1969)
Jeremy Coney	35.77 (27W) (1974-1987)
John Bracewell	35.81 (102W) (1980-1990)

BEST FIGURES IN AN INNINGS

Ajaz Patel	10/119 V India, 2021
Richard Hadlee	9/52 V Australia, 1985
Richard Hadlee	7/23 V India, 1976
Matt Henry	7/23 V South Africa, 2022
Chris Cairns	7/27 V West Indies, 1999
Neil Wagner	7/39 V West Indies, 2017
Chris Pringle	7/52 V Pakistan, 1990
Chris Cairns	7/53 V Bangladesh, 2001
Tim Southee	7/64 V India, 2012
Simon Doull	7/65 V India, 1998
Bruce Taylor	7/74 V West Indies, 1972
Lance Cairns	7/74 V England, 1983
Stephen Boock	7/87 V Pakistan, 1984
Daniel Vettori	7/87 V Australia, 2000
Danny Morrison	7/89 V Australia, 1993
Mark Craig	7/94 V Pakistan, 2014
Richard Hadlee	7/116 V Australia, 1986

BEST FIGURES IN A MATCH

Richard Hadlee	15/123 V Australia, 1985
Ajaz Patel	14/225 V India, 2021
Daniel Vettori	12/149 V Australia, 2000
Daniel Vettori	12/170 V Bangladesh, 2004
Richard Hadlee	11/58 V India, 1976
Richard Hadlee	11/102 V West Indies, 1980
Kyle Jamieson	11/117 V Pakistan, 2021
Chris Pringle	11/152 V Pakistan, 1990
Richard Hadlee	11/155 V Australia, 1985
Dion Nash	11/169 V England, 1994
Chris Martin	11/180 V South Africa, 2004
Trent Boult	10/80 V West Indies, 2013
Richard Hadlee	10/88 V India, 1988
Shane Bond	10/99 V Zimbabwe, 2005
Richard Hadlee	10/100 V England, 1978
Chris Cairns	10/100 V West Indies, 1999
Richard Hadlee	10/102 V Sri Lanka, 1984
John Bracewell	10/106 V Australia, 1986

MOST FIVE WICKETS IN AN INNINGS

Richard Hadlee	36 (1973-1990)
Daniel Vettori	20 (1997-2014)
Tim Southee	14 (2008-2022)*
Chris Cairns	13 (1989-2004)
Danny Morrison	10 (1987-1997)
Chris Martin	10 (2000-2013)
Trent Boult	10 (2011-2022)*
Niger Wagner	9 (2012-2022)*
Simon Doull	6 (1992-2000)
Lance Cairns	6 (1974-1985)
Shane Bond	5 (2001-2009)
Dick Motz	5 (1961-1969)
Kyle Jamieson	5 (2020-2022)*

NEW ZEALAND TEST SERIES RESULTS

DATE OPPONENT	RESULT (W-L-D)
1929-30 V England	0-1-3
1931 in England	0-1-2
1931-32 V South Africa	0-2-0
1932-33 V England	0-0-2
1937 in England	0-1-2
1945-46 V Australia	0-1-0
1946-47 V England	0-0-1
1949 in England	0-0-4
1950-51 V England	0-1-1
1951-52 V West Indies	0-1-1
1952-53 V South Africa	0-1-1
1953-54 in South Africa	0-4-1
1954-55 V England	0-2-0
1955-56 in Pakistan	0-2-1
1955-56 in India	0-2-3
1955-56 V West Indies	1-3-0
1958 in England	0-4-1

1958-59 V England	0-1-1
1961-62 in South Africa	2-2-1
1962-63 V England	0-3-0
1963-64 V South Africa	0-0-3
1964-65 V Pakistan	0-0-3
1964-65 in India	0-1-3
1964-65 in Pakistan	0-2-1
1965 in England	0-3-0
1965-66 V England	0-0-3
1967-68 V India	1-3-0
1968-69 V West Indies	1-1-1
1969 in England	0-2-1
1969-70 in India	1-1-1
1969-70 in Pakistan	1-0-2
1970-71 V England	0-1-1
1971-72 in West Indies	0-0-5
1972-73 V Pakistan	0-1-2
1973 in England	0-2-1
1973-74 in Australia	0-2-1

1973-74 V Australia	1-1-1
1974-75 V England	0-1-1
1975-76 V India	1-1-1
1976-77 in Pakistan	0-2-1
1976-77 in India	0-2-1
1976-77 V Australia	0-1-2
1977-78 V England	1-1-1
1978 in England	0-3-0
1978-79 V Pakistan	0-1-2
1979-80 V West Indies	1-0-2
1980-81 in Australia	0-2-1
1980-81 V India	1-0-2
1981-82 V Australia	1-1-1
1982-83 V Sri Lanka	2-0-0
1983 in England	1-3-0
1983-84 V England	1-0-2
1983-84 in Sri Lanka	2-0-1
1984-85 in Pakistan	0-2-1
1984-85 V Pakistan	2-0-1

1984-85 in West Indies	0-2-2
1985-86 in Australia	2-1-0
1985-86 V Australia	1-0-2
1986 in England	1-0-2
1986-87 V West Indies	1-1-1
1987 in Sri Lanka	0-0-1
1987-88 in Australia	0-1-2
1987-88 V England	0-0-3
1988-89 in India	1-2-0
1988-89 V Pakistan	0-0-2
1989-90 in Australia	0-0-1
1989-90 V India	1-0-2
1989-90 V Australia	1-0-0
1990 in England	0-1-2
1990-91 in Pakistan	0-3-0
1990-91 V Sri Lanka	0-0-3
1991-92 V England	0-2-1
1992-93 in Zimbabwe	1-0-1
1992-93 in Sri Lanka	0-1-1

1992-93 V Pakistan	0-1-0
1992-93 V Australia	1-1-1
1993-94 in Australia	0-2-1
1993-94 V Pakistan	1-2-0
1993-94 V India	0-0-1
1994 in England	0-1-2
1994-95 in South Africa	1-2-0
1994-95 V West Indies	0-1-1
1994-95 V South Africa	0-1-0
1994-95 V Sri Lanka	0-1-1
1995-96 in India	0-1-2
1995-96 V Pakistan	0-1-0
1995-96 V Zimbabwe	0-0-2
1995-96 in West Indies	0-1-1
1996-97 in Pakistan	1-1-0
1996-97 V England	0-2-1
1996-97 V Sri Lanka	2-0-0
1997-98 in Zimbabwe	2-0-0
1997-98 in Australia	0-2-1

1997-98 V Zimbabwe	2-0-0
1998 in Sri Lanka	1-2-0
1998-99 V India	1-0-1
1998-99 V South Africa	0-1-2
1999 in England	2-1-1
1999-2000 in India	0-1-2
1999-2000 V West Indies	2-0-0
1999-2000 V Australia	0-3-0
2000-01 in Zimbabwe	2-0-0
2000-01 in South Africa	0-2-1
2000-01 V Zimbabwe	0-0-1
2000-01 V Pakistan	1-1-1
2001-02 in Australia	0-0-3
2001-02 V Bangladesh	2-0-0
2001-02 V England	1-1-1
2002 in Pakistan	0-1-0
2002 in West Indies	1-0-1
2002-03 V India	2-0-0
2003 in Sri Lanka	0-0-2

2003-04 in India	0-0-2
2003-04 V Pakistan	0-1-1
2003-04 V South Africa	1-1-1
2004 in England	0-3-0
2004-05 in Bangladesh	2-0-0
2004-05 in Australia	0-2-0
2004-05 V Australia	0-2-1
2004-05 V Sri Lanka	1-0-1
2005 in Zimbabwe	2-0-0
2005-06 V West Indies	2-0-1
2005-06 in South Africa	0-2-1
2006-07 V Sri Lanka	1-1-0
2007-08 in South Africa	0-2-0
2007-08 V Bangladesh	2-0-0
2007-08 V England	1-2-0
2008 in England	0-2-1
2008-09 in Bangladesh	1-0-1
2008-09 in Australia	0-2-0
2008-09 V West Indies	0-0-2

2008-09 V India	0-1-2
2009 in Sri Lanka	0-2-0
2009-10 V Pakistan	1-1-1
2009-10 V Bangladesh	1-0-0
2009-10 V Australia	0-2-0
2010-11 in India	0-1-2
2010-11 V Pakistan	0-1-1
2011-12 in Zimbabwe	1-0-0
2011-12 in Australia	1-1-0
2011-12 V Zimbabwe	1-0-0
2011-12 V South Africa	0-1-2
2012 in West Indies	0-2-0
2012 in India	0-2-0
2012-13 in Sri Lanka	1-1-0
2012-13 in South Africa	0-2-0
2012-13 V England	0-0-3
2013 in England	0-2-0
2013-14 in Bangladesh	0-0-2
2013-14 V West Indies	2-0-1

2013-14 V India	1-0-1
2014 in West Indies	2-1-0
2014-15 V Pakistan[18]	1-1-1
2014-15 V Sri Lanka	2-0-0
2015 in England	1-1-0
2015-16 in Australia	0-2-1
2015-16 V Sri Lanka	2-0-0
2015-16 V Australia	0-2-0
2016 in Zimbabwe	2-0-0
2016 in South Africa	0-1-1
2016-17 in India	0-3-0
2016-17 V Pakistan	2-0-0
2016-17 V Bangladesh	2-0-0
2016-17 V South Africa	0-1-2
2017-18 V West Indies	2-0-0
2017-18 V England	1-0-1
2018-19 V Pakistan[19]	2-1-0

[18] Series played in United Arab Emirates
[19] Series played in United Arab Emirates

2018-19 V Sri Lanka	1-0-1
2018-19 V Bangladesh	2-0-0
2019 in Sri Lanka	1-1-0
2019-20 V England	1-0-1
2019-20 in Australia	0-3-0
2019-20 V India	2-0-0
2020-21 V West Indies	2-0-0
2020-21 V Pakistan	2-0-0
2021 in England	1-0-1
2021 V India[20]	1-0-0
2021-22 in India	0-1-1
2021-22 V Bangladesh	1-1-0
2021-22 V South Africa	1-1-0
2022 in England	0-3-0

[20] Played in England, this was the final of the World Test Cup

INDIA

England brought cricket to India in the 1700s, but local players were not invited to play against the English until 1877. In the early years of the twentieth century, several Indian players were selected for the England test team.

India joined the Imperial Cricket Council in 1926, and played their first test against England in London in 1932. England toured India in 1933-34, and India returned to England in 1936; but momentum was stalled by the outbreak of war in Europe in 1939.

After the war, India toured England in 1946, and Australia in the summer of 1947-48. In 1948-49, they hosted West Indies for the first time, and in 1952-53 they welcomed the new nation of Pakistan for a five test series; the first series win for India.

India played New Zealand for the first time in 1955-56, and recorded their second test series win. They would have to wait until 1967-68 to record their first away test series win, against New Zealand.

The win against New Zealand was the impetus for away series wins in England and West Indies in the early 1970s. However, they lost a home series to England in 1976-77.

In 1977-78 India lost an away series 3-2 to Australia at the height of the World Series Cricket outbreak in an epic series.

India hosted Sri Lanka for the first time in 1982-83, and toured the country in 1985. In 1992-93, India visited Zimbabwe and played a drawn test.

Since 1996-97, the prize for the winner of the test seris between India and Australia has been the Border-Gavaskar Trophy. India won the trophy with a win in the one-off test that season.

In 2000-01, India toured Bangladesh for the first time and won the only test. India steadily became a dominant force in test cricket, but lost their first chance of winning the new Pataudi Trophy when they went down 4-0 to England in 2011.

In 2018, India defeated Afghanistan in the fledgling test nation's debut. Later that year, India won the Border-Gavaskar Trophy by beating Australia on their home turf for the first time. India again left Australia victorious in 2020-21.

MOST TESTS

Sachin Tendulkar	200 (1989-2013)
Rahul Dravid	163 (1996-2012)
VVS Laxman	134 (1996-2012)
Anil Kumble	132 (1990-2008)
Kapil Dev	131 (1978-1994)
Sunil Gavaskar	125 (1971-1987)
Dilip Vengsarkar	116 (1976-1992)
Sourav Ganguly	113 (1996-2008)
Ishant Sharma	105 (2007-2021)
Harbhajan Singh	103 (1998-2015)
Virender Sehwag	103 (2001-2013)
Virat Kohli	102 (2011-2022)*
Mohammad Azharuddin	99 (1984-2000)
Cheteshwar Pujara	96 (2010-2022)*
Zaheer Khan	92 (2000-2014)
Gundappa Viswanath	91 (1969-1983)
MS Dhoni	90 (2005-2014)
Syed Kirmani	88 (1976-1986)

Ravichandran Ashwin	846(2011-2022)*
Ajinkya Rahane	82 (2013-2022)*
Ravi Shastri	80 (1981-1992)
Mohinder Amarnath	69 (1969-1988)
Bishan Bedi	67 (1966-1979)
Javagal Srinath	67 (1991-2002)
Murali Vijay	61 (2008-2018)
Ravindra Jadeja	60 (2012-2022)*
Mohammed Shami	60 (2013-2022)*
Polly Umrigar	59 (1948-1962)
Bhagwath Chandrasekhar	58 (1964-1979)
Gautam Gambhir	58 (2004-2016)
Srinivas Venkataraghavan	57 (1965-1983)
Chandu Borde	55 (1958-1969)
Vijay Manjrekar	55 (1951-1965)
Umesh Yadav	52 (2011-2022)*
Navjot Sidhu	51 (1983-1999)
Kiran More	49 (1986-1993)
Erapalli Prasanna	49 (1962-1978)

MOST RUNS

Sachin Tendulkar	15921 (1989-2013)
Rahul Dravid	13265 (1996-2012)
Sunil Gavaskar	10122 (1971-1987)
VVS Laxman	8781 (1996-2012)
Virender Sehwag	8503 (2011-2013)
Virat Kohli	8074 (2011-2022)*
Sourav Ganguly	7212 (1996-2008)
Dilip Vengsarkar	6868 (1976-1992)
Cheteshwar Pujara	6792 (2010-2022)*
Mohammad Azharuddin	6215 (1984-2000)
Gundappa Viswanath	6080 (1969-1983)
Kapil Dev	5248 (1978-1994)
Ajinkya Rahane	4931 (2013-2022)*
MS Dhoni	4876 (2005-2014)
Mohinder Amarnath	4378 (1969-1988)
Gautam Gambhir	4154 (2004-2016)
Murali Vijay	3982 (2008-2018)
Ravi Shastri	3830 (1981-1992)

Polly Umrigar	3631 (1948-1962)
Vijay Manjrekar	3208 (1951-1965)
Navot Sidhu	3202 (1983-1999)
Rohit Sharma	3137 (2013-2022)*
Chandu Borde	3061 (1958-1969)
Ravichandran Ashwin	2931 (2011-2022)*
Mansur Pataudi	2793 (1961-1975)
Syed Kirmani	2759 (1976-1986)
Farokh Engineer	2611 (1961-1975)
Kannaur Rahul	2547 (2014-2022)*
Ravindra Jadeja	2523 (2012-2022)*
Anil Kumble	2506 (1990-2008)
Pankaj Roy	2442 (1951-1960)
Shikhar Dhawan	2315 (2013-2018)
Harbhajan Singh	2224 (1998-2015)
Vijay Hazare	2192 (1946-1953)
Rishabh Pant	2123 (2018-2022)*
Ajit Wadekar	2113 (1966-1974)
Vinoo Mankad	2109 (1946-1959)

MOST WICKETS

Anil Kumble	619 (1990-2008)
Ravichandran Ashwin	442 (2011-2022)*
Kapil Dev	434 (1978-1994)
Harbhajan Singh	417 (1998-2015)
Zaheer Khan	311 (2000-2014)
Ishant Sharma	311 (2007-2021)
Bishan Bedi	266 (1966-1979)
Ravindra Jadeja	242 (2012-2022)*
Bhagwath Chandrasekhar	242 (1964-1979)
Javagal Srinath	236 (1991-2002)
Mohammed Shami	216 (2013-2022)*
Erapalli Prasanna	189 (1962-1978)
Vinoo Mankad	162 (1946-1959)
Umesh Yadav	158 (2011-2022)*
Srinivas Venkataraghavan	156 (1965-1983)
Ravi Shastri	151 (1981-1992)
Subhash Gupte	149 (1951-1961)
Jasprot Bumrah	128 (2018-2022)*

Dilip Doshi	114 (1979-1983)
Pragyan Ojha	113 (2009-2013)
Karsan Ghavri	109 (1974-1981)
Shivlal Yadav	102 (1979-1987)
Irfan Pathan	100 (2003-2008)
Venkatesh Prasad	96 (1996-2001)
Manoj Prabhakar	96 (1984-1995)
Venkatapathy Raju	93 (1990-2001)
Bapu Nadkarni	88 (1955-1968)
Maninder Singh	88 (1982-1993)
Gopu Sreesanth	87 (2006-2011)
Amit Mishra	76 (2008-2016)
Salim Surani	75 (1960-1973)
Ramakant Desai	74 (1959-1968)
Madan Lal	71 (1974-1986)
Ghulam Ahmed	68 (1948-1959)
Narendra Hirwani	66 (1988-1996)
Bhuvneshwar Kumar	63 (2013-2018)
Dattu Phadkar	62 (1947-1959)

HIGHEST SCORES

Virender Sehwag	319 V South Africa, 2008
Virender Sehwag	309 V Pakistan, 2004
Karun Nair	303* V England, 2016
Virender Sehwag	293 V Sri Lanka, 2009
VVS Laxman	281 V Australia, 2001
Rahul Dravid	270 V Pakistan, 2004
Virat Kohli	254* V South Africa, 2019
Virender Sehwag	254 V Pakistan, 2006
Sachin Tendulkar	248* V Bangladesh, 2004
Virat Kohli	243 V Sri Lanka, 2017
Mayank Agarwal	243 V Bangladesh, 2019
Sachin Tendulkar	241* V Australia, 2004
Sourav Ganguly	239 V Pakistan, 2007
Sunil Gavaskar	236* V West Indies, 1983
Virat Kohli	235 V England, 2016
Rahul Dravid	233 V Australia, 2003
Vinoo Mankad	231 V New Zealand, 1956
Vinod Kambli	227 V Zimbabwe, 1993

Vinod Kambli	224 V England, 1993
MS Dhoni	224 V Australia, 2013
Polly Umrigar	223 V New Zealand, 1955
Vinoo Mankad	223 V New Zealand, 1955
Gundappa Viswanath	222 V England, 1982
Rahul Dravid	222 V New Zealand, 2003
Sunil Gavaskar	221 V England, 1979
Sunil Gavaskar	220 V West Indies, 1971
Sanjay Manjrekar	218 V Pakistan, 1989
Sachin Tendulkar	217 V New Zealand, 1999
Rahul Dravid	217 V England, 2002
Mayank Agarwal	215 V South Africa, 2019
Sachin Tendulkar	214 V Australia, 2010
Virat Kohli	213 V Sri Lanka, 2017
Dilip Sardesai	212 V West Indies, 1971
Wasim Jaffer	212 V West Indies, 2006
Rohit Sharma	212 V South Africa, 2019
Virat Kohli	211 V New Zealand, 2016
Cheteshwar Pujara	206* V England, 2012

MOST CENTURIES

Sachin Tendulkar	51 (1989-2013)
Rahul Dravid	36 (1996-2012)
Sunil Gavaskar	34 (1971-1987)
Virat Kohli	27 (2011-2022)*
Virender Sehwag	23 (2001-2013)
Mohammad Azarhuddin	22 (1984-1990)
Cheteshwar Pujara	18 (2010-2022)*
Dilip Vengsarkar	17 (1976-1992)
VVS Laxman	17 (1996-2012)
Sourav Ganguly	16 (1996-2008)
Gundappa Viswanath	14 (1969-1983)
Polly Umrigar	12 (1948-1962)
Murali Vijay	12 (2008-2018)
Ajinkya Rahane	12 (2013-2022)*
Mohinder Amarnath	11 (1969-1988)
Ravi Shastri	11 (1981-1992)
Navjot Sidhu	9 (1983-1999)
Gautam Gambhir	9 (2004-2016)

MOST 50S (50-99)

Sachin Tendulkar	68 (1989-2013)
Rahul Dravid	63 (1996-2012)
VVS Laxman	56 (1996-2012)
Sunil Gavaskar	45 (1971-1987)
Dilip Vengsarkar	35 (1976-1992)
Sourav Ganguly	35 (1996-2008)
Gundappa Viswanath	35 (1969-1983)
MS Dhoni	33 (2005-2014)
Cheteshwar Pujara	33 (2010-2022)*
Virender Sehwag	31 (2001-2013)
Virat Kohli	28 (2011-2022)*
Kapil Dev	27 (1978-1994)
Ajinkya Rahane	25 (2013-2022)*
Mohinder Amarnath	24 (1969-1988)
Gautam Gambhir	22 (2004-2016)
Mohammad Azharuddin	21 (1984-2000)
Chandu Borde	18 (1958-1969)

MOST DISMISSALS AS WICKET KEEPER

MS Dhoni	294 (256ct, 38st) (2005-2014)
Syed Kirmani	198 (160ct, 38st) (1976-1986)
Kiran More	130 (110ct, 20st) (1986-1993)
Rishabh Pant	122 (111ct, 11st) (2018-2022)*
Nayan Mongia	107 (99ct, 8st) (1994-2001)
Wriddhiman Saha	104 (92ct, 12st) (2010-2021)
Farokh Engineer	82 (66ct, 16st) (1961-1975)
Parthiv Patel	72 (62ct, 10st) (2002-2018)
Dinesh Karthik	57 (51ct, 6st) (2004-2018)
Naren Tamhane	51 (35ct, 16st) (1955-1961)
Khokhan Sen	31 (20ct, 11st) (1948-1952)
Budhi Kunderan	28 (21ct, 7st) (1960-1967)
Nana Joshi	27 (18ct, 9st) (1951-1960)
Mannava Prasad	15 (15ct) (1999-2000)
Sameer Dighe	14 (12ct, 2st) (2001)
Chandrakant Pandit	13 (11ct, 2st) (1986-1992)
Ajay Ratra	13 (11ct, 2st) (2002)
Deep Dasgupta	13 (13ct) (2001-2002)

MOST CATCHES (FIELDER)

Rahul Dravid	209 (1996-2012)
VVS Laxman	135 (1996-2012)
Sachin Tendulkar	115 (1989-2013)
Sunil Gavaskar	108 (1971-1987)
Mohammad Azharuddin	105 (1984-2000)
Virat Kohli	102 (2011-2022)*
Ajinkya Rahane	99 (2013-2022)*
Virender Sehwag	90 (2001-2013)
Dilip Vengsarkar	78 (1976-1992)
Sourav Ganguly	71 (1996-2008)
Kapil Dev	64 (1978-1994)
Cheteshwar Pujara	64 (2010-2022)*
Gundappa Viswanath	63 (1969-1983)
Anil Kumble	60 (1990-2008)
Eknath Solkar	53 (1969-1977)
Murali Vijay	49 (2008-2018)
Kannaur Rahul	49 (2014-2022)*
Rohit Sharma	49 (2013-2022)*

BEST BATTING AVERAGES (MINIMUM 20 INNINGS)

Vinod Kambli	54.20 (21) (1993-1995)
Sachin Tendulkar	53.78 (329) (1989-2013)
Rahul Dravid	52.62 (284) (1996-2012)
Sunil Gavaskar	51.12 (214) (1971-1987)
Virat Kohli	49.53 (173) (2011-2022)*
Virender Sehwag	49.43 (178) (2001-2013)
Vijay Hazare	47.65 (52) (1946-1953)
Rohit Sharma	46.13 (77) (2013-2022)*
VVS Laxman	45.97 (225) (1996-2012)
Mohammad Azharuddin	45.03 (147) (1984-2000)
Cheteshwar Pujara	43.81 (164) (2010-2022)*
Rishabh Pant	43.32 (53) (2018-2022)*
Mohinder Amarnath	42.50 (147) (1984-2000)
Polly Umrigar	42.22 (94) (1948-1962)
Sourav Ganguly	42.17 (188) (1996-2008)
Dilip Vengsarkar	42.13 (185) (1976-1992)
Navjot Sidhu	42.13 (78) (1983-1999)
Gautam Gambhir	41.95 (104) (2004-2016)

Gundappa Viswanath	41.92 (155) (1969-1983)
Mayank Agarwal	41.33 (36) (2018-2022)*
Shikhar Dhawan	40.61 (58) (2013-2018)
Dilip Sardesai	39.23 (55) (1961-1972)
Vijay Manjrekar	39.12 (92) (1951-1965)
Ajinkya Rahane	38.52 (140) (2013-2022)*
Murali Vijay	38.28 (105) (2008-2018)
MS Dhoni	38.09 (144) (2005-2014)
Sadagoppan Ramesh	37.97 (37) (1999-2001)
Sanjay Manjrekar	37.14 (61) (1987-1996)
Sandeep Patil	36.93 (47) (1980-1984)
Ravindra Jadeja	36.56 (89) (2012-2022)*
Ravi Shastri	35.79 (121) (1981-1992)
Chandu Borde	35.59 (97) (1958-1969)
Kannaur Rahul	35.37 (74) (2014-2022)*
Mansur Pataudi	34.91 (83) (1961-1975)
Shiv Das	34.89 (40) (2000-2002)
Wasim Jaffer	34.10 (58) (2000-2008)
Yuvraj Singh	33.92 (62) (2003-2012)

BEST BOWLING AVERAGES (2000+ BALLS)

Jasprit Bumrah	21.99 (128W) (2018-2022)*
Ravichandran Ashwin	24.13 (442W) (2011-2022)*
Ravindra Jadeja	24.71 (242W) (2012-2022)*
Bhuvneshwar Kumar	26.09 (63W) (2013-2018)
Mohammed Shami	27.45 (216W) (2013-2022)*
Bishan Bedi	28.71 (266W) (1966-1979)
Bapu Nadkami	29.07 (88W) (1955-1968)
Subhash Gupte	29.55 (149W) (1951-1961)
Mohammad Siraj	29.63 (36W) (@020-2022)*
Kapil Dev	29.64 (434W) (1978-1994)
Anil Kumble	29.65 (619W) (1990-2008)
Bhagwath Chandrasekhar	29.74 (242W) (1964-1979)
Narendra Hirwani	30.10 (66W) (1988-1996)
Ghulam Ahmed	30.17 (68W) (1948-1959)
Pragyan Ojha	30.26 (113W) (2009-2013)
Erapalli Prasanna	30.38 (189W) (1962-1978)
Javagal Srinath	30.49 (236W) (1991-2002)
Amar Singh	30.64 (28W) (1932-1936)

Dilip Doshi	30.71 (114W) (1979-1983)
Venkatapathy Raju	30.72 (93W) (1990-2001)
Mohammed Siraj	30.77 (40W) (2020-2022)*
Umesh Yadav	30.80 (158W) (2011-2022)*
Irfan Pathan	32.26 (100W) (2003-2008)
Vinoo Mankad	32.32 (162W) (1946-1959)
Ishant Sharma	32.40 (311W) (2007-2021)
Harbhajan Singh	32.46 (417W) (1998-2015)
Roger Binny	32.63 (47W) (1979-1987)
Lala Amarnath	32.91 (5W) (1933-1952)
Zaheer Khan	32.94 (311W) (2000-2014)
Karsan Ghavri	33.54 (109W) (1974-1981)
Venkatesh Prasad	35.00 (96W) (1996-2001)
Arshad Ayub	35.07 (41W) (1987-1989)
Shivlal Yadav	35.09 (102W) (1979-1987)
Salim Durani	35.42 (75W) (1960-1973)
Chetan Sharma	35.45 (61W) (1984-1989)
Amit Mishra	35.72 (76W) (2008-2016)
Sunil Joshi	35.85 (41W) (1996-2000)

BEST FIGURES IN AN INNINGS

Anil Kumble	10/74 V Pakistan, 1999
Jasubhai Patel	9/69 V Australia, 1959
Kapil Dev	9/83 V West Indies, 1983
Subhash Gupte	9/102 V West Indies, 1959
Vinoo Mankad	8/52 V Pakistan, 1952
Vinoo Mankad	8/55 V England, 1952
Narendra Hirwani	8/61 V West Indies, 1988
Srinivas Vengataraghavan	8/72 V New Zealand, 1965
Narendra Hirwani	8/75 V West Indies, 1988
Erapalli Prasanna	8/76 V New Zealand, 1976
Bhagwath Chandrasekhar	8/79 V England, 1972
Harbhajan Singh	8/84 V Australia, 2001
Kapil Dev	8/85 V Pakistan, 1983
Javagal Srinath	8/86 V Pakistan, 1999
Kapil Dev	8/106 V Australia, 1985
Anil Kumble	8/141 V Australia, 2004
Maninder Singh	7/27 V Pakistan, 1987
Harbhajan Singh	7/48 V West Indies, 2002

BEST FIGURES IN A MATCH

Narendra Hirwani	16/136 V West Indies, 1988
Harbhajan Singh	15/217 V Australia, 2001
Jasubhai Patel	14/124 V Australia, 1959
Anil Kumble	14/149 V Pakistan, 1999
Vinoo Mankad	13/131 V Pakistan, 1952
Javagal Srinath	13/132 V Pakistan, 1999
Ravichandran Ashwin	13/140 V New Zealand, 2016
Anil Kumble	13/181 V Australia, 2004
Harbajan Singh	13/196 V Australia, 2001
Ravichandran Ashwin	12/85 V New Zealand, 2012
Ravichandran Ashwin	12/98 V South Africa, 2015
Bhagwath Chandrasekhar	12/104 V Australia, 1977
Vinoo Mankad	12/108 V England, 1952
Irfan Pathan	12/126 V Zimbabwe, 2005
Srinivas Venkataraghavan	12/152 V New Zealand, 1965
Ravichandran Ashwin	12/167 V England, 2016
Laxman Sivaramakrishnan	12/181 V England, 1984
Ravichandran Ashwin	12/198 V Australia, 2013

MOST FIVE WICKETS IN AN INNINGS

Anil Kumble	35 (1990-2008)
Ravichandran Ashwin	30 (2011-2022)*
Harbhajan Singh	25 (1998-2015)
Kapil Dev	23 (1978-1994)
Bhagwath Chandrasekhar	16 (1964-1979)
Bishan Bedi	14 (1966-1969)
Subhash Gupte	12 (1951-1961)
Ishant Sharma	11 (2007-2021)
Zaheer Khan	11 (2000-2014)
Erapalli Prasanna	10 (1962-1978)
Javagal Srinath	10 (1991-2002)
Ravindra Jajeda	10 (2012-2022)*
Vinoo Mankad	8 (1946-1959)
Jasprit Bumrah	8 (2018-2022)*
Irfan Pathan	7 (2003-2008)
Venkatesh Prasad	7 (1996-2001)
Pragyan Ojha	7 (2009-2013)

INDIA TEST SERIES RESULTS

DATE OPPONENT	RESULT (W-L-D)
1932 in England	0-1-0
1933-34 V England	0-2-1
1936 in England	0-2-1
1946 in England	0-1-2
1947-48 in Australia	0-4-1
1948-49 V West Indies	0-1-4
1951-52 V England	1-1-3
1952 in England	0-3-1
1952-53 V Pakistan	2-1-2
1952-53 in West Indies	0-1-4
1954-55 in Pakistan	0-0-5
1955-56 V New Zealand	2-0-3
1956-57 V Australia	0-2-1
1958-59 V West Indies	0-3-2
1959 in England	0-5-0
1959-60 V Australia	1-2-2
1960-61 V Pakistan	0-0-5

1961-62 V England	2-0-3
1961-62 in West Indies	0-5-0
1963-64 V England	0-0-5
1864-65 V Australia	1-1-1
1964-65 V New Zealand	1-0-3
1966-67 V West Indies	0-2-1
1967 in England	0-3-0
1967-68 in Australia	0-4-0
1967-68 in New Zealand	3-1-0
1969-70 V New Zealand	1-1-1
1969-70 V Australia	1-3-1
1970-71 in West Indies	1-0-4
1971 in England	1-0-2
1972-73 V England	2-1-2
1974 in England	0-3-0
1974-75 V West Indies	2-3-0
1975-76 in New Zealand	1-1-1
1975-76 in West Indies	1-2-1
1976-77 V New Zealand	2-0-1

1976-77 V England	1-3-1
1977-78 in Australia	2-3-0
1978-79 in Pakistan	0-2-1
1978-79 V West Indies	1-0-5
1979 in England	0-1-3
1979-80 V Australia	2-0-4
1979-80 V Pakistan	2-0-4
1979-80 V England	0-1-0
1980-81 in Australia	1-1-1
1980-81 in New Zealand	0-1-2
1981-82 V England	1-0-5
1982 in England	0-1-2
1982-83 V Sri Lanka	0-0-1
1982-83 in Pakistan	0-3-3
1982-83 in West Indies	0-2-3
1983-84 V Pakistan	0-0-3
1983-84 V West Indies	0-3-3
1984-85 in Pakistan	0-0-2
1984-85 V England	1-2-2

1985 in Sri Lanka	0-1-2
1985-86 in Australia	0-0-3
1986 in England	2-0-1
1986-87 V Australia	0-0-3[21]
1986-87 V Sri Lanka	2-0-1
1986-87 V Pakistan	0-1-4
1987-88 V West Indies	1-1-2
1988-89 V New Zealand	2-1-0
1988-89 in West Indies	0-3-1
1989-90 in Pakistan	0-0-4
1989-90 in New Zealand	0-1-2
1990 in England	0-1-2
1990-91 V Sri Lanka	1-0-0
1991-92 in Australia	0-4-1
1992-93 in Zimbabwe	0-0-1
1992-93 in South Africa	0-1-3
1992-93 V England	3-0-0

[21] Includes one tied test

1992-93 V Zimbabwe	1-0-0
1993 in Sri Lanka	1-0-2
1993-94 V Sri Lanka	3-0-0
1993-94 in New Zealand	0-0-1
1994-95 V West Indies	1-1-1
1995-96 V New Zealand	1-0-2
1996 in England	0-1-2
1996-97 V Australia	1-0-0
1996-97 V South Africa	2-1-0
1996-97 in South Africa	0-2-1
1996-97 in West Indies	0-1-4
1997 in Sri Lanka	0-0-2
1997-98 V Sri Lanka	0-0-3
1997-98 V Australia	2-1-0
1998-99 in Zimbabwe	0-1-0
1998-99 in New Zealand	0-1-1
1998-99 V Pakistan	1-1-0
1999 V Pakistan	0-1-0
1999 in Sri Lanka	0-0-1

1999-2000 V New Zealand	1-0-2
1999-2000 in Australia	0-3-0
1999-2000 V South Africa	0-2-0
2000-01 in Bangladesh	1-0-0
2000-01 V Zimbabwe	1-0-1
2000-01 V Australia	2-1-0
2001 in Zimbabwe	1-1-0
2001 in Sri Lanka	1-2-0
2001-02 in South Africa	0-1-1
2001-02 V England	1-0-2
2001-02 V Zimbabwe	2-0-0
2002 in West Indies	1-2-2
2002 in England	1-1-2
2002-03 V West Indies	2-0-1
2002-03 in New Zealand	0-2-0
2003-04 V New Zealand	0-0-2
2003-04 in Australia	1-1-2
2003-04 in Pakistan	2-1-0
2004-05 V Australia	1-2-1

2004-05 V South Africa	1-0-1
2004-05 in Bangladesh	2-0-0
2004-05 V Pakistan	1-1-1
2005 in Zimbabwe	2-0-0
2005-06 V Sri Lanka	2-0-1
2005-06 in Pakistan	0-1-2
2005-06 V England	1-1-1
2006 in West Indies	1-0-3
2006-07 in South Africa	1-2-0
2007 in Bangladesh	1-0-1
2007 in England	1-0-2
2007-08 V Pakistan	1-0-2
2007-08 in Australia	1-2-1
2007-08 V South Africa	1-1-1
2008 in Sri Lanka	1-2-0
2008-09 V Australia	2-0-2
2008-09 V England	1-0-1
2008-09 in New Zealand	1-0-2
2009-10 V Sri Lanka	2-0-1

2009-10 in Bangladesh	2-0-0
2009-10 V South Africa	1-1-0
2010 in Sri Lanka	1-1-1
2010-11 V Australia	2-0-0
2010-11 V New Zealand	1-0-2
2010-11 in South Africa	1-1-1
2011 in West Indies	1-0-2
2011 in England	0-4-0
2011-12 V West Indies	2-0-1
2011-12 in Australia	0-4-0
2012 V New Zealand	2-0-0
2012-13 V England	1-2-1
2012-13 V Australia	4-0-0
2013-14 V West Indies	2-0-0
2013-14 in South Africa	0-1-1
2013-14 in New Zealand	0-1-1
2014 in England	1-3-1
2014-15 in Australia	0-2-2
2015 in Bangladesh	0-0-1

2015 in Sri Lanka	2-1-0
2015-16 V South Africa	3-0-1
2016 in West Indies	2-0-2
2016-17 V New Zealand	3-0-0
2016-17 V England	4-0-1
2016-17 V Bangladesh	1-0-0
2016-17 V Australia	2-1-1
2017 in Sri Lanka	3-0-0
2017-18 V Sri Lanka	1-0-2
2017-18 in South Africa	1-2-0
2018 V Afghanistan	1-0-0
2018 in England	1-4-0
2018-19 V West Indies	2-0-0
2018-19 in Australia	2-1-1
2019 in West Indies	2-0-0
2019-20 V South Africa	3-0-0
2019-20 V Bangladesh	2-0-0
2019-20 in New Zealand	0-2-0
2020-21 in Australia	2-1-1

2020-2021 V England	3-1-0
2021 V New Zealand[22]	0-1-0
2021-22 V New Zealand	1-0-1
2021-22 in South Africa	1-2-0
2021-22 V Sri Lanka	2-0-0
2021-22 in England	2-2-1

[22] Played in England, this was the final of the World Test Cup

PAKISTAN

In 1947, at the end of the Second World War, the nation of Pakistan was created following the partition of India. Cricket was already established as many clubs participated in Indian leagues.

In 1952-53, Pakistan toured India to play their first test matches. They lost 2-1 in a five test series. In 1954, they toured England, and returned with a drawn series over four tests.

1954-55 saw Pakistan host India. The following season, Pakistan hosted New Zealand and won a test series for the first time.

Pakistan had a home win in a one-off test against Australia in 1956-57, before swapping home and away series wins with West Indies.

Pakistan had to wait until 1964-65 for another series win, when they defeated New Zealand 2-0 in a three test home series.

Pakistan's nest series win was again against New Zealand when they were on tour in 1972-73. In 1979-80 they upset Australia 1-0 during a three test away series.

In 1982, Pakistan played Sri Lanka for the first time, and won their three test series 2-0. In the mid-1980s, Pakistan were able to beat England, India, New Zealand and Australia in test series.

Pakistan were at their peak in the early 1990s, and won the World Cup in Australia in 1992. They lost just one test series between 1990-91 and 1994-95. They played their first tests against Zimbabwe in 1996-97, and Bangladesh in 2001-02.

Security issues saw Pakistan forced to play their home test matches in the United Arab Emirates from 2006. They remained competitive before returning to home in 2019-20, where they defeated Sri Lanka, Bangladesh and South Africe.

England agreed to visit Pakistan in 2021 for the first time in fifteen years, but the visit was cancelled due to the outbreak of the COVID-19 pandemic. In 2022, Australia toured Pakistan for the first time since 1999.

MOST TESTS

Javed Miandad	124 (1976-1993)
Inzamam-ul-Haq	119 (1992-2007)
Younis Khan	118 (2000-2017)
Wasim Akram	104 (1985-2002)
Saleem Malik	103 (1982-1999)
Azhar Ali	95 (2010-2021)*
Mohammad Yousuf	90 (1998-2010)
Imran Khan	88 (1971-1992)
Waqar Younis	87 (1989-2003)
Wasim Bari	81 (1967-1984)
Zaheer Abbas	78 (1969-1985)
Asad Shafiq	77 (2010-2020)
Mudassar Nazar	76 (1976-1989)
Misbah-ul-Haq	75 (2001-2017)
Moin Khan	69 (1990-2004)
Abdul Qadir	67 (1977-1990)
Majid Khan	63 (1964-1983)
Danish Kaneria	61 (2000-2010)

Ijaz Ahmed	60 (1987-2001)
Asif Iqbal	58 (1964-1980)
Mushtaq Mohammad	57 (1959-1979)
Ramiz Raja	57 (1984-1997)
Wasim Raja	57 (1973-1985)
Hanif Mohammad	55 (1952-1969)
Mohammad Hafeez	55 (2003-2018)
Saeed Anwar	55 (1990-2001)
Sarfraz Nawaz	55 (1969-1984)
Kamran Akmal	53 (2002-2010)
Mushtaq Ahmed	52 (1990-2003)
Iqbal Qasim	50 (1976-1988)
Saqlain Mushtaq	49 (1995-2004)
Sarfaraz Ahmed	49 (2010-2019)
Mohsin Khan	48 (1978-1986)
Yasir Shah	48 (2014-2022)*
Aamer Sohail	47 (1992-2000)
Intikhab Alam	47 (1959-1977)
Umar Gul	47 (2003-2013)

MOST RUNS

Younis Khan	10099 (2000-2017)
Javed Miandad	8832 (1976-1993)
Inzamam-ul-Haq	8829 (1992-2007)
Mohammad Youuf	7530 (1998-2010)
Azhar Ali	7030 (2010-2022)*
Saleem Malik	5768 (1982-1999)
Misbah-ul-Haq	5222 (2001-2017)
Zaheer Abbas	5062 (1969-1985)
Asad Shafiq	4660 (2010-2020)
Mudassar Nazar	4114 (1976-1989)
Saeed Anwar	4052 (1990-2001)
Majid Khan	3931 (1964-1983)
Hanif Mohammad	3915 (1952-1969)
Imran Khan	3807 (1971-1992)
Mohammad Hafeez	3652 (2003-2018)
Mushtaq Mohammad	3643 (1959-1979)
Asif Iqbal	3575 (1964-1980)
Ijaz Ahmed	3315 (1987-2001)

Babar Azam	3122 (2016-2022)*
Saeed Ahmed	2991 (1958-1973)
Taufeeq Umar	2963 (2001-2014)
Wasim Akram	2898 (1985-2002)
Ramiz Raja	2833 (1984-1997)
Aamer Sohail	2823 (1992-2000)
Wasim Raja	2821 (1973-1985)
Moin Khan	2741 (1990-2014)
Mohsin Khan	2709 (1978-1986)
Shoaib Mohammad	2705 (1983-1995)
Sarfaraz Ahmed	2657 (2010-2019)
Kamran Akmal	2648 (2002-2010)
Sadiq Mohammad	2579 (1969-1981)
Imran Farhat	2400 (2001-2013)
Imtiaz Ahmed	2079 (1952-1962)

MOST WICKETS

Wasim Akram	414 (1985-2002)
Waqar Younis	373 (1989-2003)
Imran Khan	362 (1971-1992)
Danish Kaneria	261 (2000-2010)
Yasir Shah	244 (2014-2022)*
Abdul Qadir	236 (1977-1990)
Saqlain Mushtaq	208 (1995-2004)
Mushtaq Ahmed	185 (1990-2003)
Shoaib Akhtar	178 (1997-2007)
Saeed Ajmal	178 (2009-2014)
Sarfraz Narwaz	177 (1969-1984)
Iqbal Qasim	171 (1976-1988)
Umar Gul	163 (2003-2013)
Fazal Mahmood	139 (1952-1962)
Intikhab Alam	125 (1959-1977)
Mohammad Amir	119 (2009-2019)
Mohammad Asif	106 (2005-2010)
Abdul Razzaq	100 (1999-2006)

Abdur Rehman	99 (2007-2014)
Shaheen Shah Afridi	99 (2018-2022)*
Tauseef Ahemd	93 (1980-1993)
Mohammad Abbas	90 (2017-2021)
Mohammad Sami	85 (2001-2012)
Wahab Riaz	83 (2010-2018)
Mushtaq Mohammad	79 (1959-1979)
Hasan Ali	77 (2017-2021)*
Junaid Khan	71 (2011-2015)
Mahmood Hussain	68 (1952-1962)
Sikander Bakht	67 (1976-1983)
Mudassar Nazar	66 (1976-1989)
Azeem Hafeez	63 (1983-1985)
Pervez Sajjad	59 (1964-1973)
Rahat Ali	58 (2013-2018)
Khan Mohammad	54 (1952-1958)
Aaqib Javed	54 (1989-1998)
Zulfiqar Babar	54 (2013-2016)
Asif Iqbal	53 (1964-1980)

HIGHEST SCORES

Hanif Mohammad	337 V West Indies, 1958
Inzamam-ul-Haq	329 V New Zealand, 2002
Younis Khan	313 V Sri Lanka, 2009
Azhar Ali	302* V West Indies, 2016
Javed Miandad	280* V India, 1983
Zaheer Abbas	274 V England, 1971
Javed Miandad	271 V New Zealand, 1989
Younis Khan	267 V India, 2005
Javed Miandad	260 V England, 1987
Wasim Akram	257* V Zimbabwe, 1996
Shoaib Malik	245 V England
Zaheer Abbas	240 V England, 1974
Saleem Malik	237 V Australia, 1994
Taufeeq Umar	236 V Sri Lanka, 2011
Zaheer Abbas	235* V India, 1978
Mudassar Nazar	231 V India, 1983
Azhar Ali	226 V Bangladesh, 2015
Mohammad Hafeez	224 V Bangladesh, 2015

Mohammad Yousuf	223 V England, 2005
Younis Khan	218 V England, 2016
Abid Ali	215* V Zimbabwe, 2021
Zaheer Abbas	215 V India, 1982
Younis Khan	213 V Australia, 2014
Javed Miandad	211 V Australia, 1988
Ijaz Ahmed	211 V Sri Lanka, 1999
Taslim Arif	210* V Australia, 1980
Qasim Umar	210 V India, 1984
Imtiaz Ahmed	209 V New Zealand, 1955
Javed Miandad	206 V New Zealand, 1976
Qasim Umar	206 V Sri Lanka, 1985
Azhar Ali	205* V Australia, 2016
Aamer Sohail	205 V England, 1992
Yousuf Youhana	204* V Bangladesh, 2002
Hanif Mohammad	203* V New Zealand, 1965
Javed Miandad	203* V Sri Lanka, 1985
Shoaib Mohammad	203* V India, 29189
Shoaib Mohammad	203* V New Zealand, 1990

MOST CENTURIES

Younis Khan	34 (2000-2017)
Inzamam-ul-Haq	25 (1992-2007)
Mohammad Yousuf	24 (1998-2010)
Javed Miandad	23 (1976-1993)
Azhar Ali	19 (2010-2021)*
Saleem Malik	15 (1982-1999)
Ijaz Ahmed	12 (1987-2001)
Hanif Mohammad	12 (1952-1969)
Zaheer Abbas	12 (1969-1985)
Asad Shafiq	12 (2010-2020)
Saeed Anwar	11 (1990-2001)
Asif Iqbal	11 (1964-1980)
Mushtaq Mohammad	10 (1959-1979)
Mohammad Hafeez	10 (2003-2018)
Mudassar Nazar	10 (1976-1989)
Misbah-ul-Haq	10 (2001-2017)
Majid Khan	8 (1964-1983)

MOST 50S (50-99)

Inzamam-ul-Haq	46 (1992-2007)
Javed Miandad	43 (1976-1993)
Misbah-ul-Haq	39 (2001-2017)
Azhar Ali	35 (2010-2022)*
Younis Khan	33 (2000-2017)
Mohammad Yousif	33 (1998-2010)
Saleem Malik	29 (1982-1999)
Asad Shafiq	27 (2010-2020)
Saeed Anwar	25 (1990-2001)
Babar Azam	23 (2016-2022)*
Ramiz Raja	22 (1984-1997)
Zaheer Abbas	20 (1969-1985)
Mushtaq Mohammad	19 (1959-1979)
Majid Khan	19 (1964-1983)
Imran Khan	18 (1971-1992)
Wasim Raja	18 (1973-1985)
Sarfaraz Ahmed	18 (2010-2019)
Mudassar Nazar	17 (1976-1989)

MOST DISMISSALS AS WICKET KEEPER

Wasim Bari	228 (201ct, 27st) (1967-1984)
Kamran Akmal	206 (184ct, 22st) (2002-2010)
Sarfaraz Ahmed	167 (146ct, 21st) (2010-2019)
Moin Khan	147 (127ct, 20st) (1990-2004)
Rashid Latif	130 (199ct, 11st) (1992-2003)
Saleem Yousif	104 (91ct, 13st) (1982-1990)
Imtiaz Ahmed	90 (74ct, 16st) (1952-1962)
Adnan Akmal	77 (66ct, 11st) (2010-2014)
Mohammad Rizwan	70 (68ct, 2st) (2016-2021)*
Anil Dalpat	25 (22ct, 3st) (1984-1995)
Ashraf Ali	22 (17ct, 5st) (1982-1997)
Zulqarnain	10 (8ct, 2st) (1986)
Taslim Arif	9 (6ct, 3st) (1980)
Naushad Ali	9 (ct) (1965)
Nadeem Abbasi	6 (6ct) (1989)

MOST CATCHES (FIELDER)

Younis Khan	139 (2000-2017)
Javed Miandad	93 (1976-1993)
Inzamam-ul-Haq	81 (1992-2007)
Asad Shafiq	77 (2010-2020)
Azhar Ali	66 (2010-2022)*
Majid Khan	65 (1964-1983)
Mohammad Yousuf	65 (1998-2010)
Saleem Malik	65 (1982-1999)
Misbah-ul-Haq	50 (2001-2017)
Mudassar Nazar	48 (1976-1989)
Mohammad Hafeez	45 (2003-2018)
Ijaz Ahmed	45 (1987-2001)
Taufeeq Umar	44 (2001-2014)
Wasim Akram	44 (1985-2002)
Iqbal Qasim	42 (1976-1988)
Mushtaq Mohammad	42 (1959-1979)
Imran Farhat	40 (2001-2013)
Hanif Mohammad	38 (1952-1969)

BEST BATTING AVERAGES (MINIMUM 20 INNINGS)

Javed Miandad	52.57 (189) (1976-1993)
Mohammad Yousuf	52.29 (156) (1998-2010)
Younis Khan	52.05 (213) (2000-2017)
Inzamam-ul-Haq	50.16 (198) (1992-2007)
Abid Ali	49.16 (26) (2019-2021)
Babar Azam	47.30 (75) (2016-2022)*
Misbah-ul-Haq	46.62 (132) (2001-2017)
Saeed Anwar	45.52 (91) (1990-2001)
Zaheer Abbas	44.79 (124) (1969-1985)
Shoaib Mohammad	44.34 (68) (1983-1995)
Hanif Mohammad	43.98 (97) (1952-1969)
Saleem Malik	43.69 (154) (1982-1999)
Azhar Ali	42.53 (169) (2010-2021)*
Mohammad Rizwan	41.06 (37) (2016-2022)*
Ahmed Shehzad	40.91 (25) (2013-2017)
Saeed Ahmed	40.41 (78) (1958-1973)
Mushtaq Mohammad	39.17 (100) (1959-1979)
Majid Khan	38.92 (106) (1964-1983)

Fawad Alam	38.88 (30) (2009-2022)*
Asif Iqbal	38.85 (99) (1964-1980)
Asad Shafiq	38.19 (128) (2010-2020)
Mudassar Nazar	38.09 (116) (1976-1989)
Taufeeq Umar	37.98 (83) (2001-2014)
Asim Kamal	37.73 (20) (2003-2005)
Imran Khan	37.69 (126) (1971-1992)
Ijaz Ahmed	37.67 (92) (1987-2001)
Mohammad Hafeez	37.64 (105) (2003-2018)
Mohsin Khan	37.10 (79) (1978-1986)
Qasim Umar	36.63 (43) (1983-1986)
Shahid Afridi	36.51 (48) (1998-2010)
Sarfaraz Ahmed	36.39 (86) (2010-2019)
Wasim Raja	36.16 (92) (1973-1985)
Umar Akmal	35.82 (30) (2009-2011)
Sadiq Mohammad	35.81 (74) (1969-1981)
Aamer Sohail	35.28 (83) (1992-2000)
Shoaib Malik	35.14 (60) (2001-2015)
Haroon Rasheed	34.77 (36) (1977-1983)

BEST BOWLING AVERAGES (2000+ BALLS)

Imran Khan	22.81 (362W) (1971-1992)
Mohammad Abbas	23.02 (90W) (2017-2021)
Shabbir Ahmed	23.03 (51W) (2003-2005)
Waqar Younis	23.56 (373W) (1989-2003)
Wasim Akram	23.62 (414W) (1985-2002)
Pervez Sajjad	23/89 (59W) (1964-1973)
Khan Mohammad	23.92 (54W) (1952-1958)
Mohammad Asif	24.36 (106W) (2005-2010)
Hasan Ali	24.57 (77W) (2017-2022)*
Fazal Mahmood	24.70 (139W) (1952-1962)
Shaheen Shah Afridi	24.86 (99W) (2018-2022)*
Shoaib Akhtar	25.69 (178W) (1997-2007)
Saeed Ajmal	28.10 (178W) (2009-2014)
Iqbal Qasim	28.11 (171W) (1976-1988)
Asif Iqbal	28.33 (53W) (1964-1980)
Mushtaq Mohammad	29.22 (79W) (1959-1979)
Abdur Rehman	29.39 (99W) (2007-2014)
Saqlain Mushtaq	29.83 (208W) (1995-2004)

Arshad Khan	30.00 (32W) (1997-2005)
Mohammad Amir	30.47 (119W) (2009-2019)
Yasir Shah	31.38 (244W) (2014-2022)*
Saleem Jaffar	31.63 (36W) (1994-2002)
Tauseef Ahmed	31.72 (93W) (1980-1993)
Junaid Khan	31.73 (71W) (2011-2015)
Sarfraz Nawaz	32.75 (177W) (1969-1984)
Abdul Qadir	32.80 (236W) (1977-1990)
Mushtaq Ahmed	32.97 (185W) (1990-2003)
Mohammad Nazir	33.05 (34W) (1969-1983)
Umar Gul	34.06 (163W) (2003-2013)
Mohammad Hafeez	34.11 (53W) (2003-2018)
Nauman Ali	34.23 (30W) (2021-2022)*
Wahab Riaz	34.50 (83W) (2010-2018)
Aaqib Javed	34.70 (54W) (1989-1998)
Danish Kaneria	34.79 (261W) (2000-2010)
Azeem Hafeez	34.98 (63W) (1983-1985)
Shahid Nazir	35.33 (36W) (1996-2007)
Shahid Afridi	35.60 (48W) (1998-2010)

BEST BOWLING FIGURES IN AN INNINGS

Abdul Qadir	9/56 V England, 1987
Sarfraz Nawaz	9/86 V Australia, 1979
Yasir Shah	8/41 V New Zealand, 2018
Sajid Khan	8/42 V Bangladesh, 2021
Imran Khan	8/58 V Sri Lanka, 1982
Imran Khan	8/60 V India, 1982
Sikander Bakht	8/69 V India, 1979
Saqlain Mushtaq	8/164 V England, 2000
Imran Khan	7/40 V England, 1987
Fazal Mahmood	7/42 V India, 1952
Iqbal Qasim	7/49 V Australia, 1980
Intikhab Alam	7/52 V New Zealand, 1973
Imran Khan	7/52 V England, 1982
Saaed Ajmal	7/55 V England, 2012
Mushtaq Ahmed	7/56 V New Zealand, 1995
Mohammad Zahid	7/66 V New Zealand, 1996
Saqlain Mohammad	7/66 V Zimbabwe, 2002
Pervez Sajjad	7/74 V New Zealand, 1969

BEST BOWLING FIGURES IN A MATCH

Imran Khan	14/116 V Sri Lanka, 1982
Yasir Shah	14/184 V New Zealand, 2018
Abdul Qadir	13/101 V England, 1987
Fazal Mahmood	13/114 V Australia, 1956
Waqar Younis	13/135 V Zimbabwe, 1993
Fazal Mahmood	12/94 V India, 1952
Danish Kaneria	12/94 V Bangladesh, 2001
Fazal Mahmood	12/99 V England, 1954
Fazal Mahmood	12/100 V West Indies, 1959
Sajid Khan	12/128 V Bangladesh, 2021
Waqar Younis	12/130 V New Zealand, 1990
Imran Khan	12/165 V Australia, 1977
Mohammad Asif	11/71 V Sri Lanka, 2006
Shoaib Akhtar	11/78 V New Zealand, 2003
Zulfiqar Ahmed	11/79 V New Zealand, 1955
Imran Khan	11/79 V India, 1982
Wasim Akram	11/110 V West Indies, 2000
Saeed Ajmal	11/111 V West Indies, 2011

MOST FIVE WICKETS IN AN INNINGS

Wasim Akram	25 (1985-2002)
Imran Khan	23 (1971-1992)
Waqar Younis	22 (1989-2003)
Yasir Shah	16 (2014-2022)*
Abdul Qadir	15 (1977-1990)
Danish Kaneria	15 (2000-2010)
Fazal Mahmood	13 (1952-1962)
Saqlain Mushtaq	13 (1995-2004)
Shoaib Akhtar	12 (1997-2007)
Saeed Ajmal	10 (2009-2014)
Mushtaq Ahmed	10 (1990-2003)
Iqbal Qasim	8 (1976-1988)
Mohammad Asif	7 (2005-2010)
Hasan Ali	6 (2017-2022)*
Junaid Khan	5 (2011-2015)
Intikhab Alam	5 (1959-1977)

PAKISTAN TEST SERIES RESULTS

DATE OPPONENT	RESULT (W-L-D)
1952-53 in India	1-2-2
1954 in England	1-1-2
1954-55 V India	0-0-5
1955-56 V New Zealand	2-0-1
1956-57 V Australia	1-0-0
1957-58 in West Indies	1-3-1
1958-59 V West Indies	2-1-0
1959-60 V Australia	0-2-1
1960-61 in India	0-0-5
1961-62 V England	0-1-2
1962 in England	0-4-1
1964-65 V Australia	0-0-1
1964-65 in Australia	0-0-1
1964-65 in New Zealand	0-0-3
1964-65 V New Zealand	2-0-1
1967 in England	0-2-1
1968-69 V England	0-0-3

1969-70 V New Zealand	0-1-2
1971 in England	0-1-2
1972-73 in Australia	0-3-0
1972-73 in New Zealand	1-0-2
1972-73 V England	0-0-3
1974 in England	0-0-3
1974-75 V West Indies	0-0-2
1976-77 V New Zealand	2-0-1
1976-77 in Australia	1-1-1
1976-77 in West Indies	1-2-2
1977-78 V England	0-0-3
1978 in England	0-2-1
1978-79 V India	2-0-1
1978-79 in New Zealand	1-0-2
1978-79 in Australia	1-1-0
1979-80 in India	0-2-4
1979-80 V Australia	1-0-2
1980-81 V West Indies	0-1-3
1981-82 in Australia	1-2-0

1981-82 V Sri Lanka	2-0-1
1982 in England	1-2-0
1982-83 V Australia	3-0-0
1982-83 V India	3-0-3
1983-84 in India	0-0-3
1983-84 in Australia	0-2-3
1983-84 V England	1-0-2
1984-85 V India	0-0-2
1984-85 V New Zealand	2-0-1
1984-85 in New Zealand	0-2-1
1985-86 V Sri Lanka	2-0-1
1985-86 in Sri Lanka	1-1-1
1986-87 V West Indies	1-1-1
1986-87 in India	1-0-4
1987 in England	1-0-4
1987-88 V England	1-0-2
1987-88 in West Indies	1-1-1
1988-89 V Australia	1-0-2
1988-89 in New Zealand	0-0-2

1989-90 V India	0-0-4
1989-90 in Australia	0-1-2
1990-91 V New Zealand	3-0-0
1990-91 V West Indies	1-1-1
1991-92 V Sri Lanka	1-0-2
1992 in England	2-1-2
1992-93 in New Zealand	1-0-0
1992-93 in West Indies	0-2-1
1993-94 V Zimbabwe	2-0-1
1993-94 in New Zealand	2-1-0
1994 in Sri Lanka	2-0-0
1994-95 V Pakistan	1-0-2
1994-95 in South Africa	0-1-0
1994-95 in Zimbabwe	2-1-0
1995-96 V Sri Lanka	1-2-0
1995-96 in Australia	1-2-0
1995-96 in New Zealand	1-0-0
1996 in England	2-0-1
1996-97 V Zimbabwe	1-0-1

1996-97 V New Zealand	1-1-0
1996-97 in Sri Lanka	0-0-2
1997-98 V South Africa	0-1-2
1997-98 V West Indies	3-0-0
1997-98 in South Africa	1-1-1
1997-98 in Zimbabwe	1-0-1
1998-99 V Australia	0-1-2
1998-99 V Zimbabwe	0-1-2
1998-99 in India	1-1-0
1998-99 in India	1-0-0
1998-99 V Sri Lanka	0-0-1
1998-99 V Sri Lanka[23]	1-0-0
1999-2000 in Australia	0-3-0
1999-2000 V Sri Lanka	1-2-0
2000 in West Indies	0-1-2
2000 in Sri Lanka	2-0-1
2000-01 V England	0-1-2

[23] Played in Bangladesh

2000-01 in New Zealand	1-1-1
2001 in England	1-1-0
2001-02 in Bangladesh	2-0-0
2001-02 V West Indies[24]	2-0-0
2001-02 V Bangladesh	1-0-0
2001-02 V Sri Lanka	0-1-0
2002 V New Zealand	1-0-0
2002-03 V Australia[25]	0-3-0
2002-03 in Zimbabwe	2-0-0
2002-03 in South Africa	0-2-0
2003 V Bangladesh	3-0-0
2003-04 V South Africa	1-0-1
2003-04 in New Zealand	1-0-1
2003-04 V India	1-2-0
2004-05 V Sri Lanka	1-1-0
2004-05 in Australia	0-3-0
2004-05 in India	1-1-1

[24] Series played in United Arab Emirates
[25] Series played in Sri Lanka & United Arab Emirates

2005 in West Indies	1-1-0
2005-06 V England	2-0-1
2005-06 V India	1-0-2
2005-06 in Sri Lanka	1-0-1
2006 in England	0-3-1
2006-07 V West Indies	2-0-1
2006-07 in South Africa	1-2-0
2007-08 V South Africa	0-1-1
2007-08 in India	0-1-2
2008-09 V Sri Lanka	0-0-2
2009 in Sri Lanka	0-2-1
2009-10 in New Zealand	1-1-1
2009-10 in Australia	0-3-0
2010 V Australia[26]	1-1-0
2010 in England	1-3-0
2010-11 V South Africa[27]	0-0-2
2010-11 in New Zealand	1-0-1

[26] Series played in England
[27] Series played in United Arab Emirates

2011 in West Indies	1-1-0
2011 in Zimbabwe	1-0-0
2011-12 V Sri Lanka[28]	1-0-2
2011-12 in Bangladesh	2-0-0
2011-12 V England[29]	3-0-0
2012 in Sri Lanka	0-1-2
2012-13 in South Africa	0-3-0
2013 in Zimbabwe	1-1-0
2013-14 V South Africa[30]	1-1-0
2013-14 V Sri Lanka[31]	1-1-1
2014 in Sri Lanka	0-2-0
2014-15 V Australia[32]	2-0-0
2014-15 V New Zealand[33]	1-1-1
2015 in Bangladesh	1-0-1
2015 in Sri Lanka	2-1-0

[28] Series played in United Arab Emirates
[29] Series played in United Arab Emirates
[30] Series played in United Arab Emirates
[31] Series played in United Arab Emirates
[32] Series played in United Arab Emirates
[33] Series played in United Arab Emirates

2015-16 V England[34]	2-0-1
2016 in England	2-2-0
2016-17 V West Indies[35]	2-1-0
2016-17 in New Zealand	0-2-0
2016-17 in Australia	0-3-0
2017 in West Indies	2-1-0
2017-18 V Sri Lanka[36]	0-2-0
2018 in Ireland	1-0-0
2018 in England	1-1-0
2018-19 V Australia[37]	1-0-1
2018-19 V New Zealand[38]	1-2-0
2018-19 in South Africa	0-3-0
2019-20 in Australia	0-2-0
2019-20 V Sri Lanka	1-0-1
2019-20 V Bangladesh	1-0-1

[34] Series played in United Arab Emirates
[35] Series played in United Arab Emirates
[36] Series played in United Arab Emirates
[37] Series played in United Arab Emirates
[38] Series played in United Arab Emirates

2020 in England	0-1-2
2020-21 in New Zealand	0-2-0
2020-21 V South Africa	2-0-0
2021 in Zimbabwe	2-0-0
2021 in West Indies	1-1-0
2021-22 in Bangladesh	2-0-0
2021-22 V Australia	0-1-2
2022 in Sri Lanka	1-1-0

SRI LANKA

Like many other nations colonised by the British, Sri Lanka embraced cricket many years before they became an independent nation.

Cricket has been played in Sri Lanka since the 1830s, and accepted visiting teams from England and Australia in the latter years of the nineteenth century. A team from New South Wales toured the island nation in 1914.

The Ceylon Cricket Association was formed in 1922. Teams from England, Australi and India toured the nation between the wars. Ceylon attempted to achieve test status after the Second World War, but suffered a setback when a 1968 tour of England was cancelled due to board infighting.

In 1972, Ceylon officially changed its name to Sri Lanka. The nation participated in the 1975 World Cup, and in 1981, they were granted full test nation status by the International Cricket Council.

Sri Lanka played their first official test match when England visited the nation in 1982. Within the next year Sri Lanka visited Pakistan, India and New Zealand. Australia played their first test against Sri Lanka when they toured in 1982-83.

In 1985, Sri Lanka won a test series for the first time when they defeated India 1-0 in a three test series on home soil.

Sri Lanka wouldn't win a test series again until 1992-93, but that season beat New Zealand and England. By the mid-1990s they were winning their share of test series, claiming victories over New Zealand, Pakistan and Zimbabwe.

In 2002, Sri Lanka welcomed Bangladesh and beat them in both test matches. In 2007-08, Australia beat Sri Lanka to claim the new Warne-Muralithiran Trophy.

Since 2015-16, Sri Lanka and West Indies have battled for the Sobers-Tissera Trophy. Sri Lanka are the current holders.

As of time of writing, Australia holds the Warne-Muralithan Trophy. Sri Lanka lost 2-0 in a home series against England in 2020-21.

MOST TESTS

Mahela Jayawardene	149 (1997-2014)
Kumar Sangakkara	134 (2000-2015)
Muttiah Muralitharan	132 (1992-2010)
Chaminda Vaas	111 (1994-2009)
Sanath Jayasuriya	110 (1991-2007)
Aravinda de Silva	93 (1984-2002)
Rangana Herath	93 (1999-2018)
Arjuna Ranatunga	93 (1982-2000)
Angelo Mathews	100 (2009-2022)*
Marvan Atapattu	90 (1990-2007)
Tillakaratne Dilshan	87 (1999-2013)
Hashan Tillakaratne	83 (1989-2004)
Dimuth Karunaratne	82 (2012-2022)*
Thilan Samaraweera	81 (2001-2013)
Suranga Lakmal	70 (2010-2022)*
Dinesh Chandimal	70 (2011-2022)*
Prasanna Jayawardene	58 (2000-2015)
Roshan Mahanama	52 (1986-1998)

MOST RUNS

Kumar Sangakkara	12400 (2000-2015)
Mahela Jayawardene	11814 (1997-2014)
Sanath Jayasuriya	6973 (1991-2007)
Angelo Mathews	6953 (2009-2022)*
Aravinda de Silva	6361 (1984-2002)
Dimuth Karunaratne	6023 (2012-2022)*
Marvan Atapattu	5502 (1990-2007)
Tillakaratne Dilshan	5492 (1999-2013)
Thilan Samaraweera	5462 (2001-2013)
Arjuna Ranatunga	5105 (1982-2000)
Dinesh Chandimal	4936 (2011-2022)*
Hashan Tillakaratne	4545 (1989-2004)
Kusal Mendis	3402 (2015-2022)*
Chaminda Vaas	3089 (1994-2009)
Roshan Mahanama	2576 (1986-1998)
Dhananjaya De Silva	2815 (2016-2022)*
Niroshan Dickwella	2750 (2014-2022)*
Asanka Gurusinha	2452 (1985-1996)

MOST WICKETS

Muttiah Muralitharan	795 (1992-2010)
Rangana Herath	433 (1999-2018)
Chaminda Vaas	355 (1994-2009)
Suranga Lakmal	171 (2010-2022)*
Dilruwan Perera	161 (2014-2021)
Lasith Malinga	101 (2004-2010)
Dilhara Fernando	100 (2000-2012)
Sanath Jayasuriya	98 (1991-2007)
Pramodya Wickramasinghe	85 (1991-2001)
Dhammika Prasad	75 (2008-2015)
Rumesh Ratnayake	73 (1983-1992)
Lasith Embuldeniya	71 (2019-2022)*
Ajantha Mendis	70 (2008-2014)
Nuwan Pradeep	70 (2011-2017)
Kumar Dharmasena	69 (1993-2004)
Lahiru Kumara	70 (2016-2022)*
Kumar Dharmasena	69 (1993-2004)
Nuwan Zoysa	64 (1997-2004)

HIGHEST SCORES

Mahela Jayawardene	374 V South Africa, 2006
Sanath Jayasuriya	340 V India, 1997
Kumar Sangakkara	319 V Bangladesh, 2014
Kumar Sangakkara	287 V South Africa, 2006
Mahela Jayawardene	275 V India, 2009
Kumar Sangakkara	270 V Zimbabwe, 2004
Aravinda de Silva	267 V New Zealand, 1991
Sanath Jayasuriya	253 V Pakistan, 2004
Marvan Atapattu	249 V Zimbabwe, 2004
Dimuth Karunaratne	244 V Bangladesh, 2021
Mahela Jayawardene	242 V India, 1999
Mahela Jayawardene	240 V Pakistan, 2009
Mahela Jayawardene	237 V South Africa, 2004
Kumar Sangakkara	232 V South Africa, 2004
Thilan Samaraweera	231 V Pakistan, 2009
Kumar Sangakkara	230 V Pakistan, 2002
Roshan Mahanama	225 V India, 1997
Marvan Atapattu	223 V Zimbabwe, 1998

Kumar Sangakkara	222* V Bangladesh, 2007
Kumar Sangakkara	221 V Pakistan, 2014
Kumar Sangakkara	219 V India, 2010
Marvan Atapattu	216* V Zimbabwe, 1999
Thilan Samaraweera	214 V Pakistan, 2009
Mahela Jayawardene	213* V England, 2007
Sanath Jayasuriya	213 V England, 1998
Kumar Sangakkara	211 V Pakistan, 2011
Marvan Atapattu	207* V Pakistan, 2000
Dinesh Chandimal	206* V Australia, 2022
Aravinda de Silva	206 V Bangladesh, 2002
Hashan Tillakaratne	204* V West Indies, 2001
Mahela Jayawardene	203* V Bangladesh, 2014
Kumar Sangakkara	203 V New Zealand, 2015
Brendon Kuruppu	201* V New Zealand, 1987
Marvan Atapattu	201* V England, 2001
Marvan Atapattu	201 V Bangladesh, 2001
Kumar Sangakarra	200* V Bangladesh, 2007
Angelo Mathews	200* V Zimbabwe, 2020

MOST CENTURIES

Kumar Sangakkara	38 (2000-2015)
Mahela Jayawardine	34 (1997-2014)
Aravinda de Silva	20 (1984-2002)
Tillakaratne Dilshan	16 (1999-2013)
Marvan Atapattu	16 (2990-2007)
Thilan Samaraweera	14 (2001-2013)
Sanath Jayasuriya	14 (1991-2007)
Dimuth Karunaratne	14 (2012-2022)*
Dinesh Chandimal	13 (2011-2022)*
Angelo Mathews	13 (2009-2022)*
Hashan Tillakaratne	11 (1989-2004)
Dhananjaya de Silva	9 (2016-2021)*
Asanka Gurusinha	7 (1985-1996)
Kusal Mendis	7 (2015-2022)*

MOST 50S (50-99)

Kumar Sangakkara	52 (2000-2015)
Mahela Jayawardine	50 (1997-2014)
Arjuna Ranatunga	38 (1982-2000)
Angelo Mathews	38 (2009-2022)*
Dimuth Karunaratne	31 (2012-2022)*
Sanath Jayasuriya	31 (1991-2007)
Thilan Samaraweera	30 (2001-2013)
Dinesh Chandimal	24 (2011-2022)*
Tillakaratne Dilshan	23 (1999-2013)
Niroshan Dickwella	22 (2014-2022)*
Aravinda de Silva	22 (1984-2002)
Hashan Tillakaratne	20 (1989-2004)
Marvan Atapattu	17 (1990-2007)
Kusal Mendis	15 (2015-2022)*
Chaminda Vaas	13 (1994-2009)
Kaushal Silva	12 (2011-2018)
Roshan Mahanama	11 (1986-1998)
Tharanga Paranavitana	11 (2009-2012)

MOST DISMISSALS AS WICKET KEEPER

Niroshan Dickwella	157 (130ct, 27st) (2014-2022)*
Prasanna Jayawardene	156 (124ct, 32st) (2000-2015)
Kumar Sangakkara	151 (131ct, 20st) (2000-2015)
Romesh Kaluwitharana	119 (93ct, 26st) (1992-2004)
Dinesh Chandimal	73 (63ct, 10st) (2011-2022)*
Hashan Tillakaratne	35 (33ct, 2st) (1989-2004)
Amal Silva	34 (33ct, 1st) (1983-1988)
Pubudu Dassanayake	24 (19ct, 5st) (1993-1994)
Guy de Alwis	23 (21ct, 2st) (1983-1988)
Kusal Perera	22 (14ct, 8st) (2015-2021)*

MOST CATCHES AS FIELDER

Mahela Jayawardene	205 (1997-2014)
Hashan Tillakaratne	89 (1989-2004)
Sanath Jayasuriya	78 (1991-2007)
Tillakaratne Dilshan	77 (1999-2013)
Kusal Mendis	74 (2015-2022)*
Muttiah Muralitharan	70 (1992-2010)
Angelo Mathews	70 (2009-2022)*
Marvan Atapattu	58 (1990-2007)
Roshan Mahanama	56 (1986-1998)
Dimuth Karunaratne	55 (2012-2022)*
Dhananjaya de Silva	53 (2016-2022)*
Russel Arnold	51 (1997-2004)
Kumar Sangakkara	51 (2000-2015)
Arjuna Ranatunga	47 (1982-2000)
Thilan Samaraweera	45 (2001-2013)
Aravinda de Silva	43 (1984-2002)
Lahiru Thirimanne	36 (2011-2022)

BEST BATTING AVERAGES (MINIMUM 20 INNINGS)

Kumar Sangakkara	57.40 (233) (2000-2015)
Mahela Jayawardene	49.84 (252) (1997-2014)
Thilan Samaraweera	48.76 (132) (2001-2013)
Angelo Mathews	45.14 (178) (2009-2022)*
Dinesh Chandimal	43.29 (127) (2011-2022)*
Aravinda de Silva	42.97 (159) (1984-2002)
Hashan Tillakaratne	42.87 (131) (1989-2004)
Tillakaratne Dilshan	42.87 (131) (1989-2004)
Sanath Jayasuriya	40.07 (188) (1991-2007)
Dimuth Karunaratne	39.62 (158) (2012-2022)*
Marvan Atapattu	39.02 (156) (1990-2007)
Asanka Gurusinha	38.92 (70) (1985-1996)
Dhananjaya de Silva	37.53 (81) (2016-2022)*
Michael Vandort	36.90 (33) (2001-2008)
Roy Dias	36.71 (36) (1982-1987)
Oshada Fernando	35.82 (33) (2019-2022)*
Arjuna Ranatunga	35.69 (155) (1982-2000)
Malinda Warnapura	35.69 (24) (2007-2009)

Roshen Silva	35.10 (23) (2017-2019)
Kusal Mendis	34.36 (103) (2015-2022)*
Tharanga Paranavitana	32.58 (60) (2009-2012)
Upul Tharanga	31.89 (58) (2005-2017)
Duleep Mendis	31.64 (43) (1982-1988)
Niroshan Dickwella	31.60(94) (2014-2022)*
Kusal Perera	30.97 (41) (2015-2021)
Chandika Hathurusingha	29.62 (44) (1991-1999)
Prasanna Jayawardene	29.50 (83) (2000-2015)
Ranjan Madugalle	29.40 (39) (1982-1988)
Roshan Mahanama	29.27 (89) (1986-1998)
Sidath Wettimuny	29.07 (43) (1982-1987)
Kaushal Silva	28.36 (74) (2011-2018)
Russel Arnold	28.01 (69) (1997-2004)
Upul Chandana	26.78 (24) (1999-2005)
Lahiru Thirimanne	26.43 (85) (2011-2022)*
Romesh Kaluwitharana	26.12 (78) (1992-2004)
Ravi Ratnayeke	25.21 (38) (1982-1989)

BEST BOWLING AVERAGES (2000+ BALLS)

Muttiah Muralitharan	22.67 (795W) (1992-2010)
Kasun Rajitha	27.92 (39W) (2018-2022)*
Rangana Herath	28.07 (433W) (1999-2018)
Ramesh Mendis	28.39 (46W) (2021-2022)*
Chaminda Vaas	29.58 (355W) (1994-2009)
Jayananda Warnaweera	31.90 (32W) (1986-1994)
Lasith Malinga	33.15 (101W) (2004-2010)
Lasith Embuldeniya	33.30 (62W) (2019-2021)*
Nuwan Zoysa	33.70 (64W) (1997-2004)
Sanath Jayasuriya	34.34 (98W) (1991-2007)
Lakshan Sandakan	34.48 (37W) (2016-2018)
Ajantha Mendis	34.77 (70W) (2008-2014)
Rumesh Ratnayake	35.10 (73W) (1983-1992)
Ravi Ratnayake	35.21 (56W) (1982-1989)
Dilruwan Perera	35.90 (161W) (2014-2021)*
Dhammika Prasad	35.97 (75W) (2008-2015)
Somachandra de Silva	36.40 (37W) (1982-1984)
Suranga Lakmal	36.44 (171W) (2010-2022)*

Lasith Embuldeniya	36.77 (71W) (2019-2022)*
Ashantha de Mel	36.94 (59W) (1982-1986)
Nuwan Kulasekara	37.37 (48W) (2005-2014)
Shaminda Eranga	37.50 (57W) (2011-2016)
Suraj Randiv	37.51 (43W) (2010-2012)
Don Anurasiri	37.75 (41W) (1986-1998)
Dilhara Fernando	37.84 (100W) (2000-2012)
Vishwa Fernando	38.27 (43W) (2016-2022)*
Lahiru Kumara	38.48 (70W) (2016-2022)*
Ravindra Pushpakumara	38.65 (58W) (1994-2001)
Dushmantha Chameera	41.28 (32W) (2015-2021)
Chanaka Welegedara	41.32 (55W) (2007-2014)
Upul Chandana	41.48 (37W) (1999-2005)
Aravinda de Silva	41.65 (29W) (1984-2002)
Pramodya Wickramasinghe	41.87 (85W) (1991-2001)
Kumar Dharmasena	42.31 (69W) (1993-2004)
Champaka Ramanayake	42.72 (44W) (1988-1993)
Nuwan Pradeep	42.90 (70W) (2011-2017)
Tillakaratne Dilshan	43.87 (39W) (1999-2013)

BEST BOWLING FIGURES IN AN INNINGS

Muttiah Muralitharan	9/51 V Zimbabwe, 2002
Muttiah Muralithatan	9/65 V England, 1998
Rangana Herath	9/127 V Pakistan, 2014
Muttiah Muralitharan	8/46 V West Indies, 2005
Rangana Herath	8/63 V Zimbabwe, 2016
Muttiah Muralitharan	8/70 V England, 2006
Ravi Ratnayeke	8/83 V Pakistan, 1985
Muttiah Muralitharan	8/87 V India, 2001
Muttiah Muralitharan	7/46 V England, 2003
Rangana Herath	7/48 V India, 2015
Rangana Herath	7/64 V Australia, 2016
Chaminda Vaas	7/71 V West Indies, 2001
Muttiah Muralitharan	7/84 V South Africa, 2000
Rangana Herath	7/89 V Bangladesh, 2013
Muttiah Muralitharan	7/94 V Zimbabwe, 1998
Muttiah Muralitharan	7/97 V South Africa, 2006
Muttiah Muralitharan	7/100 V India, 2005

BEST BOWLING FIGURES IN A MATCH

Muttiah Muralitharan	16/220 V England, 1998
Rangana Herath	14/184 V Pakistan, 2014
Chaminda Vaas	14/191 V West Indies, 2001
Muttiah Muralitharan	13/115 V Zimbabwe, 2002
Rangana Herath	13/145 V Australia, 2016
Rangana Herath	13/152 V Zimbabwe, 2016
Muttiah Muralitharan	13/171 V South Africa, 2000
Muttiah Muralitharan	12/82 V Bangladesh, 2007
Muttiah Muralitharan	12/117 V Zimbabwe, 1998
Rangana Herath	12/157 V Bangladesh, 2013
Rangana Herath	12/171 V England, 2012
Prabath Jayasuriya	12/177 V Australia, 2022
Muttiah Muralitharan	12/225 V South Africa, 2006

MOST FIVE WICKETS IN AN INNINGS

Muttiah Muralitharan	67 (1992-2010)
Rangana Herath	34 (1999-2018)
Chaminda Vaas	12 (1994-2009)

SRI LANKA TEST SERIES RESULTS

DATE OPPONENT	RESULT (W-L-D)
1981-82 V England	0-1-0
1981-82 in Pakistan	0-2-1
1982-83 in India	0-0-1
1982-83 in New Zealand	0-2-0
1982-83 V Australia	0-1-0
1983-84 V New Zealand	0-2-1
1984 in England	0-0-1
1985 V India	1-0-2
1985-86 in Pakistan	0-2-1
1985-86 V Pakistan	1-1-1
1986-87 in India	0-2-1
1987 V New Zealand	0-0-1
1987-88 in Australia	0-1-0
1988 in England	0-1-0
1989-90 in Australia	0-1-1
1990-91 in India	0-1-0
1990-91 in New Zealand	0-0-3

1991 in England	0-1-0
1991-92 in Pakistan	0-1-2
1992 V Australia	0-1-2
1992-93 V New Zealand	1-0-1
1992-93 V England	1-0-0
1993 V India	0-1-2
1993 V South Africa	0-1-2
1993-94 V West Indies 0-0-1	
1993-94 in India	0-3-0
1994 V Pakistan	0-2-0
1994-95 in Zimbabwe	0-0-3
1994-95 in New Zealand	1-0-1
1995-96 in Pakistan	2-1-0
1995-96 in Australia	0-3-0
1996 V Zimbabwe	2-0-0
1996-97 in New Zealand	0-2-0
1996-97 V Pakistan	0-0-2
1997 in West Indies	0-1-1
1997 V India	0-0-2

1997-98 in India	0-0-3
1997-98 V Zimbabwe	2-0-0
1997-98 in South Africa	0-2-0
1998 V New Zealand	2-1-0
1998 in England	1-0-0
1998-99 V India	0-0-1
1998-99 in Pakistan	0-0-1
1998-99 V Pakistan[39]	0-1-0
1999 V Australia	1-0-2
1999-2000 in Zimbabwe	1-0-2
1999-2000 in Pakistan	2-1-0
2000 V Pakistan	0-2-1
2000 V South Africa	1-1-1
2000-01 in South Africa	0-2-1
2000-01 V England	1-2-0
2001 V India	2-1-0
2001-02 V West Indies 3-0-0	
2001-02 V Zimbabwe	3-0-0

[39] Test played in Bangladesh

2001-02 V Bangladesh	1-0-0
2001-02 in Pakistan	1-0-0
2002 in England	0-2-1
2002 V Bangladesh	0-2-0
2002-03 in South Africa	0-2-0
2003 V New Zealand	0-0-2
2003 in West Indies	0-1-1
2003-04 V England	1-0-2
2003-04 V Australia	0-3-0
2004 in Zimbabwe	2-0-0
2004 in Australia	0-1-1
2004 V South Africa	1-0-1
2004-05 in Pakistan	1-1-0
2004-05 in New Zealand	0-1-1
2005 V West Indies	2-0-0
2005 V Bangladesh	2-0-0
2005-06 in India	0-2-1
2005-06 in Bangladesh	2-0-0
2005-06 V Pakistan	0-1-1
2006 in England	1-1-1

2006 V South Africa	2-0-0
2006-07 in New Zealand	1-1-0
2007 V Bangladesh	3-0-0
2007-08 in Australia	0-2-0
2007-08 V England	1-0-2
2007-08 in West Indies 1-1-0	
2008 V India	2-1-0
2008-09 in Bangladesh 2-0-0	
2008-09 in Pakistan	0-0-2
2009 V Pakistan	2-0-1
2009 V New Zealand	2-0-0
2009-10 in India	0-2-1
2010 V India	1-1-1
2010-11 V West Indies 0-0-3	
2011 in England	0-1-2
2011 V Australia	0-1-2
2011-12 V Pakistan[40]	0-1-2
2011-12 in South Africa	1-2-0
2011-12 V England	1-1-0

[40] Series played in United Arab Emirates

2012 V Pakistan 1-0-2

2012-13 V New Zealand 1-1-0

2012-13 in Australia 0-3-0

2012-13 V Bangladesh 1-0-1

2013-14 V Pakistan[41] 1-1-1

2013-14 in Bangladesh 1-0-1

2014 in England 1-0-1

2014 V South Africa 0-1-1

2014 V Pakistan 2-0-0

2014-15 in New Zealand 0-2-0

2015 V Pakistan 1-2-0

2015 V India 1-2-0

2015-16 V West Indies 2-0-0

2015-16 in New Zealand 0-2-0

2016 in England 0-2-1

2016 V Australia 3-0-0

2016-17 in Zimbabwe 2-0-0

2016-17 in South Africa 0-3-0

2016-17 V Bangladesh 1-1-0

2017 V Zimbabwe 1-0-0

---

[41] Series played in United Arab Emirates

2017 V India	0-3-0
2017-18 V Pakistan[42]	2-0-0
2017-18 in India	0-1-2
2017-18 in Bangladesh 1-0-1	
2018 in West Indies	1-1-1
2018 V South Africa	2-0-0
2018-19 V England	0-3-0
2018-19 in New Zealand	0-1-1
2018-19 in Australia	0-2-0
2018-19 in South Africa	2-0-0
2019 V New Zealand	1-1-0
2019-20 in Pakistan	0-1-1
2019-20 in Zimbabwe	1-0-1
2020-21 in South Africa	0-2-0
2020-21 V England	0-2-0
2020-21 in West Indies0-0-2	
2021 V Bangladesh	1-0-1
2021-22 V West Indies 2-0-0	
2021-22 in India	0-2-0
2022 in Bangladesh	1-0-1
2022 V Australia	1-1-0
2022 V Pakistan	1-1-0

[42] Series played in United Arab Emirates

ZIMBABWE

The complicated history of Zimbabwe, formerly known as Rhodesia, is linked with both England and South Africa. The British South Africa Company was formed in 1889 in an area known as Zambezia, which was renamed Rhodesia in 1895.

Cricket had been played in a small pocket in the south of the country; mostly against teams from South Africa. A representative team featured sporadically in South Africa's provincial Currie Cup competition between 1904 and 1932.

At the end of the Second World War, Rhodesia was a more regular competitor, and a handful of their players were selected in the South African national team to tour England in the 1950s.

By 1965, the area where cricket was played was known as Southern Rhodesia. They declared independence from Great Britain, but had to wait fifteen years to truly break ties.

Zimbabwe became a member of the International Cricket Council in 1981. They participated in the 1983 World Cup, and played their first test in 1992, at home against India.

MOST TESTS

Grant Flower	67 (1992-2004)
Heath Streak	65 (1993-2005)
Andy Flower	63 (1992-2002)
Alistair Campbell	60 (1992-2002)
Guy Whittall	46 (1993-2002)
Hamilton Masakadza	38 (2001-2018)
Stuart Carlisle	37 (1995-2005)
Brendan Taylor	34 (2004-2021)*
Henry Olonga	30 (1995-2002)
Dion Ebrahim	29 (2001-2005)
Tatenda Taibu	28 (2001-2012)
Craig Wishart	27 (1995-2005)
Bryan Strang	26 (1995-2001)
Paul Strang	24 (1994-2001)
Gavin Rennie	23 (1997-2002)
Regis Chakabva	22 (2011-2021)*
Dave Houghton	22 (1992-1997)
Ray Price	22 (1999-2013)

MOST RUNS

Andy Flower	4794 (1992-2002)
Grant Flower	3457 (1992-2004)
Alistair Campbell	2858 (1992-2002)
Brendan Taylor	2320 (2004-2021)*
Hamilton Masakadza	2223 (2001-2018)
Guy Whittall	2207 (1993-2002)
Heath Streak	1990 (1993-2005)
Stuart Carlisle	1615 (1995-2005)
Tatenda Taibu	1546 (2001-2012)
Dave Houghton	1464 (1992-1997)
Murray Goodwin	1414 (1998-2000)
Dion Ebrahim	1225 (2001-2005)
Craig Ervine	1208 (2011-2020)*
Sikandar Raza	1187 (2013-2021)*
Craig Wishart	1098 (1995-2005)
Regi Chakabva	1061 (2011-2021)*
Sean Williams	1034 (2013-2021)*

MOST WICKETS

Heath Streak	216 (1993-2005)
Ray Price	80 (1999-2013)
Paul Strang	70 (1994-2001)
Henry Olonga	68 (1995-2002)
Graeme Cremer	57 (2005-2017)
Bryan Strang	56 (1995-2001)
Andy Blignaut	53 (2001-2005)
Guy Whittall	51 (1993-2002)
Kyle Jarvis	46 (2011-2020)
Sikandar Raza	34 (2013-2021)*
Mpumelelo Mbangwa	32 (1996-2000)
Tainashe Panyangara	31 (2004-2014)
David Brain	30 (1992-1995)
Chris Mpofu	29 (2005-2017)
Eddo Brandes	26 (1992-1999)
Donald Tiripano	26 (2014-2021)*

HIGHEST SCORES

Dave Houghton	266 V Sri Lanka, 1994
Andy Flower	232* V India, 2000
Guy Whittall	203* V New Zealand, 1997
Grant Flower	201* V Pakistan, 1995
Andy Flower	199* V South Africa, 2001
Guy Whittall	188* V New Zealand, 2000
Andy Flower	183* V India, 2000
Brendan Taylor	171 V Bangladesh, 2013
Murray Goodwin	166* V Pakistan, 1998
Tino Mawoyo	163* V Pakistan, 2011
Craig Ervine	160 V Sri Lanka, 2017
Hamilton Masakadza	158 V Bangladesh, 2014
Grant Flower	156* V Pakistan, 1998
Andy Flower	156 V Pakistan, 1995
Tatenda Taibu	153 V Bangladesh, 2005
Sean Willaims	151* V Afghanistan, 2021
Grant Flower	151 V New Zealand, 1997
Murray Goodwin	148* V England, 2000

Hamilton Masakadza	147 V West Indies, 2017
Craig Ervine	146 V New Zealand, 2016
Dave Houghton	142 V Sri Lanka, 1994
Andy Flower	142 V South Africa, 2001
Andy Flower	129 V Sri Lanka, 1999
Heath Streak	127* V West Indies, 2003
Sikandar Raza	127 V Sri Lanka, 2017
Dave Houghton	121 V India, 1992
Guy Whittall	119 V Bangladesh, 2001
Hamilton Masakadza	119 V West Indies, 2001
Sean Williams	119 V New Zealand, 2016
Stuart Carlisle	118 V Australia, 2003
Mark Vermeulen	118 V West Indies, 2003
Brendan Taylor	117 V New Zealand, 2011
Andy Flower	115 V India, 1993
Andy Flower	114* V Bangladesh, 2001
Craig Wishart	114 V Bangladesh, 2001
Guy Whittall	113* V Pakistan, 1995
Andy Flower	113* V West Indies, 2000

MOST CENTURIES

Andy Flower	12 (1992-2002)
Brendan Taylor	6 (2004-2021)*
Grant Flower	6 (1992-2004)
Hamilton Masakadza	5 (2001-2018)
Dave Houghton	4 (1992-1997)
Guy Whittall	4 (1993-2002)
Sean Williams	4 (2013-2021)*

MOST 50S (50-99)

Andy Flower	27 (1992-2002)
Alistair Campbell	18 (1992-2002)
Grant Flower	15 (1992-2004)
Brendan Taylor	12 (2004-2021)*
Tatenda Taibu	12 (2001-2012)
Heath Streak	11 (1993-2005)
Guy Whittall	10 (1993-2002)
Dion Ebrahim	10 (2001-2005)

MOST DISMISSALS AS WICKET KEEPER

Andy Flower	151 (142ct, 9st) (1992-2002)
Tatenda Taibu	60 (55ct, 5st) (2001-2012)
Regis Chakabva	50 (45ct, 5st) (2011-2021)*
Richmond Mutumbami	19 (17ct, 2st) (2013-2014)
Wayne James	16 (16ct) (1993-1994)

MOST CATCHES AS FIELDER

Alistair Campbell	60 (1992-2002)
Grant Flower	43 (1992-2004)
Stuart Carlisle	34 (1995-2005)
Hamilton Masakadza	29 (2001-2018)
Brendan Taylor	27 (2004-2021)*
Guy Whittall	19 (1993-2002)
Dave Houghton	17 (1992-1997)
Heath Streak	17 (1993-2005)
Vusi Sibanda	16 (2003-2014)
Craig Ervine	16 (2011-2020)*

BEST BATTING AVERAGES (MINIMUM 20 INNINGS)

Andy Flower	51.54 (112) (1992-2002)
Dave Houghton	43.05 (36) (1992-1997)
Murray Goodwin	42.84 (37) (1998-2000)
Sean Williams	41.36 (27) (2013-2021)*
Brendan Taylor	36.25 (58) (2004-2021)*
Sikandar Raza	35.96 (33) (2013-2021)*
Craig Ervine	35.52 (36) (2011-2020)*
Tatenda Taibu	30.31 (54) (2001-2012)
Hamilton Masakadza	30.04 (76) (2001-2018)
Grant Flower	29.54 (123) (1992-2004)
Guy Whittall	29.42 (82) (1993-2002)
Tino Mawoyo	29.28 (22) (2011-2016)
Alistair Campbell	27.21 (109) (1992-2002)
Regis Chakabva	27.20 (43) (2011-2021)*
Paul Strang	27.06 (41) (1992-2001)
Stuart Carlisle	26.91 (66) (1995-2005)
Andy Blignaut	26.84 (36) (2001-2005)

BEST BOWLING AVERAGES (2000+ BALLS)

Heath Streak	28.14 (216W) (1993-2005)
Kyle Jarvis	29.43 (46W) (2011-2020)
Mpumelelo Mbangwa	31.43 (32W) (1996-2000)
Paul Strang	36.02 (70W) (1994-2001)
Ray Price	36.06 (80W) (1999-2013)
Andy Blignaut	37.05 (53W) (2001-2005)
Henry Olonga	38.52 (68W) (1995-2002)
Bryan Strang	39.33 (56W) (1995-2001)
Guy Whittall	40.94 (51W) (1993-2002)
Sikandar Raza	42.38 (34W) (2013-2021)*
Travis Friend	43.60 (25W) (2001-2004)
Graeme Cremer	45.68 (57W) (2005-2017)
Donald Tiripano	47.96 (26W) (2014-2021)*
Chris Mpofu	48.00 (29W) (2005-2017)

BEST BOWLING FIGURES IN AN INNINGS

Paul Strang	8/109 V New Zealand, 2000
Sikandar Raza	7/113 V Sri Lanka, 2020
Douglas Hondo	6/59 V Bangladesh, 2005
Ray Price	6/73 V West Indies, 2003
Heath Streak	6/73 V India, 2005
Heath Streak	6/87 V England, 2000
Heath Streak	6/90 V Pakistan, 1995
Adam Huckle	6/109 V New Zealand, 1997
Ray Price	6/121 V Australia, 2003
Heath Streak	5/27 V West Indies, 2000
Travis Friend	5/31 V Bangladesh, 2001
David Brain	5/42 V Pakistan, 1993
Elton Chigumbura	5/54 V Bangladesh, 2005
Kyle Jarvis	5/54 V West Indies, 2013
Heath Streak	5/56 V Pakistan, 1993
Tinashe Panyangara	5/59 V Bangladesh, 2014
Brian Vitori	5/61 V Pakistan, 2013
Tendai Chatara	5/61 V Pakistan, 2013

BEST BOWLING FIGURES IN A MATCH

Adam Huckle	11/255 V New Zealand, 1997
Paul Strang	10/158 V New Zealand, 2000
Ray Price	10/161 V West Indies, 2003
Heath Streak	9/72 V West Indies, 2000
Heath Streak	9/105 V Pakistan, 1995
Ray Price	9/235 V West Indies, 2003
Graeme Cremer	9/275 V Sri Lanka, 2017
Grant Flower	8/104 V Bangladesh, 2001
Heath Streak	8/105 V Pakistan, 1995
Andy Blignaut	8/110 V Bangladesh, 2001
Heath Streak	8/114 V Pakistan, 1993
Andy Blignaut	8/160 V Pakistan, 2002
Sikandar Raza	8/176 V Sri Lanka, 2020
Graeme Cremer	8/178 V West Indies, 2017

MOST FIVE WICKETS IN AN INNINGS

Heath Streak	7 (1993-2005)
Ray Price	5 (1999-2013)

ZIMBABWE TEST SERIES RESULTS

DATE OPPONENT	RESULT (W-L-D)
1992-93 V India	0-0-1
1992-93 V New Zealand	0-1-1
1992-93 in India	0-1-0
1993-94 in Pakistan	0-2-1
1994-95 V Sri Lanka	0-0-3
1994-95 V Pakistan	1-2-0
1995-96 V South Africa	0-1-0
1995-96 in New Zealand	0-0-2
1996 in Sri Lanka	0-2-0
1996-97 in Pakistan	0-1-1
1996-97 V England	0-0-2
1997-98 V New Zealand	0-0-2
1997-98 in Sri Lanka	0-2-0
1997-98 in New Zealand	0-2-0
1997-98 V Pakistan	0-1-1
1998-99 V India	1-0-0
1998-99 in Pakistan	1-0-2

1999-2000 V Australia	0-1-0
1999-2000 in South Africa	0-1-0
1999-2000 V South Africa	0-1-0
1999-2000 V Sri Lanka	0-1-2
1999-2000 in West Indies	0-2-0
2000 in England	0-1-1
2000-01 V New Zealand	0-2-0
2000-01 in India	0-1-1
2000-01 in New Zealand	0-0-1
2000-01 V Bangladesh	2-0-0
2001 V India	1-1-0
2001 V West Indies	0-1-1
2001-02 V South Africa	0-1-1
2001-02 in Bangladesh	1-0-1
2001-02 in Sri Lanka	0-3-0
2001-02 in India	0-2-0
2002-03 V Pakistan	0-2-0
2003 in England	0-2-0
2003-04 in Australia	0-2-0

2003-04 V West Indies	0-1-1
2003-04 V Bangladesh	1-0-1
2004 V Sri Lanka	0-2-0
2004-05 in Bangladesh	0-1-1
2004-05 in South Africa	0-2-0
2005 V New Zealand	0-2-0
2005 V India	0-2-0
2011 V Bangladesh	1-0-0
2011 V Pakistan	0-1-0
2011-12 V New Zealand	0-1-0
2011-12 in New Zealand	0-1-0
2012-13 in West Indies	0-2-0
2013 V Bangladesh	1-1-0
2013 V Pakistan	1-1-0
2014 V South Africa	0-1-0
2014-15 in Bangladesh	0-3-0
2016 V New Zealand	0-2-0
2016-17 V Sri Lanka	0-2-0
2017 in Sri Lanka	0-1-0
2017-18 V West Indies	0-1-1

2017-18 in South Africa	0-1-0
2018-19 in Bangladesh	1-1-0
2019-20 V Sri Lanka	0-1-1
2019-20 in Bangladesh	0-1-0
2020-21 V Afghanistan[43]	1-1-0
2021 V Pakistan	0-2-0
2021 V Bangladesh	0-1-0

[43] Played in United Arab Emirates

BANGLADESH

The British East India Company introduced cricket into the area known as Bengal in the late eighteenth century. The game gained popularity very slowly, as the area was mostly insulated for the next century.

A representative team played against an English touring squad in 1889; and Bengal took part in a provincial tournament in India in 1923.

Bengal played the touring Australian team in 1935, and continued to play in Indian competitions until the outbreak of the Second World War.

After the war, Bengal was split in two, with the western part in India, and the eastern part in the new nation of East Pakistan. East Bengal did not have any formal competition until the mid-1950s.

Teams from East Pakistan played in the Pakistani domestic competition between 1954 and 1971. East Bengal was devastated by a cyclone in 1970, which indirectly led to a declaration of independence in 1971.

Bangladesh endured much hardship in its early years of independence, and had to wait until 1977 to have a national team. They hosted several visiting teams before competing in the World Cup for the first time in 1999. They played their first test the following year, at home against India.

MOST TESTS

Mushfiqur Rahim	82 (2005-2022)*
Tamim Iqbal	69 (2008-2022)*
Shakib Al Hasan	63 (2007-2022)*
Mohammad Ashraful	61 (2001-2013)
Mominul Haque	54 (2013-2022)*
Habibul Bashar	50 (2000-2008)
Mahmudullah	50 (2009-2021)
Khaled Mashud	44 (2000-2007)
Javed Omar	40 (2001-2007)
Imrul Kayes	39 (2008-2019)
Taijul Islam	38 (2014-2022)*
Shahadat Hossain	38 (2005-2015)
Mashrafe Mortaza	36 (2001-2009)
Mehidy Hasan Miraz	35 (2016-2022)*
Liton Das	35 (2015-2022)*
Mohammad Rafique	33 (2000-2008)
Rubel Hossain	27 (2009-2020)
Rajin Saleh	24 (2003-2008)
Shahriar Nafees	24 (2005-2013)

MOST RUNS

Mushfiqur Rahim	5235 (2005-2022)*
Tamim Iqbal	5082 (2008-2022)*
Shakib Al Hasan	4251 (2007-2022)*
Mominul Haque	3529 (2013-2022)*
Habibul Bashar	3026 (2000-2008)
Mahmudullah	2914 (2009-2021)
Mohammad Ashraful	2737 (2001-2013)
Liton Das	2112 (2015-2022)*
Imrul Kayes	1797 (2008-2019)
Javed Omar	1720 (2001-2007)
Khaled Mashud	1409 (2000-2007)
Shahriar Nafees	1267 (2005-2013)
Rajin Saleh	1141 (2003-2008)
Mehidy Hasan MIraz	1089 (2016-2022)*
Mohammad Rafique	1059 (2000-2008)
Nasir Hossain	1044 (2011-2017)

MOST WICKETS

Shakib Al Hasan	225 (2007-2022)*
Taijul Islam	158 (2014-2022)*
Mehidy Hasan Miraz	135 (2016-2022)*
Mohammad Rafique	100 (2000-2008)
Mashrafe Mortaza	78 (2001-2009)
Shahadat Hossain	72 (2005-2015)
Enamul Haque Jnr	44 (2003-2013)
Mahmudallah	43 (2009-2021)
Sohag Gazi	38 (2012-2014)
Tapash Baisya	36 (2002-2005)
Rubel Hossain	36 (2009-2020)
Nayeem Hasan	31 (2018-2022)*
Mustafizur Rahman	31 (2015-2022)*
Ebadot Hossain	31 (2019-2022)*
Abu Jayed	30 (2018-2021)
Manjural Islam	28 (2001-2004)
Abdur Razzak	28 (2006-2018)
Robiul Islam	25 (2010-2014)
Taskin Ahmed	25 (2017-2022)*

HIGHEST SCORES

Mushfiqur Rahim	219* V Zimbabwe, 2018
Shakib Al Hasan	217 V New Zealand, 2017
Tamim Iqbal	206 V Pakistan, 2015
Mushfiqur Rahim	203* V Zimbabwe, 2020
Mushfiqur Rahim	200 V Sri Lanka, 2013
Mohammad Ashraful	190 V Sri Lanka, 2013
Mominul Haque	181 V New Zealand, 2013
Mominul Haque	176 V Sri Lanka, 2018
Mushfiqur Rahim	175* V Sri Lanka, 2022
Najmal Hossain Shanto	163 V Sri Lanka, 2021
Mominul Haque	161 V Zimbabwe, 2018
Mushfiqur Rahim	159 V New Zealand, 2017
Mohammad Ashraful	158* V India, 2004
Tamim Iqbal	151 V India, 2010
Mahmudallah	150* V Zimbabwe, 2021
Imrul Kayes	150 V Pakistan, 2015
Soumya Sarkar	149 V New Zealand, 2019
Mahmudallah	146 V New Zealand, 2019
Aminul Islam	145 V India, 2000

MOST CENTURIES

Mominul Haque	11 (2013-2022)*
Tamim Iqbal	10 (2008-2022)*
Mushfiqur Rahim	9 (2005-2022)*
Mohammad Ashraful	6 (2001-2013)
Shakib Al Hasan	5 (2007-2021)*
Mahmudallah	5 (2009-2021)

MOST 50S (50-99)

Tamim Iqbal	31 (2008-2022)*
Shakib Al Hasan	29 (2007-2022)*
Mushfiqur Rahim	25 (2005-2022)*
Habibul Bashar	24 (2000-2008)
Mahmudallah	16 (2009-2020)
Mominul Haque	15 (2013-2022)*
Liton Das	14 (2015-2022)*
Mohammad Ashraful	8 (2001-2013)
Javed Omar	8 (2001-2007)

MOST DISMISSALS AS WICKET KEEPER

Mushfiqur Rahim	113 (98ct, 15st) (2005-2022)*
Khaled Mashud	87 (78ct, 9st) (2000-2007)
Liton Das	59 (53ct, 6st) (2015-2022)*

MOST CATCHES AS FIELDER

Mahmudallah	38 (2009-2021)
Mominul Haque	34 (2013-2022)*
Imrul Kayes	30 (2008-2019)
Shakib Al Hasan	26 (2007-2022)*
Mohammad Ashraful	25 (2001-2013)
Soumya Sarkar	23 (2015-2019)
Habibul Bashar	22 (2000-2008)
Mehidy Hasan Miraz	22 (2016-2022)*
Shahriar Nafees	19 (2005-2013)
Tamim Iqbal	19 (2008-2022)*
Taijul Islam	19 (2014-2022)*

BEST BATTING AVERAGES (MINIMUM 20 INNINGS)

Tamim Iqbal	39.09 (132) (2008-2022)*
Shakib Al Hasan	39.00 (116) (2007-2022)*
Mushfiqur Rahim	37.93 (151) (2005-2022)*
Mominul Haque	37.54 (100) (2013-2022)*
Lito Das	35.79 (60) (2015-2022)*
Nasir Hossain	34.80 (32) (2011-2017)
Mahmudallah	33.49 (94) (2009-2021)
Habibul Bashar	30.87 (99) (2000-2008)
Soumya Sarkar	27.70 (30) (2015-2019)
Shahriar Nafees	26.39 (48) (2005-2013)
Junaid Siddique	26.18 (37) (2008-2012)
Najmul Hossain Shanto	26.08 (36) (2017-2022)*
Rajin Saleh	25.93 (46) (2003-2008)
Imrul Kayes	24.28 (76) (2008-2019)
Sabbir Rahman	24.05 (22) (2016-2018)
Mohammad Ashraful	24.00 (119) (2001-2013)
Nafees Iqbal	23.54 (22) (2004-2006)
Shadman Islam	23.29 (25) (2018-2022)*
Al Shahriar	22.76 (30) (2000-2003)

BEST BOWLING AVERAGES (2000+ BALLS)

Shakib Al Hasan	31.32 (225W) (2007-2022)*
Taijul Islam	33.08 (158W) (2014-2022)*
Mehidy Hasan Miraz	34.15 (135W) (2016-2022)*
Mustafizur Rahman	36.73 (30W) (2015-2021)*
Enamul Haque Jnr	40.61 (44W) (2003-2013)
Mohammad Rafique	40.76 (100W) (2000-2008)
Mashrafe Mortaza	41.52 (78W) (2001-2009)
Sohag Gazi	42.07 (38W) (2012-2014)
Mahmudallah	45.32 (43W) (2009-2021)

BEST BOWLING FIGURES IN AN INNINGS

Taijul Islam	8/39 V Zimbabwe, 2014
Shakib Al Hasan	7/36 V New Zealand, 2008
Mehidy Hasan Miraz	7/58 V West Indies, 2018
Enamul Haque Jnr	7/95 V Zimbabwe, 2005
Taijul Islam	7/116 V Pakistan, 2021
Shahadat Hossain	6/27 V South Africa, 2008
Shakib Al Hasan	6/33 V West Indies, 2018
Taijul Islam	6/33 V West Indies, 2018

BEST BOWLING FIGURES IN A MATCH

Mehidy Hasan Miraz	12/117 V West Indies, 2018
Mehidy Hasan Miraz	12/159 V England, 2016
Enamul Haque Jnr	12/200 V Zimbabwe, 2005
Taijul Islam	11/170 V Zimbabwe, 2018
Shakib Al Hasan	10/124 V Zimbabwe, 2014
Shakib Al Hasan	10/153 V Australia, 2017
Taijul Islam	9/81 V Zimbabwe, 2014
Shahadat Hossain	9/97 V South Africa, 2008
Shakib Al Hasan	9/115 V New Zealand, 2008
Mehidy Hasan Miraz	9/148 V Zimbabwe, 2021
Nayeem Hasan	9/152 V Zimbabwe, 2020
Robiul Islam	9/155 V Zimbabwe, 2013
Mohammad Rafique	9/160 V Australia, 2006
Taijul Islam	9/202 V South Africa, 2022
Sohag Gazi	9/219 V West Indies, 2012

MOST FIVE WICKETS IN AN INNINGS

Shakib Hasan	19 (2007-2022)*
Taijul Islam	10 (2014-2022)*

BANGLADESH TEST SERIES RESULTS

DATE OPPONENT	RESULT (W-L-D)
2000-01 V India	0-1-0
2000-01 in Zimbabwe	0-2-0
2001-02 in Pakistan	0-1-0
2001-02 in Sri Lanka	0-1-0
2001-02 V Zimbabwe	0-1-1
2001-02 in New Zealand	0-2-0
2001-02 V Pakistan	0-2-0
2002 in Sri Lanka	0-2-0
2002-03 in South Africa	0-2-0
2002-03 V West Indies	0-2-0
2003 V South Africa	0-2-0
2003 in Australia	0-2-0
2003-04 V England	0-2-0
2003-04 in Zimbabwe	0-1-1
2004 in West Indies	0-1-1
2004-05 V New Zealand	0-2-0
2004-05 V India	0-2-0
2004-05 V Zimbabwe	1-0-1

2005 in England	0-2-0
2005 in Sri Lanka	0-2-0
2005-06 V Sri Lanka	0-2-0
2005-06 V Australia	0-2-0
2007 V India	0-1-1
2007 in Sri Lanka	0-3-0
2007-08 in New Zealand	0-2-0
2007-08 V South Africa	0-2-0
2008-09 V New Zealand	0-1-1
2008-09 in South Africa	0-2-0
2008-09 V Sri Lanka	0-2-0
2009 in West Indies	2-0-0
2009-10 V India	0-2-0
2009-10 in New Zealand	0-1-0
2009-10 V England	0-2-0
2010 in England	0-2-0
2011 in Zimbabwe	0-1-0
2011-12 V West Indies	0-1-1
2011-12 V Pakistan	0-2-0
2012-13 V West Indies	0-2-0

2012-13 in Sri Lanka	0-1-1
2013 in Zimbabwe	1-1-0
2013-14 V New Zealand	0-0-2
2013-14 V Sri Lanka	0-1-1
2014 in West Indies	0-2-0
2014-15 V Zimbabwe	3-0-0
2015 V Pakistan	0-1-1
2015 V India	0-0-1
2015 V South Africa	0-0-2
2016-17 V England	1-1-0
2016-17 in New Zealand	0-2-0
2016-17 in India	0-1-0
2016-17 in Sri Lanka	1-1-0
2017 V Australia	1-1-0
2017-18 in South Africa	0-2-0
2017-18 V Sri Lanka	0-1-1
2018 in West Indies	0-2-0
2018-19 V Zimbabwe	1-1-0
2018-19 V West Indies	2-0-0
2018-19 in New Zealand	0-2-0

2019 V Afghanistan	0-1-0
2019-20 in India	0-2-0
2019-20 V Zimbabwe	1-0-1
2019-20 in Pakistan	0-1-1
2020-21 V West Indies	0-2-0
2021 in Sri Lanka	0-1-1
2021 in Zimbabwe	1-0-0
2021-22 V Pakistan	0-2-0
2021-22 in New Zealand	1-1-0
2021-22 in South Africa	0-2-0
2022 V Bangladesh	0-1-1
2022 in West Indies	0-2-0

AFGHANISTAN

Cricket in Afghanistan has had to battle oppressive government opposition, and an ongoing debilitating war to survive.

The sport gained popularity among Afghan refugees living in Pakistan in the mid 1990s. The sport, like all others, was banned by the Taliban regime in Afghanistan; although the Afghanistan Cricket Board was formed in 1995.

The Taliban lifted their ban in 2000, and a team from Afghanistan was invited to play in Pakistan's domestic competition. They toured England to play second tier regional sides in 2006, and narrowly missed out on qualifying for the 2011 World Cup.

In 2012, Afghanistan played their first official One Day International match against Pakistan. They played Australia later that year; and participated in the 2015 World Cup.

Afghanistan played their first test match in June 2018, against India. They defeated Ireland in early 2019, and later that year recorded an unlikely test victory against Bangladesh. Their lost the sole test against West Indies in 2019, before playing a drawn series (1-1) against Zimbabwe in the UAE in 2020-21.

Afghanistan underwent a regime change in 2021, and their future in test cricket is uncertain.

MOST TESTS

Asghar Afghan	6 (2018-2021)*
Rahmat Shah	6 (2018-2021)*
Rashid Khan	5 (2018-2021)*
Yamin Ahmadzai	5 (2018-2021)*
Afsar Zazai	5 (2018-2021)*
Hashmatalluh Shahidi	5 (2018-2021)*

MOST RUNS

Asghar Afghan	440 (2018-2021)*
Rahmat Shah	385 (2018-2021)*
Ibrahim Zadran	356 (2019-2021)*
Hashmatullah Shahidi	353 (2018-2021)*
Afsar Zazai	172 (2018-2021)*
Javed Ahmadi	113 (2018-2021)*
Ihsanullah	110 (2019)
Rashid Khan	106 (2018-2021)*

MOST WICKETS

Rashid Khan	34 (2018-2021)*
Amir Hamza	16 (2019-2021)*
Yamin Ahmadzai	11 (2018-2021)*
Mohammad Nabi	8 (2018-2019)
Zahir Khan	7 (2019-2021)*

HIGHEST SCORES

Hasmatulaah Shahidi	200* V Zimbabwe, 2021
Asghar Afghan	164 V Zimbabwe, 2021
Rahmat Shah	102 V Bangladesh, 2019
Rahmat Shah	98 V Ireland, 2019
Asghar Afghan	92 V Bangladesh, 2019
Ibrahim Zadran	87 V Bangladesh, 2019
Rahmat Shah	76 V Ireland, 2019
Ibrahim Zadran	76 V Zimbabwe, 2021
Ibrahim Zadran	72 V Zimbabwe, 2021
Asghar Afghan	67 V Ireland, 2019
Ihsanullah	65* V Ireland, 2019

MOST DISMISSALS AS WICKET KEEPER

Afsar Zazai	10 (9ct, 1st) (2018-2021)*
Ikram Alikhil	5 (4ct, 1st) (2019)

MOST CATCHES AS FIELDER

Ibrahim Zadran	6 (2019-2021)*
Ihsanullah	4 (2019)
Rahmat Shah	4 (2018-2021)*

BEST BOWLING FIGURES IN AN INNINGS

Rashid Khan	7/137 V Zimbabwe, 2021
Rashid Khan	6/49 V Bangladesh, 2019
Amir Hamzra	6/75 V Zimbabwe, 2021

BEST BOWLING FIGURES IN A MATCH

Rashid Khan	11/104 V Bangladesh, 2019
Rashid Khan	11/275 V Zimbabwe, 2021

IRELAND

The English introduced cricket to Ireland in the early nineteenth century. The game spread quickly, and an Irish representative side faced the Marylebone Cricket Club in 1858.

The Land War of the 1880s saw British games banned in Ireland, and cricket fell away. Irish teams still played sporadically, but their players were banned from other sports such as Gaelic Football. The ban wasn't lifted until 1970, although an annual match between Ireland and Scotland was allowed to proceed from 1924 onwards.

Ireland became an associate member of the International Cricket Council in 1993. They played their first One Day International match, against England, in 2006; and participated in the 2007 World Cup, making it into the final eight.

Ireland played at the World Cup again in 2011 and 2015. They gained full membership of the ICC in 2017, and played their first test match the following year, going down to Pakistan.

In March 2019, Ireland lost to fellow test minnows Afghanistan. Their third and final test to date was a loss to England in July 2019.

MOST TESTS

Andy Balbirnie	3 (2018-2019)*
Tim Murtagh	3 (2018-2019)*
Kevin O'Brien	3 (2018-2019)*
William Porterfield	3 (2018-2019)*
Paul Stirling	3 (2018-2019)*
Stuart Thompson	3 (2018-2019)*

MOST RUNS

Kevin O'Brien	258 (2018-2019)*
Andy Balbirnie	146 (2018-2019)*
Tim Murtagh	109 (2018-2019)*
Paul Stirling	104 (2018-2019)*
James McCollum	73 (2018-2019)*
George Dockrell	64 (2019)*
Stuart Thompson	64 (2018-2019)*
William Porterfield	58 (2018-2019)*

MOST WICKETS

Tim Murtagh	13 (2018-2019)*
Stuart Thompson	10 (2018-2019)*
Boyd Rankin	7 (2018-2019)*
Mark Adair	6 (2019)*

HIGHEST SCORES

Kevin O'Brien	118 V Pakistan, 2018
Andy Balbirnie	82 V Afghanistan, 2019
Kevin O'Brien	56 V Afghanistan, 2019
Andy Balbirnie	55 V England, 2019
Tim Murtagh	54* V Afghanistan, 2019
Stuart Thompson	53 V Pakistan, 2018

MOST DISMISSALS AS WICKET KEEPER

Gary Wilson	6 (6ct) (2018-2019)*

MOST CATCHES AS FIELDER

Paul Stirling	4 (2018-2019)*
Andy Balbirnie	3 (2018-2019)*

BEST BOWLING FIGURES IN AN INNINGS

Tim Murtagh	5/13 V England, 2019
Tim Murtagh	4/45 V Pakistan, 2018

BEST BOWLING FIGURES IN A MATCH

Tim Murtagh	6/65 V England, 2019
Mark Adair	6/98 V England, 2019
Tim Murtagh	6/100 V Pakistan, 2018

WORLD TEST RECORDS

MOST TESTS

Sachin Tendulkar (IND)	200 (1989-2013)
James Anderson (ENG)	175 (2003-2022)*
Ricky Ponting (AUS)	168 (1995-2012)
Steve Waugh (AUS)	168 (1985-2004)
Jacques Kallis (SAF)	166 (1995-2013)
Shivnarine Chanderpaul (WI)	164 (1994-2015)
Rahul Dravid (IND)	164 (1996-2012)
Alastair Cook (ENG)	161 (2006-2018)
Stuart Broad (ENG)	159 (2007-2022)*
Allan Border (AUS)	156 (1978-1994)
Mahela Jayawardene (SL)	149 (1997-2014)
Mark Boucher (SAF)	147 (1997-2012)
Shane Warne (AUS)	145 (1992-2007)
VVS Laxman (IND)	134 (1996-2012)
Kumar Sangakkara (SL)	134 (2000-2015)
Muttiah Muralitharan (SL)	133 (1992-2010)
Alec Stewart (ENG)	133 (1990-2003)
Anil Kumble (IND)	132 (990-2008)

Courtney Walsh (WI)	132 (1984-2001)
Kapil Dev (IND)	131 (1978-1994)
Brian Lara (WI)	131 (1990-2006)
Mark Waugh (AUS)	128 (1991-2002)
Sunil Gavaskar (IND)	125 (1971-1987)
Hashim Amla (SL)	124 (2004-2019)
Javed Miandad (PAK)	124 (1976-1993)
Glenn McGrath (AUS)	124 (1993-2007)
Joe Root (ENG)	124 (2012-2022)*
Viv Richards (WI)	121 (1974-1991)
Inzamam-ul-Haq (PAK)	120 (1992-2007)
Ian Healy (AUS)	119 (1988-1999)
Ian Bell (ENG)	118 (2004-2015)
Graham Gooch (ENG)	118 (1975-1995)
Younis Khan (PAK)	118 (2000-2017)
David Gower (ENG)	117 (1978-1992)
Graeme Smith (SAF)	117 (2002-2014)
Desmond Haynes (WI)	116 (1978-1994)
Dilip Vengsarkar (IND)	116 (1976-1992)

MOST RUNS

Sachin Tendulkar (IND)	15921 (1989-2013)
Ricky Ponting (AUS)	13378 (1995-2012)
Jacques Kallis (SAF)	13289 (1995-2013)
Rahul Dravid (IND)	13288 (1996-2012)
Alastair Cook (ENG)	12472 (2006-2018)
Kumar Sangakkara (SL)	12400 (2000-2015)
Brian Lara (WI)	11953 (1990-2006)
Shivanrine Chanderpaul (WI)	11867 (1994-2015)
Mahela Jayawardene (SL)	11814 (1997-2014)
Allan Border (AUS)	11174 (1978-1994)
Steve Waugh (AUS)	10927 (1985-2004)
Joe Root (ENG)	10504 (2012-2022)*
Sunil Gavaskar (IND)	10122 (1971-1987)
Younis Khan (PAK)	10099 (2000-2017)
Hashim Amla (SAF)	9282 (2004-2019)
Graeme Smith (SAF)	9265 (2002-2014)
Graham Gooch (ENG)	8900 (1975-1995)
Javed Miandad (PAK)	8832 (1976-1993)
Inzamam-ul-Haq (PAK)	8830 (1992-2007)

VVS Laxman (IND)	8781 (1996-2012)
AB de Villiers (SAF)	8765 (2004-2018)
Michael Clarke (AUS)	8643 (2004-2015)
Matthew Hayden (AUS)	8625 (1994-2009)
Virender Sehwag (IND)	8586 (2001-2013)
Viv Richards (WI)	8540 (1974-1991)
Alec Stewart (ENG)	8463 (1990-2003)
David Gower (ENG)	8231 (1978-1992)
Kevin Pietersen (ENG)	8181 (2005-2014)
Steve Smith (AUS)	8161 (2010-2022)*
Geoffrey Boycott (ENG)	8114 (1964-1982)
Virat Kohli (IND)	8074 (2011-2022)*
Garfield Sobers (WI)	8032 (1954-1974)
Mark Waugh (AUS)	8029 (1991-2002)
David Warner (AUS)	7817 (2011-2022)*
Mike Atherton (ENG)	7728 (1989-2001)
Ian Bell (ENG)	7727 (2004-2015)
Justin Langer (AUS)	7696 (1993-2007)
Ross Taylor (NZ)	7683 (2007-2022)
Colin Cowdrey (ENG)	7624 (1954-1975)

MOST WICKETS

Muttiah Muralitharan (SL)	800 (1992-2010)
Shane Warne (AUS)	708 (1992-2007)
James Anderson (ENG)	667 (2003-2022)*
Anil Kumble (IND)	619 (1990-2008)
Stuart Broad (ENG)	566 (2007-2022)*
Glenn McGrath (AUS)	563 (1993-2007)
Courtney Walsh (WI)	519 (1984-2001)
Ravichandran Ashwin (IND)	442 (2011-2022)*
Dale Steyn (SAF)	439 (2004-2019)
Nathan Lyon (AUS)	438 (2011-2022)*
Kapil Dev (IND)	434 (1978-1994)
Rangana Herath (SL)	433 (1999-2018)
Richard Hadlee (NZ)	431 (1973-1990)
Shaun Pollock (SAF)	421 (1995-2008)
Harbhajan Singh (IND)	417 (1998-2015)
Wasim Akram (PAK)	414 (1985-2002)
Curtly Ambrose (WI)	405 (1988-2000)
Makhaya Ntini (SAF)	390 (1998-2009)
Ian Botham (ENG)	383 (1977-1992)

Malcolm Marshall (WI)	376 (1978-1991)
Waqar Younis (PAK)	373 (1989-2003)
Imran Khan (PAK)	362 (1971-1992)
Daniel Vettori (NZ)	362 (1997-2014)
Dennis Lillee (AUS)	355 (1971-1984)
Chaminda Vaas (SL)	355 (1994-2009)
Tim Southee (NZ)	347 (2008-2022)*
Alan Donald (SAF)	330 (1992-2002)
Bob Willis (ENG)	325 (1971-1984)
Trent Boult (NZ)	317 (2011-2022)*
Mitchell Johnson (AUS)	313 (2007-2015)
Ishant Sharma (IND)	311 (2007-2021)
Zaheer Khan (IND)	311 (2000-2014)
Brett Lee (AUS)	310 (1999-2008)
Morne Morkel (SAF)	309 (2006-2018)
Lance Gibbs (WI)	309 (1958-1976)
Fred Trueman (ENG)	307 (1952-1965)
Derek Underwood (ENG)	297 (1966-1982)
Jacques Kallis (SAF)	292 (1995-2013)
Craig McDermott (AUS)	291 (1984-1996)

HIGHEST SCORES

Brian Lara (WI)	400* V England, 2004
Matthew Hayden (AUS)	380 V Zimbabwe, 2003
Brian Lara (WI)	375 V England, 1994
Mahela Jayawardene (SL)	374 V South Africa, 2006
Garfield Sobers (WI)	365* V Pakistan, 1958
Len Hutton (ENG)	364 V Australia, 1938
Sanath Jayasuriya (SL)	340 V India, 1997
Hanif Mohamma (PAK)	337 V West Indies, 1958
Wally Hammond (ENG)	336* V New Zealand, 1933
David Warner (AUS)	335* V Pakistan, 2019
Mark Taylor (AUS)	334* V Pakistan, 1998
Don Bradman (AUS)	334 V England, 1930
Graham Gooch (ENG)	333 V India, 1990
Chris Gayle (WI)	333 V Sri Lanka, 2010
Michael Clarke (AUS)	329* V India, 2012
Inzamam-ul-Haq (PAK)	329 V New Zealand, 2002
Andy Sandham (ENG)	325 V West Indies, 1930
Virender Dehwag (IND)	319 V South Africa, 2008
Kumar Sangakkara (SL)	319 V Bangladesh, 2014
Chris Gayle (WI)	317 V South Africa, 2005

Younis Khan (PAK)	313 V Sri Lanka, 2009
Hashim Amla (SAF)	311* V South Africa, 2012
Bob Simpson (AUS)	311 V England, 1964
John Edrich (ENG)	310* V New Zealand, 1965
Virender Sehwag (IND)	309 V Pakistan, 2004
Bob Cowper (AUS)	307 V England, 1966
Don Bradman (AUS)	304 V England, 1934
Karun Nair (IND)	303* V England, 2016
Azhar Ali (PAK)	302* V West Indies, 2016
Lawrence Rowe (WI)	302 V England, 1974
Brendon McCullum (NZ)	302 V India, 2014
Don Bradman (AUS)	299* V South Africa, 1932
Martin Crowe (NZ)	299 V Sri Lanka, 1991
Alastair Cook (ENG)	294 V India, 2011
Virender Sehwag (IND)	293 V Sri Lanka, 2009
Viv Richards (WI)	291 V England, 1976
Ramnaresh Sarwan (IND)	291 V England, 2009
Ross Taylor (NZ)	290 V Australia, 2015
Reg 'Tip' Foster (ENG)	287 V Australia, 1903
Kumar Sangakkara (SL)	287 V South Africa, 2006

MOST CENTURIES

Sachin Tendulkar (IND)	51 (1989-2013)
Jacques Kallis (SAF)	45 (1995-2013)
Ricky Ponting (AUS)	41 (1995-2012)
Kumar Sangakkara (SL)	38 (2000-2015)
Rahul Dravid (IND)	36 (1996-2012)
Younis Khan (PAK)	34 (2000-2017)
Sunil Gavaskar (IND)	34 (1971-1987)
Brian Lara (WI)	34 (1990-2006)
Mahela Jayawardene (SL)	34 (1997-2014)
Alastair Cook (ENG)	33 (2006-2018)
Steve Waugh (AUS)	32 (1985-2004)
Matthew Hayden (AUS)	30 (1994-2009)
Shivnarine Chanderpaul (WI)	30 (1994-2015)
Don Bradman (AUS)	29 (1928-1948)
Michael Clarke (AUS)	28 (2004-2015)
Hashim Amla (SAF)	28 (2004-2019)
Steve Smith (AUS)	28 (2010-2022)*
Joe Root (ENG)	28 (2012-2022)*
Virat Kohli (IND)	27 (2011-2022)*

Graeme Smith (SAF)	27 (2002-2014)
Allan Border (AUS)	27 (1978-1994)
Garfield Sobers (WI)	26 (1954-1974)
Inzamam-ul-Haq (PAK)	25 (1992-2007)
Kane Williamson (NZ)	24 (2010-2022)*
Greg Chappell (AUS)	24 (1970-1984)
Mohammad Yousuf (PAK)	24 (1998-2010)
David Warner (AUS)	24 (2011-2022)*
Viv Richards (WI)	24 (1974-1991)
Virender Sehwag (IND)	23 (2001-2013)
Kevin Pietersen (ENG)	23 (2005-2014)
Justin Langer (AUS)	23 (1993-2007)
Javed Miandad (PAK)	23 (1976-1993)
Wally Hammond (ENG)	22 (1927-1947)
Mohammad Azharuddin (IND)	22 (1984-2000)
Colin Cowdrey (ENG)	22 (1954-1975)
AB de Villiers (SAF)	22 (2004-2018)
Geoffrey Boycott (ENG)	22 (1964-1982)
Ian Bell (ENG)	22 (2004-2015)

MOST 50S (50-99)

Sachin Tendulkar (IND)	68 (1989-2013)
Shivnarine Chanderpaul (WI)	66 (1994-2015)
Rahul Dravid (IND)	63 (1996-2012)
Allan Border (AUS)	63 (1978-1994)
Ricky Ponting (AUS)	62 (1995-2012)
Jacques Kallis (SAF)	58 (1995-2013)
Alastair Cook (ENG)	57 (2006-2018)
VVS Laxman (IND)	56 (1996-2012)
Joe Root (ENG)	54 (2012-2022)*
Kumar Sangakkara (SL)	52 (2000-2015)
Mahela Jayawardene (SL)	50 (1997-2014)
Steve Waugh (AUS)	50 (1985-2004)
Brian Lara (WI)	48 (1990-2006)
Mark Waugh (AUS)	47 (1991-2002)
Inzamam-ul-Haq (PAK)	46 (1992-2007)
AB de Villiers (SAF)	46 (2004-2018)
Ian Bell (ENG)	46 (2004-2015)
Graham Gooch (ENG)	46 (1975-1995)
Mike Atherton (ENG)	46 (1989-2001)

Stephen Fleming (NZ)	46 (1994-2008)
Sunil Gavaskar (IND)	45 (1971-1987)
Viv Richards (WI)	45 (1974-1991)
Alec Stewart (ENG)	45 (1990-2003)
Javed Miandad (PAK)	43 (1976-1993)
Geoffrey Boycott (ENG)	42 (1064-1982)
Hashim Amla (SAF)	41 (2004-2019)
Mark Taylor (AUS)	40 (1989-1999)

MOST DISMISSALS AS WICKET KEEPER

Mark Boucher (SAF)	555 (532ct, 23st) (1997-2012)
Adam Gilchrist (AUS)	416 (379ct, 37st) (1999-2008)
Ian Healy (AUS)	395 (366ct, 29st) (1988-1999)
Rod Marsh (AUS)	355 (343ct, 12st) (1970-1984)
MS Dhoni (IND)	294 (256ct, 38st) (2005-2014)
Brad Haddin (AUS)	270 (262ct, 8st) (2008-2015)
Jeff Dujon (WI)	270 (265ct, 5st) (1981-1991)
Alan Knott (ENG)	269 (250ct, 19st) (1967-1981)
BJ Watling (NZ)	265 (257ct, 8st) (2009-2021)
Matt Prior (ENG)	256 (243ct, 13st) (2007-2014)
Alec Stewart (ENG)	241 (227ct, 14st) (1990-2003)
Quinton de Kock (SAF)	232 (221ct, 11st) (2014-2021)
Wasim Bari (PAK)	228 (201ct, 27st) (1967-1984)
Ridley Jacobs (WI)	219 (207ct, 12st) (1998-2004)
Godfrey Evans (ENG)	219 (173ct, 46st) (1946-1959)
Denesh Ramdin (WI)	217 (205ct, 12st) (2005-2016)
Kamran Akmal (PAK)	206 (184ct, 22st) (2002-2010)
Adam Parore (NZ)	201 (194ct, 7st) (1990-2002)

MOST CATCHES AS FIELDER

Rahul Dravid (IND)	210 (1996-2012)
Mahela Jayawardene (SL)	205 (1997-2014)
Jacques Kallis (SAF)	200 (1995-2013)
Ricky Ponting (AUS)	196 (1995-2012)
Mark Waugh (AUS)	181 (1991-2002)
Alastair Cook (ENG)	175 (2006-2018)
Stephen Fleming (NZ)	171 (1994-2008)
Graeme Smith (SAF)	169 (2002-2014)
Brian Lara (WI)	164 (1990-2006)
Joe Root (ENG)	163 (2012-2022)*
Ross Taylor (NZ)	163 (2007-2022)
Mark Taylor (AUS)	157 (1989-1999)
Allan Border (AUS)	156 (1978-1994)
Steve Smith (AUS)	141 (2010-2022)*
Younis Khan (PAK)	139 (2000-2017)
VVS Laxman (IND)	135 (1996-2012)
Michael Clarke (AUS)	134 (2004-2015)
Matthew Hayden (AUS)	128 (1994-2009)
Shane Warne (AUS)	125 (1992-2007)

BEST BATTING AVERAGES (MINIMUM 20 INNINGS)

Don Bradman (AUS)	99.94 (80) (1928-1948)
Adam Voges (AUS)	61.87 (31) (2015-2016)
Graeme Pollock (SF)	60.97 (41) (1963-1970)
George Headley (WI)	60.83 (40) (1930-1954)
Herb Sutcliffe (ENG)	60.73 (84) (1924-1935)
Steve Smith (AUS)	60.00 (154) (2010-2022)*
Eddie Paynter (ENG)	59.23 (31) (1931-1939)
Ken Barrington (ENG)	58.67 (131) (1955-1968)
Everton Weekes (WI)	58.61 (81) (1948-1959)
Wally Hammond (ENG)	58.45 (140) (1927-1947)
Garfield Sobers (WI)	57.78 (160) (1954-1974)
Marnus Labuschagne (AUS)	57.76 (41) (2018-2022)*
Kumar Sangakkara (SL)	57.40 (233) (2000-2015)
Jack Hobbs (ENG)	56.94 (102) (1908-1930)
Clyde Walcott (WI)	56.68 (74) (1948-1960)
Len Hutton (ENG)	56.67 (138) (1937-1955)
Jacques Kallis (SAF)	55.37 (280) (1995-2013)
Ernest Tyldesley (ENG)	55.00 (20) (1921-1929)

BEST BOWLING AVERAGES (2000+ BALLS)

George Lohmann (ENG)	10.75 (112W) (1886-1896)
JJ Ferris (AUS/ENG)	12.70 (61W) (1887-1892)
Billy Barnes (ENG)	15.54 (51W) (1880-1890)
Billy Bates (ENG)	16.42 (50W) (1881-1887)
Sydney Barnes (ENG)	16.43 (189W) (1901-1914)
Charlie Turner (AUS)	16.53 (101W) (1887-1895)
Bobby Peel (ENG)	16.98 (101W) (1884-1896)
Johnny Briggs (ENG)	17.75 (118W) (1884-1899)
Bert Ironmonger (AUS)	17.97 (74W) (1928-1933)
Fred Spofforth (AUS)	18.41 (94W) (1877-1887)
Frank Tyson (ENG)	18.56 (76W) (1954-1959)
Colin Blythe (ENG)	18.63 (100W) (1901-1910)
Kyle Jamieson (NZ)	19/45 (72W) (2020-2022)*
Ollie Robinson (ENG)	19.80 (51W) (2021-2022)*
Johnny Wardle (ENG)	20.39 (102W) (1948-1957)
George Ulyett (ENG)	20.40 (50W) (1877-1890)
Alan Davidson (AUS)	20.53 (186W) (1953-1963)
Frank Foster (ENG)	20.57 (45W) (1911-1912)
Ken Higgs (ENG)	20.74 (71W) (1965-1968)

BEST BOWLING FIGURES IN AN INNINGS

Jim Laker (ENG)	10/53 V Australia, 1956
Anil Kumble (IND)	10/74 V Pakistan, 1999
Ajaz Patel (NZ)	10/119 V India, 2021
George Lohmann (ENG)	9/28 V South Africa, 1896
Jim Laker (ENG)	9/37 V Australia, 1956
Muttiah Muralitharan (SL)	9/51 V Sri Lanka, 2002
Richard Hadlee (NZ)	9/52 V Australia, 1985
Abdul Qadir (PAK)	9/56 V England, 1987
Devon Malcolm (ENG)	9/57 V South Africa, 1994
Muttiah Muralitharan (SL)	9/65 V England, 1998
Jasubhai Patel (IND)	9/69 V Australia, 1959
Kapil Dev (IND)	9/83 V West Indies, 1983
Sarfraz Nawaz (PAK)	9/86 V Australia, 1979
Jack Noreiga (WI)	9/95 V India, 1971
Subhash Gupte (IND)	9/102 V West Indies, 1958
Sydney Barnes (ENG)	9/103 V South Africa, 1913
Hugh Tayfield (SAF)	9/113 V England, 1957
Arthur Mailey (AUS)	9/121 V England, 1921
Rangana Herath (SL)	9/127 V Pakistan, 2014

BEST BOWLING FIGURES IN A MATCH

Jim Laker (ENG)	19/90 V Australia, 1956
Sydney Barnes (ENG)	17/159 V South Africa, 1913
Narendra Hirwani (IND)	16/136 V West Indies, 1988
Bob Massie (AUS)	16/137 V England, 1972
Muttiah Muralitharan (SL)	16/220 V England, 1998
Johnny Briggs (ENG)	15/28 V South Africa, 1889
George Lohmann (ENG)	15/45 V South Africa, 1896
Colin Blythe (ENG)	15/99 V South Africa, 1907
Hedley Verity (ENG)	15/104 V Australia, 1934
Richard Hadlee (NZ)	15/123 V Australia, 1985
Wilfred Rhodes (ENG)	15/124 V Australia, 1904
Harbhajan Singh (IND)	15/217 V Australia, 2001
Fred Spofforth (AUS)	14/90 V England, 1882
Alec Bedser (ENG)	14/99 V Australia, 1953
Billy Bates (ENG)	14/102 V Australia, 1883
Imran Khan (PAK)	14/116 V Sri Lanka, 1982
Jasubhai Patel (IND)	14/124 V Australia, 1959
Sydney Barnes (ENG)	14/144 V South Africa, 1914
Michael Holding (WI)	14/149 V England, 1976

MOST FIVE WICKETS IN AN INNINGS

Muttiah Muralitharan (SL)	67 (1992-2010)
Shane Warne (AUS)	37 (1992-2007)
Richard Hadlee (NZ)	36 (1973-1990)
Anil Kumble (IND)	35 (1990-2008)
Rangana Herath (SL)	34 (1999-2018)
James Anderson (ENG)	32 (2003-2022)*
Ravichandran Ashwin (IND)	30 (2011-2022)*
Glenn McGrath (AUS)	29 (1993-2007)
Ian Botham (ENG)	27 (1977-1992)
Dale Steyn (SAF)	26 (2004-2019)
Wasim Akram (PAK)	25 (1985-2002)
Harbhajan Singh (IND)	25 (1998-2015)
Sydney Barnes (ENG)	24 (1901-1914)
Dennis Lillee (AUS)	23 (1971-1984)
Imran Khan (PAK)	23 (1971-1992)
Kapil Dev (IND)	23 (1978-1994)
Waqar Younis (PAK)	22 (1989-2003)
Malcolm Marshall (WI)	22 (1978-1991)
Curtly Ambrose (WI)	22 (1988-2000)
Courtney Walsh (WI)	22 (1984-2001)

Printed in Great Britain
by Amazon

20341836R00181

I[illegible]ng Discourse

80 Situations for Teaching Meaningful Conversation to Children

by Marion Blank, Ph.D., and M. Ann Marquis, M.S.

Communication Skill Builders®
3830 E. Bellevue/P.O. Box 42050
Tucson, Arizona 85733
(602) 323-7500

DUPLICATING

You may prefer to copy the designated reproducible materials by using stencils or spirit masters. It is not necessary to tear pages out of this book. Make a single photocopy of the desired page. Use that photocopy to make a stencil or spirit master on a thermal copier.

Communication Skill Builders, Inc.®
3830 E. Bellevue/P.O. Box 42050
Tucson, Arizona 85733
(602) 323-7500

ISBN 0-88450-217-1 Catalog No. 7403

10 9 8 7 6 5 4 3 2
Printed in the United States of America

Excerpts on pages 2-16 from "The Next Stage of Intervention" by Dr. Marion Blank in *Language Perspectives* (in press) are reprinted with permission from PRO-ED, Austin, Texas.

ABOUT THE AUTHORS

Marion Blank is the Director of Developmental Neuropsychology Service at Children's Hearing Institute, New York City; a member of the faculty of the Department of Psychiatry at Columbia University; and has her own private practice. She received her master's degree in Education from the City College of New York and her Ph.D. in Medical Psychology from Cambridge University in England.

Her impressive background includes teaching at Rutgers Medical School, Albert Einstein College of Medicine, the University of London, Hebrew University in Jerusalem, Stanford University, and Monash University in Australia. Dr. Blank has been a consultant to a number of publishing companies, educational institutions and child development centers and committees. She has been associated as editor and author with numerous journals and publications including *Behavioral and Brain Sciences, Child Development, Journal of Experimental Child Psychology, Journal of Educational Psychology, Journal of Applied Psycholinguistics,* and *Topics in Learning and Learning Disabilities.* For over two decades Dr. Blank's books and articles have played an important role in the fields of child development, linguistics, psychology, and education.

M. Ann Marquis is a Speech-Language Pathologist in a program for communicatively disordered students in Albuquerque, New Mexico. She is also Communication Consultant to the Albuquerque Public Schools and the University of New Mexico. She received a bachelor's degree in Spanish from Florida International University and a master's degree in Communicative Disorders from the University of New Mexico. In 1978, she was awarded the C.C.C. from the American Speech-Language-Hearing Association.

Ms. Marquis' professional positions have included Clinical Supervisor and Instructor in the Departments of Special Education and Communicative Disorders at the University of New Mexico, consultant to rehabilitation programs and Head Start, and associate to private educational agencies. For several years, she has been developing games and activities for use in language therapy with young children and adolescents. She is currently on the Author Advisory Board of Communication Skill Builders.

FOREWORD

In 1980 I presented a paper entitled "I don't care who said it or what it means, just tell me what to do." The paper was a reaction address that was given after a panel of distinguished speakers finished discussing their research in language, learning, and reading disabilities. I began by stating the title for my talk, which did not appear on the program. The reaction was amazing: The audience clapped loudly and with great enthusiasm! While ego-gratifying on certain levels, I found this reaction quite disconcerting. I am certain the audience was disappointed because the point of my presentation was to show how a strong theoretical base was needed for language intervention to make sense. I went on to say that, as I saw it, people just wanted to *know what to do* with very little understanding of *what it is.* The *what it is* involved an understanding of language development as well as an understanding of cognitive and social development, information-processing theory, and the influence of context and material on children's performances.

We have come a very long way even from 1980. The research in language, communication, metalinguistics, and metacognition has been tremendous. The work in narrative development, classroom discourse, and conversational interaction has also given us an enormous theoretical base from which language intervention and remediation ideas may be gleaned.

Clinical and educational application still lag behind theoretical advances. This is not new. We have all been touched by the pragmatics revolution in child language and we are indeed much more sensitive to the changes in philosophy that have affected both research and clinical and educational goals. However, we still have difficulty bringing the research to life in our classrooms, resource rooms, and clinics. As we move further away from a focus on specific skills manifested by infamous color-naming drills, "-ing" lessons, classification activities, sentence repetition, and other variations, we are challenged to present children with opportunities to become better communicators. As we move toward the development of pragmatic and conversational taxonomies that seem overwhelmingly broad, we are tempted to take a slightly different approach from the *Tell me what to do* one that was stated in 1980. Now the question is *Where do I begin?*

Blank and Marquis provide an innovative approach for teaching conversation to children that begins to answer that question. By focusing on discourse and its various levels, the authors bring to life some of the how-tos without making their lesson formats unrealistically cumbersome and without, as they put it, creating conversations that have the "bizarre quality" often unknowingly encouraged in some of the popular prepackaged programs.

Directing Discourse represents a strong and potentially powerful prototype for discourse development from a number of perspectives, but it does not pretend, as some books and programs do, to encompass all human verbal interaction. Nevertheless, it is quite comprehensive because it provides a model rather than a series of intervention bandages. Its strength is manifested in a number of ways. The invervention suggestions come from a solid theoretical framework discussed in earlier works by Blank and her colleagues (Blank, Rose, and Berlin 1978a). Blank and Marquis talk about current issues in language pragmatics and show readers how their ideas relate to many concepts being discussed today. *Directing Discourse* is a refreshing change from workbooks that approach language intervention with a *try a little bit of this and a little bit of that* philosophy. It is the only resource available that helps teachers and clinicians structure conversations by carefully considering the conceptual level of both questions and comments. We are encouraged to take a hard look at the truisms we have held for so long. Some of the truisms challenged by Blank and Marquis are "Say less to children," "Encourage them to talk about anything they like," and "Repeat questions a number of times to facilitate verbal processing." *Directing Discourse* also shows us how to make conversations more relevant. Blank and Marquis ask us to think about the differences between *relevance* and validity when making language-intervention decisions. They present numerous examples that demonstrate how irrelevant some classroom and language therapy sessions really are. Readers of *Directing Discourse* will recognize many of the examples. We are challenged to think about the relevance of lessons derived from category-based topics such as fruits, clothing, and animals. We are asked to think about exercises that focus on word-opposites, and activities that require children to talk about size, color, shape, and composition of objects. Blank and Marquis suggest we ask ourselves whether children really believe these tasks represent the core of conversation.

Although Blank and Marquis challenge many traditional approaches to language intervention and remediation, they offer powerful alternatives. They also show us how to modify and expand the knowledge we already have about language, communicative competence, and cognitive competence. The lesson plans presented in *Directing Discourse* not only make the sequences and conversational tasks explicit but also provide a broad organizational framework. The conversational levels are applicable to a wide range of children and cover diverse topics. The procedures outlined help us integrate contextual, instructional, and child variables. This book represents a tremendous link between theory and practice. Its creative and innovative approach to discourse development is an exciting beginning for those of us in the business of helping children become better communicators. We can only hope that Blank and Marquis continue their work in the area and provide us with additional installments of this work.

Geraldine P. Wallach, Ph.D.
Professor of Communication Disorders
Emerson College

CONTENTS

DISCOURSE AND PRAGMATICS

For a number of decades, speech-language professionals who studied language development focused primarily on the areas of semantics and syntax (Prutting 1982). More recently, research on language has shifted to pragmatics; that is, the way language is used in purposeful communication. Led by investigators such as Bates (1976), Spekman (1983), and Rees (1978), it is now recognized that "successful communication requires that the speaker learn what to talk about and under what circumstances, as well as how to say it" (Spekman 1983, 157).

This shift is exciting, but at the same time overwhelming for it essentially extends therapy to encompass all of human verbal interaction. As such, the clinician or teacher who wishes to foster pragmatic development is faced with a potentially endless array of behaviors. If progress is to be made, this near-infinite field must be delineated into a manageable array of well-defined domains.

The purpose of this book is to present a way of approaching discourse, or the sustained analysis and development of an idea through language. It contains many complex components with one of the chief ones being topic maintenance. This point is stressed because many topics do not require sustained development. For example, two- and three-turn greeting exchanges do not demand such development even though they call upon a range of pragmatic skills (eye contact, tone of voice, and conveying intentions). While these areas are central in human interaction, they are not the ones of concern here. Rather, the topics of this book, much like stories, contain underlying themes that evolve with each turn in the conversation. In trying to conceptualize this type of discourse, it is useful to borrow the idea of *text,* a term commonly associated with written language. As noted by Halliday and Hasan, text is a meaningful way to describe "any passage, spoken or written, of whatever length, that does form a meaningful whole" (1976, 1). Thus, as in written texts, oral texts can be conceptualized as containing sequenced sets of words, phrases, and sentences that work together to create a meaningful unity.

THE ORGANIZATION OF ORAL TEXTS

With the surge of interest in pragmatics, a wide variety of new behaviors has come under study. Unfortunately, the issue of topic selection and development has not yet received the detailed attention it merits. To the degree that it has been studied, the ideas have commonly been framed in terms of the *children's behavior.* They have included such skills as the ability to initiate and terminate a topic, to respond appropriately, and to demonstrate situational appropriateness (Damico 1985, Roth and Spekman 1984). *The issue of the topics offered to the children by the adults* has been almost unnoticed. It seems to have been assumed that the topics raised by adults do not require analysis. It is this assumption that deserves serious scrutiny.

An anecdote reported by Rees (1978) highlights this concern. She describes a "mentally retarded girl" who had received "psycholinguistic training." In the described incident, the girl upon being handed a cup says, "It's a cup, it's pink, it's plastic, you drink out of it." The utterance clearly has a "bizarre quality." But Rees points out that of even greater interest is that the bizarre quality is a direct consequence of the teaching the child has experienced. The teaching has "led the student to use language in ways that are not simply different, but also inappropriately different, from those of the average person." (Blank, in press)

When one looks at current classroom texts, the reasons for the girl's "failure" become clear. This is seen in the following segment of dialogue from a typical preschool program (Blank, in press). The instructor is teaching the concept of texture by having the children group rough objects in one circle (Mr. Rough's Circle) and smooth ones in another circle (Mr. Smooth's Circle).

Teacher: Well, let's see, Steven. Would you like to go into the box and pick out something?

Steven: (selects a ball)

Teacher: What's that? You just look at it. What's that?

Steven: A ball.

Teacher: What do you use a ball for, Peter?

Peter: Bouncing up and down and throwing up.

Teacher: And would it just be boys and girls that use the ball?

Peter: Yes.

Teacher: Is it? No one else at all?

Peter: Nope.

Teacher: No? What colors are in the ball, Pauline?

Pauline: Blue and yellow and red and orange.

Teacher: Pauline, Mr. Rough (referring to a puppet) wants you to decide if that ball is smooth like Mr. Smooth or is it rough like Mr. Rough? Would you like to feel it against your cheek? Put it up against your cheek with your hands.

Pauline: (rubs ball against cheek)

Teacher: Is it smooth or is it rough?

Pauline: Smooth.

Teacher: It's smooth. Well. Mr. Rough has a rough ring here and Mr. Smooth has a smooth ring here and he wants Peter and Steven and Laura Ann to put the articles that are either smooth or rough into the right one. Pauline, you said it was smooth—so what one are you going to put it in?

Pauline: (puts ball in smooth ring)

Teacher: The smooth one! So Mr. Smooth has got one. Right. Peter, would you like to get into the box, please?

Peter: (takes out grater) (Laura Ann spontaneously says, "That one's for Mr. Rough.")

Teacher: Now, what's that? Can you tell us what that is?

Laura: A grater.

Teacher: A grater. What do you use a grater for?

Pauline: Grating cheese.

Teacher: Grate cheese. Anything else?

Steven: Carrots.

Teacher: What do you grate carrots for?

Steven: Eat.

Teacher: What foods would you be eating if you were grating carrots?

Laura: Soup?

Teacher: Soup. Oh, we have lovely soup in the wintertime. Well, who does the grater belong to?

Steven: (pointing to an object in the box) That's for the winter.

Teacher: For the winter and that's when we have soup as well.

Laura: Mr. Rough! Mr. Rough!

Teacher: Well, are we going to put it in Mr. Rough's ring?

Peter: (puts it in the circle for Mr. Rough)

Teacher: So each one has one thing.

> This type of dialogue is so familiar in classrooms that it takes on the quality of most familiar patterns; that is, it feels both appropriate and comfortable. Yet, it is nearly identical to the language intervention dialogues that led the mentally retarded girl to produce the "pink, plastic cup" example cited earlier. . . . Like the children in [the preschool], and like the children in hundreds of classrooms around the world, for years she had been told to cite the name, size, color, shape, and composition of objects; and she now quite reasonably believes that this type of label and attribute description form the core of a conversation. (Blank, in press)

Of particular importance is the fact that the girl's *"bizarre" response was not the result of poor learning, but rather of effective learning.* She learned what she had been taught.

If more effective discourse is to be developed, it is essential to change what she and other children are being taught. To this end, it is essential to examine the range of topics being offered to children. Rather, clear guidelines must be established that permit the development of effective topics of conversation.

In achieving this goal, the following two issues are central:

1. The relevance of an utterance in a text
2. The connections between the successive utterances in a text.

The Relevance of Utterance

Texts involving meaningful topics are not simply extended sequences of language. Instead, all the components within the extended sequence must relate to the basic underlying topic. *Thus, one reasonably expects that a conversation about preparing food will differ markedly from one concerned with shopping for food, even though food is present in both conversations.* In the former conversation, one could imagine hearing about the dishes one will need, the recipe that might be followed, and the ingredients that will be used. In the latter, one might hear about the amount of money needed for the purchase, the availability of certain foods and whether or not a shopping cart is necessary. The topic essentially determines the relevance or irrelevance of any bit of information raised.

"The issue of relevance (i.e., the meaningfulness of an idea) should not be confused with the issue of validity (i.e., the truth of an idea)" (Blank, in press). In school dialogue, such confusion is not uncommon

> and it is often the factor responsible for inappropriate conversation. The Mr. Rough—Mr. Smooth dialogue presented earlier is an example of the failure to make the distinction between relevance

> and validity. The teacher has ostensibly set the concept of texture as the topic. In this context, all of the questions that she asks represent valid characteristics of the objects being discussed (i.e., each object does have a color, a function, etc.). (Blank, in press)

Nevertheless, few of the questions are relevant to the topic of texture.

> The ball's smoothness does not depend upon its being red or blue or any other color; similarly, the fact that carrots can be put into soups has nothing to do with the roughness of the grater.
>
> The linking of irrelevance and validity is responsible for providing children with incorrect information about the organization and purpose of dialogue. Its importance can be gauged from the fact that it is probably the key factor in determining our feelings about the inappropriateness of the "conversation" about the pink plastic cup. Pink and plastic and cup are all valid characteristics of the cup, but that fact does not make them relevant items for conversation. (Blank, in press)

The schism in school dialogue between relevance and validity seems to be a consequence of the ideas that have been selected for discussion. Schools have long emphasized verbal categories. From the earliest ages, "texts and lesson plans abound with category-based topics such as CLOTHING, ANIMALS, FOOD and WEATHER" (Blank, in press). The preschool discussion presented earlier is clearly of this type. "The teacher selected the category of TEXTURE as her topic, but she could just as easily have chosen SIZE or COLOR or SHAPE" (Blank, in press).

These sorts of categories can be useful, particularly when the goal is the storage and retrieval of information. For example, if one went to a library to find some material on birds, the search would be fruitless without a classification system. *However, such systems are not what conversation can or should be about.*

The inappropriateness of using categories as the basis of conversation is highlighted in a joke about a person known for his lack of social skill. He was given a telephone book to read and, upon completing his assignment, was asked, "What did you think of it?" He replied, "It didn't have much plot, but it did have a great cast of characters."

Just as there is not much to converse about in a phone book, there is also not much one can say about the traditional topics of conversation used in schools. The teacher in the earlier texture lesson senses this and, in an effort to expand the discussion, she resorts to the standard set of questions about color, use and association. Thus, by using unsuitable topics, all conversations begin to look alike. As a consequence, the children receive misleading models about the diverse nature of meaningful dialogue.

Predicating a Concept

These comments ought not be interpreted to mean that the typical school topics are without value. They represent appealing, concrete material children can understand. But if material is to be of value, it must be fitted to the structure of meaningful oral text.

> The adaptation can be achieved by a process that might best be termed *predicating the concept*. In brief, this process means that the topic selected for discussion is represented not simply by a noun (e.g., colors, numbers, food, etc.), but rather by a relevant predicate that modifies the noun. (Blank, in press)

Perhaps the easiest way to see how a predicated concept constrains a text is to think of a newspaper headline involving the concept of a *baboon*. Like all concepts, this one involves a rich set of associations (primates, climbing trees, wild animals, etc.). However, if the headline reads *Baby receives baboon's heart* the reader's associations are both altered and organized. The typical associations to baboon fade while others come to the fore. For example, one expects information about medical details and ethical issues.

The idea of predicating a concept applies to all the lessons in this book. The development of a predicated concept will vary according to the domain being discussed. For example, text that evolves around a story will differ from the text that evolves around constructing a puzzle. The models will intentionally be varied so the children will achieve the important realization that the pattern of discourse changes according to the type of topic under discussion. At the same time, a limited and manageable number of models will be presented so the children will not be inundated with diversity.

Predicated concepts provide a number of additional benefits. First, in contrast to a straightforward description of objects or pictures, they offer motivating activities that encourage more active participation in dialogue. It is difficult for even the most non-verbal children to resist washing a doll or making chocolate pudding. Second, predicated concepts by definition have a reasonably predictable sequential development. For example, after washing a doll, it is natural to expect to dry and clothe it. *In offering predictability, predicated concepts provide an avenue for attaining one of the major goals in pragmatics, helping the child anticipate and interpret the intentions and expectations of the other person.*

Typically, intentions and expectations have been thought of as being social in nature and, of course, they are. But it is equally true that they contain what are conceived of as more cognitive components. Specifically, if one has a meaningful, logically evolving text, then one can begin to anticipate what the other person will be thinking and saying. Essentially, predicated concepts provide the basis for the much desired "shared focus of attention," ensuring a greater likelihood that the child will become a more active participant in the verbal flow.

This predicated topic approach gives a different view of children's spontaneous talk than is found in many other approaches. Relevant, spontaneous speech is highly desirable, but often the method of its attainment is not clear. Frequently, the hope is that it can be fostered by placing a child in a relatively undefined situation where the child is seemingly free to say whatever comes to mind. Despite its appeal, this setting does not provide the security necessary for productive dialogue. Rather, particularly for children in difficulty, it often provokes the anxiety that follows when clear guidelines are not available. By contrast, a child, like all of us, will begin to talk freely and appropriately when comfortable and secure. Familiarity with motivating topics based on predicated concepts can help to provide that comfort and security.

The Connections Between Successive Utterances in a Text

An essential feature to text unity is *coherence,* or the linking of individual utterances so that they relate to each other in an orderly manner. Like many other components of communication, the attainment of coherence is by no means easy or assured (Dorval and Eckerman 1984; Friel-Patti and Conti-Ramsden 1984; Westby 1984). An understanding of the difficulty can be gained by examining a relatively simple text. The segment that follows is from an English nursery story (Uttley 1980) in which Hare, who lives with Grey Rabbit, is speaking about his chilblain (frostbite):

> "Ow, ow!" exclaimed Hare, rubbing his toe. "Do think of something, Grey Rabbit, you don't know how it hurts."
>
> "Moldy Warp once told me to use some snow," said Grey Rabbit. "I'll get some." She ran outside and scraped the frost from the grass. Then she rubbed Hare's foot till the chilblain disappeared. (Uttley 1980)

The text, written for young children, seems relatively simple. Nevertheless, it has many characteristics of any sustained text. While there is an overall unity to the ideas, the sentences contain enormous changes from one to the other in practically every aspect of language—syntactic structures, number of words, specific concepts covered, and the basic message of each sentence. For example, in terms of speaker intent—a major pragmatic variable—the first utterance contains a least three speech acts: a complaint, a direct request, and an implied request.

For those who are skilled in language, the rapid shifts across sentences go almost unnoticed and the text is perceived as coherent. However, the reason for the coherence is not based directly on what is stated. It is achieved by a subtle and complex meshing of explicit and implicit information. For instance, the request by Hare and the response by Grey Rabbit can be related only if the reader interpolates a range of unstated ideas such as (a) *Grey Rabbit has recognized that Hare is complaining and* (b) *that his complaint has a basis in reality.* (c) *He plans to grapple with the problem.* (d) *The way he is going to offer help is to rely on some information provided by another animal.* (e) *That animal is Moldy Warp.*

For those who do not make these implicit connections, the two sentences stand as separate ideas that happen to be close to one another.

> For example, if one could ask the nonverbally sophisticated child, "Which sentence is a more logical one in the exchange between Hare and Grey Rabbit, 'She ran outside and scraped the frost from the grass' or 'She ran outside and made some snowballs for throwing,'" it is unclear whether the child would see one as preferable to the other. Indeed, the latter might be seen as better since it both connects more directly to the word *snow* in the previous sentence and it reflects a more desirable activity. (Blank, in press)

Making the Implicit Explicit

> In helping children gain a sense of the vital, but elusive, component of coherence, it is useful to employ a technique that might best be termed making the implicit explicit. Essentially, it involves the adult filling in the missing links so that the language disabled child is offered a model of how connected discourse is constructed. Of course, no text can be totally explicit. If the gaps are fairly small, however, children can cope more effectively. A narrow gap might be exemplified by the following: After Hare says, "You don't know how it hurts," Grey Rabbit might have said, "Oh, it does hurt and I will help you so that it stops hurting." The redundancy of the information and the closer semantic links (hurt = help) allow the child to avoid dealing with high levels of implicit information. (Blank, in press)

Illustrations of making the implicit explicit are in the expanded lessons at the beginning of each area. The following basic principles underly this process:

1. The adult's verbalizations are more elaborate than is commonly the case and they contain a number of comments surrounding any question or problem posed. For example, in making orange juice, the adult may have led a child to the point of recognizing that the orange needs to be cut. Rather than say, "Get a knife," the adult might say, "If we're going to cut it, we need something that will be able to do that. One of the things we could use is a knife. Go get one."
2. The adult's elaborating comments help make explicit the ideas underlying the topic being discussed. They help the students to connect what the adult has been saying and to connect what the children themselves have been saying so that a much more integrated discussion takes place.
3. The effect of the comments is that the adult's utterances contain considerable redundancy. These are restatements of bits of information in slightly varying form so that each statement builds slowly on the preceding one ("The orange needs to be cut; a knife is good for cutting, get a knife.")

> These characteristics by themselves are not particularly striking. Nevertheless, their implementation effects dramatic changes in the dialogue. For instance, one consequence concerns in the amount of language used by teachers. In contrast to the frequent suggestion that instructors ought to reduce their language output, the ideas proposed here lead to a substantial increase in teacher utterances. However, if their effects are to be positive, the increase cannot be indiscriminate; rather, the greater verbalization occurs primarily through the introduction of information in comment as opposed to question form. As a result, the rate of questioning should dip dramatically relative to the total amount of teacher verbalization.
>
> The alteration in the teacher's pattern of language has definite advantages, particularly for language disabled children. As noted above, the expanded verbalization is largely redundant. As a result, if children attend, they have the opportunity to have the information reinforced. By contrast, if their attention wavers, they still have the opportunity to hear the message that might have been missed. In addition, the expanded messages provide children with more time between questions, thereby meeting their need to have longer periods in which to process information. Finally, in making the implicit explicit, the demands for inferential reasoning on the children's part are reduced, thereby bringing the conversation within manageable proportions. (Blank, in press)

CONCEPTUAL LEVELS OF DISCOURSE

A predictable topic provides the framework for a meaningful discussion. However, its use alone does not assure a successful lesson. The course of the discussion must be at a level that the child can conceptually follow the ideas that arise. For example, imagine two children in a supermarket. One is quite limited and can understand the idea of money only as the transfer of some particular pieces of paper and coins between the shopper and the person at the cash register. The other child is far more sophisticated and can even compute (within limits) the amount to be paid and the amount of change to be received. It seems clear that although both children might be in a discussion on the predicated concept of buying food, the level of the discussion will and ought to be markedly different for each one. The demands on the former child must be restricted to relatively simple tasks that focus on the immediately evident objects and events such as "Who are you going to give the money to?" and "Give him this." By contrast, the demands on the latter child can include more complex requests along with simple ones such as "Is that item one we had on our shopping list?" and "Will we have enough money to buy it along with all the other items?" The conversation with the more sophisticated child should not be limited to higher-level demands. Simpler demands must also be included. A continuously high level conversation is artificial and overly demanding and, therefore, should never be used.

Interacting with children on an appropriate conceptual level reinforces their comfort with the interaction. If children understand the topic and are comfortable with the adult language level, they are more likely to feel free to initiate elements into the conversation. A child who is able to predict what is relevant in a dialogue has the opportunity to contribute to it.

Determination of simple versus complex demands is not an easy matter and the elaboration of this issue exceeds the material that can be presented here. Interested readers may refer to Blank (1983) and Blank, Rose, and Berlin (1978a and b) for a model and an extended discussion of this issue.

The material in *Directing Discourse* is arranged to take account of the vital role played by children's different levels of functioning. Specifically, each lesson is formulated at a conceptually simple level and at a conceptually complex level. In general, the simple level is appropriate for children whose language functioning is equivalent to that of normal children approximately three to five years of age, while the complex level is appropriate for children whose language functioning is equivalent to that of children about five to eight years of age.

Simple versus complex applies only to the actual *demands* being put to the children. The *comments* surrounding the demands, even for the more restricted child, can be at any level of complexity. This allows the children to attend to, and possibly glean meaning from, the surrounding verbal material. If they do not fully comprehend the comments, they can still respond appropriately to the demands, thereby promoting success and avoiding failure. By making more complex language available children are helped to become accustomed to hearing higher levels of language without experiencing the failure that has been such a part of their lives. Complex language thereby becomes a more familiar and more comfortable part of their environment.

In deciding which level is suitable, a formal or informal assessment of each student is useful. A checklist for informal assessment is on pages 228-229. Some possible formal assessment measures include:

Preschool Language Assessment Instrument (PLAI) (1978)

Token Test for Children (1978)

Porch Index of Communicative Ability in Children (PICAC) (1979)

Weschlser Intelligence Scale for Children—Revised (WISC-R)—Vocabulary Subtest (1974)

Weschsler Preschool and Primary Scale of Intelligence (WPPSI)—Vocabulary Subtest (1967)

Clinical Evaluation of Language Functions (CELF) (1980)

AREAS OF LANGUAGE ACTIVITY

The lessons in *Directing Discourse* are grouped into the following five major areas:

1. Organization of Objects and Materials
2. Transformation of Material
3. Perceptual Analysis of Material
4. Games and Motor Activities
5. Dramatic and Written Representation

Texts can vary greatly from one context to another. For example, a discussion about planning a trip will have a different course and content than a discussion about the rules for playing a game. These five areas will provide the children with some insight into the variability of discourse and the way in which different content areas are responsible for the variability. Each area contains predicated topics that allow and require sustained analysis of a sequentially evolving activity. Without this feature, there is no need for extended discourse. The lessons should not be presented by areas. From day to day, the selection should vary from one area to another. This allows the child to become familiar with variability and also increases motivation.

Organization of Objects and Materials

This area is based on the idea that certain objects and materials can be created from parts or can be separated into parts (a dollhouse, a tool set). It is designed to help children analyze the complexity inherent in common material that is usually taken for granted. To achieve this, a situation might be set up where a broken chair has to be repaired. Lessons are structured so that students are led to solve problems at each point in the sequence.

Different concepts would be used according to the content or materials under consideration. For example, if parts are emphasized, the parts in building a house will be doors, windows, and a roof, while the parts in sewing a dress would be sleeves, collars, and buttons. Similarly, if means-end relationships are emphasized, the relevant ones in building a house might be nails and hammer and in sewing a dress they might be needles and thread.

To illustrate, in a lesson concerned with repairing a chair the following materials might be used:

1. Bits of wood cut into shapes for the seat, back, and legs
2. A simple chair or a picture of a simple chair as a model to guide the student's construction
3. Material or objects that would be inappropriate for constructing a chair (paper, rocks, cup) to contrast with appropriate material
4. Material for combining the parts (glue, hammer, nails, or strong tape) (see Blank 1983).

Transformation of Material

Lessons in Organization of Objects and Material focus on objects that can be taken apart or put together. The component parts do not lose their identity. By contrast, in Transformation of Material lessons, the substances undergo changes so that the original components are no longer recognizable (flour and water becomes dough, fruit becomes juice, corn kernels become popcorn). Language in this area focuses on talking about cause and effect relationships that are present when materials are combined to form a new whole, as in making cookies.

This area is important for children who are often not able to comprehend the sequence of actions that occur when the beginning and end products show marked changes. For example, water melted from snow is frequently seen as independent of the snow, even when the child has observed the melting process from start to finish. Transformation of Materials lessons can help children bring order to what they may have perceived as isolated, incoherent bits of information.

Perceptual Analysis of Material

This area requires that the child analyze perceptual material to become aware of its various features and their relationships. Lessons in this area involve making puzzles, creating gameboards, and drawing a room plan. These activities tend to involve language that focuses on the analysis of the perceptual input (which pieces fit and the characteristics of the pieces that are difficult to place).

Games and Motor Activities

Games and Motor Activities present excellent motivational settings for facilitating language interaction. Activities such as bowling or basketball encourage language associated with the establishment of rules, the sequence of play and methods of keeping score. By bringing games into a cognitive domain, the added advantage exists of showing a child that almost any activity can be subjected to analysis—should one choose to do so. The general format is such that as the student sets up the activity and starts playing, language is interwoven with the actions. For example, after the students unbox a game of croquet, they can identify the game parts, distribute the hoops according to a diagram, and engage in a conversation about how to angle the ball through the hoops. This type of material can be extended to help students use a written symbol system to keep score in a game.

Dramatic and Written Representation

This area, which is traditionally associated with language activities, involves reading books, dramatizing plays and poems, and creating stories. While literature can be highly motivating, the usual means of story representation is often beyond the capabilities of a language-handicapped child. Problems arise in large measure because the children experience a story as a random collection of independent facts rather than as a series of events linked into a sequence.

For purposes of language development during Dramatic and Written Representation lessons, books are not read in the traditional way of telling a story. Instead, the story is the vehicle for creating a dialogue that gives the child insight into the organization of written text. This is often accomplished by bringing a story to life with dolls and other materials. In addition, the child may be asked to explain the actions in the story, to predict outcomes, or to act out a scene or story. The idea of bringing the story to life may be greatly expanded by creating and performing age-appropriate plays. Many metalinguistic activities are naturally appropriate (analyzing words, offering synonomous rephrasing, and altering a sequence of words). The lesson format allows metalinguistic concepts to be interlaced into discourse in a relevant and cohesive manner.

Relationship of Preschool to School Curriculum

Because each area tends to emphasize different ideas and material, together they encompass many of the prerequisites to the curriculum for a school-age child. For instance, Organization of Objects and Materials and Transformation of Material include what is frequently termed "science" for the young child. Dramatic and Written Representation is highly related to language arts. Through stories, children deal with the comprehension of verbal material, while Perceptual Analysis of Material is related to skills needed for learning a written symbol system. Games and Motor Activities covers a wide area that can be used for a variety of purposes. For example, a lesson that includes keeping score is useful for understanding written codes while a lesson focused on shapes (for example, placement of the lines on a basketball court) emphasizes perceptual analysis.

Although the different areas have different emphases, lessons from particular areas are not to be viewed as representing firm categories.

> . . . any lesson can easily drift across areas. For example, in a lesson on cooking, it might be useful to introduce drawing (e.g., drawing a fried egg) to help the child focus on the different parts of an object. In addition, some lessons do not fit easily into any category. Thus, introductory lessons with timid children frequently are based upon undemanding, non-threatening situations such as the doll play traditionally associated with play therapy. While it is possible to use such lessons for cognitive development, (e.g., "let's fill the pan with water," "where did you put the doll's clothes?" etc.) the lesson does not appear readily to fit into any of the defined categories. Thus, rather than viewing the categories as rigid areas, they can be seen as flexible frameworks in which to cover almost any idea that can be meaningfully raised with a young child. (Blank 1983, 279).

THE TREATMENT OF WRONG RESPONSES

When discourse is organized to match children's conceptual level, they will be able to effectively handle the majority of demands imposed. Nevertheless, some degree of error will invariably occur and the adult must be prepared to cope with these errors in a way that permits the child (1) to avoid the shame of failure, and (2) to experience a more effective way of handling the problem.

One of the most effective means for achieving these goals is to use "simplification techniques" (Blank 1983). Specifically, the problem the child could not cope with is simplified to a point the child can deal with. For example, imagine a situation where the adult asks, "Why do you think we couldn't get this sponge into the [too small] cup and we could fit in the soap?" The child responds, "Because it's a sponge." Should this occur, the adult simplifies, "Okay, I'll cut this sponge into two. Now it's still a sponge. Why does it go into the cup now?" Extended discussions and illustrations of simplifications are in Blank (1983) and Blank, Rose, and Berlin (1978a).

Further, the lessons in *Directing Discourse* contain examples of various simplification techniques for use when the child encounters difficulty. The one major area that is not "simplified" is labeling objects. If a child does not know or recall a particular label, it is simply provided by the adult.

LESSONS FOR DIRECTING DISCOURSE

Directing Discourse provides speech-language pathologists and teachers with context-appropriate activities that take the guesswork out of language teaching. This sourcebook provides the topics of conversation and the sequences for presenting ideas that lead children to higher levels of language functioning.

The lessons are at two levels: The Simple Level is suitable for language ages 3-5 years, and the Complex Level is intended for language ages 5-8 years. Level of abstract language, of vocabulary, and of language complexity vary between the two levels.

Language activities are divided among five areas:

1. Organization of Objects and Materials
2. Transformation of Material
3. Perceptual Analysis of Material
4. Games and Motor Activities
5. Dramatic and Written Representation

Eight lessons from each area are included for each level, making a total of eighty lessons. A list of additional lesson ideas are included for each area.

Two expanded lessons (one from the simple level and one from the complex level) provide a more complete model of discourse for each area. In addition to the eighty lessons, a list of additional lesson ideas is included at the end of each area.

How to Use the Lessons

These lessons are based on the principles presented in previous sections of this book. Each lesson is written as if it were being conducted with one child. However, the lessons can easily be used with a group.

Instructors are not expected to memorize the lessons, but they must gain a sense of how the discourse should flow for particular activities. The layout of the lessons is arranged to be previewed with ease. Specifically, each lesson is designed to communicate three to five major points to the child. These points are identified by the capital letters A, B, C, D, and E. The points need never be stated directly by the adult. They are transmitted through tasks identified by numbers (1, 2, 3, etc.).

The lessons are a framework of the adult's verbalizations and polite components of speech such as *please* and *thank you* have not been explicitly noted. They should be added to the discussions whenever appropriate. As with any part of the lessons, spontaneous adult interjections that are relevant to the topic move the interaction from a rigid format to comfortable discourse.

The lessons show the adult's verbalizations to the child. The adult's verbalizations are not restricted to questions and commands. They include many comments that serve several purposes, including (1) providing a child with a more natural and richer language sample, (2) offering a verbal context that allows easier understanding of the demand being made, and (3) allowing the pace of the questions to be slower than usual, thereby providing the greater processing time many children need to follow the dialogue. *To aid in distinguishing between comments and demands on the child, commands and questions are in italics.* The comments must be contextually appropriate and coherent, but they can be at any level of conceptual difficulty. The commands and questions are designed to be at the child's level.

The first lesson (both simple and complex) in each area is in a complete form, that is, it contains all the comments, demands, and questions that an adult might direct to a child (except those that arise spontaneously). In the abbreviated lessons (Lessons 2-8), questions, demands and comments are focal points. When used in actual interchange, they require elaboration. Lessons are expanded primarily by incorporating children's spontaneous comments and questions into the dialogue and also by offering verbalizations that contain redundancy. Restating information in a slightly varying form gives children more opportunity to understand the language demand directed toward them. (For example, "You've talked about two important persons in the story. Who were the two important persons?"). All lessons, even the initial expanded ones, can be elaborated further, depending on time and the skill of the child.

The discourse lessons are designed to last 15-30 minutes, depending on the topic and the children's abilities and attention spans. Details or materials for a particular topic can be changed whenever appropriate.

Lessons

The area of language activity for each lesson is indicated on each left-hand page in the upper left corner. The lessons are identified as *Simple* or *Complex* in the upper right corner of the right-hand page.

PROCEDURE

1. Assess each child's language to determine if the Simple Level or the Complex Level is the appropriate level of discourse.

2. Choose a topic and read the lesson through before gathering the materials needed. To carry out a topic successfully, have all the materials at hand.

3. Have many non-relevant materials available to help the child focus and recognize the distinction between relevant and non-relevant materials and ideas.

4. Comment as much as you question.

Making A House Out of a Cardboard Box

Materials
Books with pictures of houses and parts of houses, paper or plastic shapes (square, triangle, rectangle, and oval) cardboard box, triangular blocks, ball, crayons, scissors, tape

A. Establishing the Shape of a House

1. We've make lots of things here, but we've never made a house. I thought today we could do that—we could make a house. First, though, we have to make sure what a house looks like so that ours will be right. There's a house in this book and it's on the page where the piece of paper is.

   [Pointing to a bookmark.]

   Open the book to where the paper is.

2. Great. *Now look at all the pictures on the page and find the one that is a house.*

3. Look over here at these things.

   [Referring to the square, triangle, rectangle, and oval.]

   None of these shapes is a house, but one of them looks a lot like the shape of the house in the book. *Which one looks most like the shape of the house?*

4. That's right. It looks a lot like that. That shape is called a "rectangle." *Say "rectangle."*

5. Let's look at this page.

   [Exposing a page with a lot of houses on it.]

   Find a house. Is it shaped like a rectangle?

6. *Point to another. Is it shaped like a rectangle?*

7. *And just one more.*

   [Pointing.]

   Is this shaped like a rectangle?

B. Selecting Materials and Identifying the Parts of a House

1. All the houses we looked at had a rectangular shape so I think our house ought to be shaped like that. *Go over to the table.*

   [The table contains items such as a cardboard box, triangular blocks, and a ball.]

   Find something that has that kind of shape so we can use it to make the house.

2. That's a perfect choice, but it isn't a house yet. A house has all kinds of things on it and ours doesn't have anything on it yet. Look at the picture again and let's see what things are on houses.

   [Referring to the first picture.]

   And tell me what this is.

   [Pointing to a window.]

3. *And this.*

   [Pointing to a roof.]

4. *And this.*

   [Pointing to a door.]

5. Now look at the box that you brought over. *Does it have windows?*

6. *Or a roof?*

7. *Or a door?*

C. Creating the Parts on the House

1. Well, I guess we've got to put those things on our house. I think we should start with the windows. I'll take this crayon and draw one window here. Now, *you draw another window over here*. But wait, *do you want to use the same color crayon I used or do you want to use a different color?*

2. Okay, here's a different (same) color crayon. *Go ahead and draw the window.*

3. These windows look nice, but if people want to look out of them, we'll have to get this cardboard out of the way. We're going to have to cut it out. *What can we use to cut the cardboard out so that the windows will be more like windows?*

   [Offer choice of scissors, a ruler, and a cup.]

4. Scissors will be fine. *Remember, when you cut with the scissors, keep them on the line* so the window stays the way we drew it.

5. *Now let's cut the other window.* I'll start again and *here, you finish it.*

D. Making a Door

1. We've done the windows, but look over here.

   [Referring to the picture of the house again.]

   What is this?

2. That's right. It's a door, *but does our house have a door?*

3. I think we ought to make one. It's necessary to have a door. *Where would you like to put it? Here or here?*

   [Either placement should be suitable for a door.]

4. Now you can draw the door. *Do you remember what you used to draw the window?*

5. That's right. A crayon. In fact, you used this color for drawing the window. *Do you want to use the same one again or would you like a different color this time?*

   [Accept child's choice.]

6. *Ok, go ahead and draw the door.*

7. That's very good. Now we have to do the same thing to the door that we did with the windows. *What did we do to the windows that we drew on the box?*

8. Ok, we have to cut it. *Do you want to do the cutting or should I?*

E. Attaching the Door

1. Now we have a door, but there is a problem. This door is not staying on the house. It's in our hands (or "on the table"). Look at the door in this room. See, it's attached. It's not off like our door. It's holding onto the wall. *Go over to the door and move it.*

2. See, no matter how much you move it, it still stays on the wall. I think we should fix our door so it holds onto the wall of the house. I think this tape would be good for that. *Tear off a piece of tape.*

3. *Put it over here.*

   [Pointing to a spot on the wall and door.]

4. Let's do that again so that the door will have more support. *Let's tear off another piece of tape.*

5. *Put it here.*

   [Pointing to a second spot on the wall and door.]

6. Great. See, the door is holding onto the house. You say that. *The door is holding onto the house.*

Concluding Comments to the Child

You did a wonderful job. You made the whole house. It has windows and a door. It's a great house. You can take it home if you like.

Have nonrelevant materials available to help the child recognize the distinction between relevant and nonrelevant materials and ideas.

Making A House Out of a Cardboard Box

In all complex lessons, simple commands are mixed with complex commands. To mirror the language of everyday discourse, all ranges of language complexity must be included.

Word-finding problems are common in language-disabled children. The technique used below in A-5 is designed to deal with the problem in a way that will not stop the flow of the lesson.

Materials
Relevant pictures of houses, paper, scissors, knife, cardboard box, paper, crayons (paints), pieces of cardboard, mirror.

A. Establishing the Shape of the House

1. We've made lots of things here, but we've never made the thing that people live in. What things do people live in?

   [Accept all reasonable responses including trailer, mobile home, tent, etc.]

2. That's right, they live in houses.

   [To take account of the child's verbalization, the adult's verbalization must be modified in this and all subsequent relevant cases. Thus, if the child says "A tent," the adult will say, "That's right, and they also live in houses. It would be nice to make a tent, but I don't have those materials here today. I do have things to make a house and I thought that is what we could make."]

   I thought we could make one today. If we do that, we need something that's the shape of a house. So before we begin, let's make sure what the shape is. *Take this paper and draw the shape of a house.*

3. Let's check if you're right.

   [Offering a book.]

   On these pages are some pictures of houses. *Find at least three and see if they are the same shape that you have drawn.*

4. *Is the shape you drew like the ones in the book?*

5. *That shape is called a __________.*

   [Pause, giving the child time to fill in the sentence. If the child fails to do so, complete it and ask child to repeat what you have said.]

B. Selecting Material and Identifying the Parts of a House

1. We're going to need something that has a rectangular shape to make our house. Look over at the table and *name something that is a rectangular shape and can be used for making a house.*

   [Table should contain some rectangular objects that cannot be used for making a house such as a mirror.]

2. A box is a great choice. But there were other things on the table that were rectangles and you didn't pick those. Look at this mirror. It's a rectangle. *Why didn't you pick that for the house?*

3. That's right. It might break (or whatever relevant term the child used), but that's not true of the box. It will make a fine house. But it can't be a house just as it is. It needs parts. It needs the part that allows people to go in and out of a house. *What part is that?*

4. And it needs the part that allows light to come into a house. *What part is that?*

5. And it needs the part that prevents rain from dripping in on people. *What part is that?*

6. Great, you've named three major parts of a house. *Tell me the three that you've named.*

C. Creating the Parts of a House

1. First, let's decide about the doors. *How many would you like?*

   [In this or other situations, a totally inappropriate answer such as "Seven" is a sign that this level dialogue is too complex and the child should continue at the simple level.]

2. *Where would you like to put it (them)?*

3. That's fine. That's a good place for a door. You put it so its bottom is touching the ground. *Why did you put it there and not up here?*

   [Pointing to a place high on the house.]

4. You have the place for a door, but you have another problem. *What are you going to use so that place begins to look like a door?*

5. OK. *Go on and draw it (paint it).*

6. Remember you named two other parts of a house. One is similar in some ways to a door, but it's usually smaller. *What is it?*

7. *Now draw that.*

8. The last part you mentioned can't be drawn.

   [Referring to the roof.]

   You need to make it out of some other material. *What is it?*

9. OK. *Find some materials over there that we could use for the roof.*

   [Paper or cardboard should be available.]

10. *Now go ahead and put on the roof.*

D. Cutting the Doors and Windows

1. Things are going great. You've got all the parts, but they're not quite working the way they should yet. For example, doors work to allow people to do certain things. *What do doors in a house allow people to do?*

2. But no one can go in and out of our door (Use whatever words the child used) the way it is now. *Why can't they?*

3. *What do we have to do so the door(s) can be used?*

4. OK. Let's cut it (them) out. You can use the scissors or the knife. *Which do you want?*

5. The house we're making is made out of cardboard. *If it were made out of something else, like brick, would we be able to cut it the way you are doing?*

6. *Why not?*

7. That's terrific! Now I'm going to ask you an even harder question. We can't cut brick with scissors or a knife, but we can cut this cardboard that way. *What do you think cardboard is made of that allows it to be cut?*

   [If the child does not know that cardboard is made out of paper, demonstrate by taking a small piece of cardboard and showing how layers of paper can be pulled off.]

8. Let's get back to the house now. *Cut the windows the way you did the door.*

E. Reviewing the Course of the Lesson

1. You've really worked hard on this. Before you go, I'd like you to go over the things you've done here today. *First, tell me what you made.*

2. *Now tell me its parts and the functions of each part.*

3. *Tell me how you made each of those parts.*

4. You've made a great house, but of course, it's not a real house. At least not a real house for people. *Name two ways that this house is different from a real house.*

Concluding Comment to the Child
You did a wonderful job. You can take the house home if you like.

Comments in conversation are vital. Be sure to comment as frequently as you question.

Potting a Plant

Materials

Plant cutting ready to pot (should have leaves, stem, and roots), parent plant, other plants, pot with drainage holes, styrofoam cup, soil in an unopened plastic bag in a paper bag, water, trowel or large spoon

A. Identifying a Plant

1. *A plant has a lot of parts. Tell me what this whole thing is.*

   [Holding up a plant cutting.]

2. *Tell me the name of this part.*

   [Pointing to the leaves.]

   This part

   [Pointing to the roots.]

   And this part.

   [Pointing to the stem.]

3. *Can you find the plant that this came from?*

4. *Now find two other plants that are different from the one you just showed me.*

B. Recognizing the Need for Soil

1. This plant is just by itself.

   [Referring to a cutting.]

   It's not in anything. Look at those other plants. They are in something. *What are they in?*

2. *So what do we need for this plant?*

3. We have something like a pot. It's over there. *Bring it here.*

   [Referring to the styrofoam cup.]

4. Some soil (dirt) is in a paper bag under the table. *Bring that here.*

5. *What two things did you bring?*

C. Putting Soil Into the Pot

1. *Now open the paper bag.*

2. *Is there soil there?*

3. *Take out the soil.*

4. *Now cut open the plastic bag so we can reach the soil.*

5. I don't want to use our hands to take out the soil. *Which one of these things could we use instead?*

   [Offer a choice that includes a trowel or a large spoon.]

6. *When you take out the soil, where are you going to put it?*

7. *Go ahead and take out three spoonfuls.*

8. Now I'll have a turn. *Tell me how many spoonfuls to take out.*

D. Putting the Plant in the Soil

1. We have enough soil. Let's go back and get the plant.

2. We need a hole in the soil. I'll make one.

   [Model the hole and replace the soil.]

   Now you do it.

3. This part of the plant has to go into the soil.

   [Pointing to the roots.]

   Which part did I just show you?

4. *Now put it in.*

5. *Push the soil around it so the plant stays straight.*

E. Making Holes for Drainage

1. Let's look at the bottom of this.

   [Lifting the clay pot.]

   What are these?

   [Pointing to the drainage holes.]

2. Let's pour some water in this plant and see what happens. *What's happening?*

[Excess water is coming out.]

3. Let's look at our plant. *Does it have holes to let out the extra water?*
[Referring to plant in styrofoam cup.]

4. Let's make some holes. *You can use these scissors.*

5. *Make the holes over here.*

[Making two marks.
Carefully supervise the use of scissors
to make holes in the cup.]

Potting a Plant

Materials
A plant cutting, parent plant, another plant, soil, styrofoam cup, large spoon, water

A. Identifying a Plant

1. There are things that grow in the ground. *What are some of them?*

2. Here is one.

   [Holding up plant cutting.]

   Is this one of the things you named?

3. This one

   [Referring to cutting.]

   came from the plant. *How can I tell it's from this plant?*

4. It didn't come from this plant, but it still is similar in some ways to this plant. *In what ways is it similar?*

B. Recognizing the Need for Soil

1. A plant like this can grow for a certain time in water, but to be healthy, it needs something else. *What else does it need?*

2. There are places outside this room where lots of soil is found. *Tell me where there is some soil near here.*

3. *What would we have to do if we wanted to get that soil?*

4. We can't go outside and get the soil. Instead, I brought some in.

   [Showing bag of soil.]

   Do you know where I might have gotten this soil?

C. Putting Soil in the Pot

1. Look at this cup—it's for the plant—and look at the amount of soil. *Can we use all the soil in this cup?*

2. *Why not?*

3. So we only need a portion of the soil. *Do you know what "portion" means?*

4. *Take a guess at how many spoonfuls of soil we'll use to get the portion we'll need for the cup.*

5. Let's see if you're right. *Count the spoonfuls you put in.*

6. *How close was your guess?*

D. Putting the Plant in the Soil

1. We're going to be putting the plant in the soil. *Which part of the plant will go into the soil?*

2. *Why don't we put it in this way?*

   [Demonstrating leaves in first.]

3. Right, now there doesn't seem to be enough space to put the plant in. *What could we do?*

4. *Go ahead and do it.*

E. Making Holes for Drainage

1. There's one thing that is still missing. Look carefully at this plant.

   [Pointing to another plant.]

   Find something it has that ours doesn't.

2. *What do you think the holes are for?*

3. When you let the extra water out, it's called drainage. Something you know very well also has drainage. It's the pipes in a sink. *Why do you think there are drains in sinks? What would happen if there were no drains?*

4. Now we'll put some holes in our cup to allow for drainage. Go ahead and do it.

   [Carefully supervise the use of scissors to make holes in the cup.]

Making a Sock Puppet

Materials

Pictures of items including puppets and dolls, socks (big enough to fit over a child's hand), shredded paper (the paper may be already shredded or the shredding may be done by the child), pieces of string, assortment of small objects including buttons, needle, thread, paste, pieces of wool or yarn for hair

This lesson can be expanded at the start by comparing dolls from different cultures and showing how the dolls reflect each culture.

A. Identifying the Class of Dolls

1. There are things in this room that are just objects, or things. *Name some.*

2. There are things in this room that are not objects, or things. They're people. *Name some.*

3. And of course, your class is full of people. *Who are some of the people in your class?*

4. People can do very special things. They can talk, they can dance, they can laugh, they can cry. And there are things that look like people, but they can't do any of these things. *Look at these pictures and find two things that look like people but can't do what people do.*

B. Making a Puppet with a Sock

1. One of the things you found was a puppet. I thought we would make one today. We'll make it of something special. We'll make it out of a sock. *Find me a sock over there.*

2. The sock is just flat. If it's going to be a puppet, it needs to be filled with something. We can fill it with this paper. *But first, let's cut the paper into small pieces.*

3. *Now put the paper in the sock.*

4. The paper's going to fall out if we leave the sock open like this.

   [Holding up sock.]

   If we take the string and tie a knot that won't happen. Let me show you how to do it.

C. Putting a Face on the Puppet

1. Dolls and puppets can't do what people do, but at least they look a little bit like people.

   [Looking at pictures.]

   What things are on the faces of these dolls and puppets that are on the faces of people?

2. So our puppet needs eyes. *Which of these things could we use for eyes?*

3. *Let's sew them on.*

   [Help child as necessary.]

4. [Repeat in a similar manner for the nose and mouth. Materials can vary so that the mouth is pasted on rather than sewn on. If time allows, wool or yarn hair can be put on.]

Restating information in a slightly varying form gives the child more opportunity to understand the language demand and more time to process language.

Making a Sock Puppet

Materials
Hand puppet, socks (big enough to fit over child's hand), shredded paper, pieces of string, assortment of small objects including buttons, needle, thread, wool or yarn for hair, paste

A. Identifying the Class of Dolls

1. Children all over the world like toys. *Name some of the kinds of toys that you know.*

2. One very special class of toys are things that look like people, but they're not people. *Do you know what class of toys I'm thinking of?*

3. I said before that these types of toys are like people in certain ways. *Name some of the ways in which they are alike.*

4. But they are also different from real people. *How are they different?*

5. A lot of the differences have to do with the idea of being able to do things. Real people can laugh, can jump, can pull, and things like that. But dolls can't do those things.

B. Making a Puppet with a Sock

1. There's one kind of doll that can't quite do those things either. But it's designed to sort of do them. Here, look at this puppet.

   [Showing a hand puppet.]

   What are some things it can do, or rather, what it can be made *to do?*

2. *So in what way is a puppet different from other dolls?*

3. I thought we would make a puppet. We can make it out of this sock. The sock though, is flat. *What can we do so that it won't be flat?*

4. *Find something over there that we can stuff it with.*

5. *Go ahead and do it.*

6. The way you've done it, the stuffing could fall out. *Why could it?*

7. *What could we do so this doesn't happen?*

8. *Let's go ahead and do it.*

C. Putting a Face on the Puppet

1. We've made something like the head of the puppet, but it doesn't have the features of a face. *What things are missing?*

2. You know, not only do dolls and people have those features, but lots of things do. *Name some other things that have eyes and mouths.*

3. *What things over there could we use for the eyes, nose, and mouth?*

4. *How are you going to get them to stay on the puppet?*

5. OK, *let's go ahead and do that.*

When a child working at the complex level gives a high percentage of inappropriate responses, continue the topic by moving the lesson to the simple level.

Making a Doll's Dress

Materials

Dolls, pieces of cloth for clothes in various colors, piece of metal or other hard material, paper, pencil, scissors, assortment of small items for decoration and accessories (sequins, ribbons, paper or plastic flowers, etc.), paste

A. Recognizing the Presence of Clothes

1. One of the things people use a lot of is clothing. *Name some clothes that the people in this room are wearing.*

2. Not only do people have clothes, but even dolls can have clothes. *Find a doll on the table and name some of the clothes that she has on.*

3. [Repeat above with another doll.]

4. *Look in the carriage (box, etc.) and see if you can find a doll there.*

5. *Does that doll have any clothes?*

6. *So what does she need?*

B. Establishing the Material for Clothing

1. We have no clothing for her. We have to make it. *Which one of these could we use to make some clothing?*

   [Give choice between cloth and hard unusable material such as metal.]

2. You picked some red material, but I also have some material in other colors. It's in a box in the corner. *Go get the box.*

3. *Now open the box.*

4. *Which would you like to use, the one you originally picked,*

   [Pointing]

   or one of these?

5. OK, we'll use that. *Put the others away.*

C. Cutting Out the Dress

1. I thought we would use this material to make a dress for the doll. There's an easy way to do it by using a circle. *Finish drawing the circle that I started on this paper.*

2. Now we'll cut out the circle. *What could we use to cut it out?*

3. *Go ahead and do it.*

4. *Let's put the circle on the material.*

5. *What did I say we were making out of the material?*

D. Fitting the Dress

1. You've cut the dress very well, but it still isn't a dress. If it's to be a dress, it has to go over the doll. It needs a hole for her head to go through. Let me draw a circle and you can cut it out to make a hole. OK, *now cut it.*

2. The dress has to have a hole not only for her head. It also has to have a hole for these.

   [Pointing to doll's arms.]

   What are these?

3. I'll make one hole here and *you make one there.*

4. Let's see if the dress fits. To do that you have to put it on her. *What are you going to do?*

5. OK. *Go ahead and do it.*

6. [If time allows, add a belt, ornaments, and accessories.]

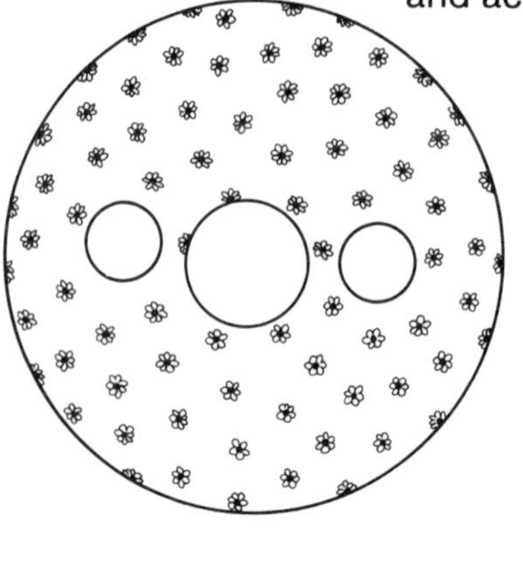

Making a Doll's Dress

Materials
Dolls, pieces of cloth in various colors, sandpaper, tissue paper, piece of metal, 1″ square fabric swatch, doll's dress, pencil, scissors

A. Recognizing the Presence of Clothes

1. We're going to be making some clothing today. *Do you know what clothing is?*

   [If child says no, explain.]

2. We have different kinds of clothing for different parts of our body. *Clothing on our legs is called __________.*

3. *And on our heads __________.*

4. *And on our hands __________.*

5. I said we are going to make some clothing, but it's not going to be for a person. There is something on the table that could use some clothing but doesn't have any. *Go find out what that might be.*

B. Establishing the Material for Clothing

1. Here's a bunch of stuff. Some can be used for clothing and some can't.

   [Hold up a piece of sandpaper.]

   This wouldn't be good for clothing. *Why not?*

2. [Repeat this exchange with the tissue paper (too fragile) and metal (unbendable).]

3. But we can use this.

   [Holding up cloth.]

   Why is this good?

4. I have another piece of that material.

   [Holding up swatch.]

   Would we be able to use this to make a dress for this doll?

5. *Why not?*

C. Cutting Out the Dress

1. Here, I have a dress.

   [Holding up a dress.]

   How is it different from the piece of material that isn't a dress yet?

2. *What could we do so that this*

   [Pointing to material.]

   becomes like this?

3. Before we cut it, we have to have the places marked. *Where are we going to cut it? How can we do that?*

4. OK, *go ahead and do that.*

D. Fitting the Dress

1. You told me before that there were three holes in the dress. *What do you think the three holes are for?*

2. The one hole for the head is bigger than the other two holes. *Why do you think it was made to be bigger?*

3. If you want to be sure that the size of the holes are going to be right, you could use the dress as a model. *How could you use the model to help you?*

4. *Go ahead and do it.*

5. *Now fit the dress on the doll.*

6. We made a very simple dress only by cutting. That is not the way most clothing is made. *Do you know what is also done to make it into clothing?*

   [If child does not know, show seams, thread, gathers, tucks, etc., of some items of clothing.]

Making a Beanbag

Materials

Beanbag, hollow ball, knife, scissors, empty beanbag with one side open, beans, spoon, thread, pencil, rubber band, needle

A. Directing Attention to a Beanbag

1. I have something here whose name you may or may not know.

   [Show a beanbag.]

   Do you know what this is called?

   [If child does not know, provide label.]

2. You can do some of the same things with this that you do with a ball. You can throw a ball. *Try throwing the beanbag.*

3. *Were you able to throw it?*

4. You can catch a ball. You can also catch a beanbag. *Throw it to me* and let's see if I can catch it.

5. I'll do the same with you. *I'm going to throw it and now you're the one who has to* __________.

6. So you can play with this thing a little bit like you can play with a ball. *Do you remember what this thing is called?*

B. Recognizing Constituents of a Beanbag

1. A beanbag is like a ball in certain ways, but not in all ways. The insides are different. Here, *shake the ball. Do you hear anything?*

2. *Shake the beanbag. Do you hear anything?*

3. One of these has something inside and one doesn't. *Which one do you think has something inside?*

4. Let's see if you're right. If we cut open this ball, *what do you think will be inside?*

5. *Let's do that. You can try cutting it with a knife.*

   [Supervising closely.]

6. *What's inside?*

7. If we cut open the beanbag, *what do you think will be inside?*

8. *Let's do it.*

9. *Do you know what these are called?*

   [Showing a handful of beans.]

10. And that's why it's called a beanbag. *It's a bag that has what inside?*

C. Making a Beanbag

1. I thought you might like to have a beanbag to take home and I started making one for you. But it's not finished.

   [Holding up small bag that has three sides sewn.]

   What's missing?

2. *Go get the beans. They're on my desk.*

3. *Do you want to put the beans in the bag with the spoon or do you want to use your hands?*

4. *Do it the way you said you wanted to.*

5. It's filled, but there's a problem. If I turn it over, *what's going to happen to the beans?*

   [Demonstrate if necessary.]

6. We don't want that to happen. To prevent it from happening, we have to close the hole. I thought we could close it by sewing it with some thread. *Say, "We could close it with thread."*

D. Sewing the Beanbag

1. To sew it, I first have to put the thread through a needle. *Which one of these things is a needle?*

   [The needle should be in group of clearly incorrect alternatives such as a pencil and rubber band.]

2. *Now what am I doing?*

   [Putting thread in needle.]

3. Let's start sewing. I'll do some. *Now you put it through here.*

4. [Repeat the sewing process until the opening is closed.]

5. And I'll knot it to make sure it stays closed.

   [Make a knot.]

   Show me where the knot is.

The most demanding part of the lesson should occur during the first half of the therapy session. If the child tires during the last half of the session, the demands may be simplified and reduced.

Making a Beanbag

Materials
A beanbag, scissors, empty beanbag with one side open, ball, knife, 3 different size (measuring) cups filled with beans, scissors, thread, pin, needle

A. Directing Attention to a Beanbag

1. You know, children love to play games. Some games you can play just by yourselves without any help from any objects—like the game of tag. *What do you do in tag?*

2. *Do you use any objects?*

3. But many games you play need objects. When you play jump rope you need an object. *What object do you need in jump rope?*

4. And you can play softball. *What object do you need in softball?*

5. Here I have an object that can be used for playing.

   [Showing beanbag.]

   Do you know what this is called?

6. A beanbag is sort of the same size as a small ball and you can do some of the same things with it that you can do with a ball. *Think of some things you could do with it that you could do with a ball.*

7. There are also some things you can do with a ball that you can't do with a bean bag. *What do you think these might be?*

B. Recognizing the Constituents of a Beanbag

1. This is called a *beanbag* for a very special reason. *Why do you think it's called a* beanbag?

2. If this beanbag weren't filled with beans but were filled with pebbles, *what do you think we could call it?*

3. *What could we do to see if, in fact, there are beans inside the bag? Go ahead and do it.*

4. Before, you said a beanbag and a ball were alike in certain ways. You can throw them both and you can catch them both. *But are they alike in all ways?* We just cut open the beanbag and found there were beans inside. If we cut open a ball, *what do you think we would find inside?*

5. *Go ahead and do it.*

C. Making the Beanbag

1. I thought you might like to have a beanbag to take home. You know, we can make one. Now you took a beanbag apart and it had two parts. *What were the two major parts of the beanbag?*

2. If you're going to make a beanbag, we need some cloth (or whatever word the child used). There's one that I started on the desk. *Go get it.*

3. If we fill this with beans

   [Referring to partly sewn bag]

   and leave it this way, *will it work?*

4. *Why not?*

5. *What do we have to do to prevent that?*

6. Before we sew it, we have to put in the beans.

   [Give a choice of three cups of notably different sizes that are filled with different amounts of beans.]

   Which of these cups looks like it's holding the amount of beans that would fill this bag?

7. *Let's see if you are right.*

8. *Were you right?* (If the child was wrong, say, "What's wrong? Go fix it.")

D. Sewing the Beanbag

1. Now we have to do what you said to make the beanbag work. *What is it we have to do?*

2. We are going to have to sew it. If we're going to have to sew it, we have to somehow get the thread through. *Can we get the thread through by itself?*

3. *Why not?*

4. *What do we need?*

5. Look at this.

   [Holding up a pin.]

   It's a lot like the needle. *Why can't we use the pin instead of the needle? What does the needle have that the pin doesn't?*

6. *Why don't you go ahead and try threading the needle.*

   [Make sure the eye of the needle is big enough.]

7. Let me start it, then you can continue. See these little things being made by the thread?

   [Referring to the stitches.]

   Do you know what they are called?

   [Provide the label if necessary.]

8. Many, many things have stitches. Look at your shirt and look at my shirt. *See if you can find some stitches.*

9. *Let's go back and finish stitching the beanbag.* Good job.

Any play activity that lends itself to sequenced development can form the basis of a lesson. The lesson plans in this book can be used as models to frame the new lesson.

Repairing a Chair

Materials

Dollhouse, 6 pictures of rooms that have only furniture and no people, box with plastic doll furniture including a broken chair and unrelated items (paper clip, eraser, pencil sharpener), glue.

A. Focusing on Furniture

1. Here is a dollhouse I thought we could play with today. Right now, there's nothing in the rooms of the dollhouse. But most rooms have things inside. Look at this picture

   [Showing picture of a room]

   and *tell me some of the things that it has.*

2. [Repeat with three other pictures.]

3. *Does our dollhouse have any chairs, tables (use whatever words child has used) or other furniture?*

4. *What do you think we should do?*

B. Recognizing the Chair is Broken

1. It's a good idea to put furniture in, but we can't just use any furniture. This furniture is too big.

   [Pointing to furniture in the therapy room]

   So why can't we use this furniture?

2. The box over there has furniture that isn't too big. *Bring it over here.*

   [Box should have non-furniture as well as furniture items.]

3. *Look in the box and tell me if you see a table.*

4. *Take it out and put it in the house.*

5. *Tell me if you see some chairs. Take them out and put them in the house.*

6. Oh, something's wrong with one of the chairs! *Can you see which one has something wrong?*

   [If the child has spontaneously recognized the broken chair, follow that lead.]

7. *What's wrong with the chair?*

8. Watch what happens if I move this chair,

   [Moving an intact chair]

   and watch what happens when I move this chair.

   [Moving the broken chair.]

   One of the chairs was wobbly and shaky. *Which one was it?*

C. Fixing the Chair

1. It's really not good to have a wobbly chair. We'd better fix it. The chair needs a leg. *Show me a leg on the chair.*

2. It needs one more of those. *Which one of these things could we use for a leg?*

3. We can put the leg in place, but it doesn't stay. See, it keeps falling off. *Say, "It keeps falling off."*

4. Some glue could keep it on. *What did I say could keep it on?*

5. *Go over there*

   [Pointing]

   and get the glue.

6. It would be good to squeeze the glue on here and here.

   [Indicating points on leg.]

   You do it.

7. *Where are you going to put the leg?*

8. *OK, do it.*

9. *Let's leave the chair to dry.* We'll come back in a little while to see if it's fixed.

   [Go back a few minutes later and demonstrate that the chair is now usable.]

Repairing a Chair

Materials

Dollhouse, paper, pencil, plastic doll furniture, glue

A. Focusing on Furniture

1. Here is a house that is empty. People can actually live in empty houses. For example, you could sleep on the floor even if the house was empty. But we usually don't sleep on the floor. *What do we sleep on?*

2. People could also eat sitting on the floor, but we usually don't eat that way. *What do we usually use when we are eating?*

3. So far, you've mentioned beds and tables and chairs. There are other things like that that you can put in a room. *Can you think of anything else?*

4. *What are all those different things called that you put in rooms?*

B. Recognizing the Chair Is Broken

1. I thought that it would be good to put some furniture in this dollhouse. Here is some of the furniture we could use. Before you put it in, I thought we could draw a plan of how you are going to arrange the furniture. Take this piece of paper. It's the same shape as the room you are going to put furniture in. *Which room are you going to put furniture in?*

2. *Draw where you are going to do that.*

3. [Repeat this process for several pieces of furniture.]

4. OK, *arrange the room the way your plan is laid out.*

5. You've done a great job, but one of the pieces of furniture has a problem. *Can you identify which one it is and what's wrong with it?*

C. Fixing the Chair

1. I think it's a good idea to repair the chair. *Do you know what I mean by the word "repair?"*

[Provide the definition if necessary.]

2. This is doll furniture and we are going to repair it in a very special way. But if it were real furniture—a real chair—*what might you do to repair it?*

3. That idea is fine for real furniture, but it wouldn't work for this furniture. *Why would we NOT do that with this furniture?* (It's too small, or it's plastic, etc.).

4. Nevertheless, it's broken. *What could we use to fix this plastic chair?*

5. OK, *where will you put the glue so it will hold and fix the leg of the chair.*

6. *Why wouldn't you put the glue over here?*

   [Pointing to an inappropriate place.]

7. *Go ahead and put the glue where you said you would.*

8. It will take some time for the glue to dry. *Where would you like to put the chair so it can dry?*

Have nonrelevant materials available to help the child recognize the distinction between relevant and nonrelevant materials and ideas.

Making a Potato Ink Stamp

Materials

Drawings made in different media (paints, crayons, pencils), bag of rubber stamps, stamp pads, ink of a different color than the rubber stamps, paper, potatoes, pen, knife

A. Recognizing Materials for Writing

1. See the drawings over there? One was made by using paints. *Find me that one.*

2. One was made by using crayons. *Find that one.*

3. One was made by using pencils. *Find that one.*

4. Crayons and paints and pencils are the usual way of writing or drawing, but I have another way. *Go to that bag and take out what's inside.*

   [Several rubber stamps are in the bag.]

5. *Do you know what these are?*

   [If the child does not know, explain.]

B. Understanding the Use of an Ink Stamp

1. These ink stamps can be used to make designs or marks, but you can't use them just this way. Let me show you what I mean. Here, *press one on the paper.*

2. *Did anything happen? Is there any mark on the paper?*

3. [Repeat steps 1 and 2 with two other ink stamps.]

4. You can make marks and designs but you can't do it by just pressing down. You have to get some ink on the stamps so they'll make a mark. Here is an ink pad that has ink in it. *And what did I say the stamp needs?*

5. That's right, it needs ink and you can press the stamp on the ink pad and it will pick up the ink. *Go ahead and do it.*

6. Look at the stamp. *Does it have any ink on it?*

7. *Now press the stamp on some paper.*

8. *Did it leave a mark?*

9. *Try other stamps. Do you think they will leave a mark if you press them in the ink?*

10. *Go ahead and try.*

C. Making a Stamp Out of a Potato

1. The stamps we have been using are made out of rubber. But there are lots of other things they can be made out of. You can even make them out of a potato. *Do you see a potato over there?*

   [Pointing to objects on the table.]

2. *Go get it.*

3. To make the stamp, we first have to cut the potato to get to the inside white part. I'll make a mark where you can cut it. *Go ahead and do it.*

   [Supervising the cutting closely.]

4. The stamps we were using had different designs. *Do you remember what some of the designs were?*

5. To make the potato into a stamp, we have to put a design on it. Here's a pen. *Draw a design on the potato.*

   [Indicating cut white area.]

6. Now I'll cut away the parts around the design.

   [Cutting away the potato.]

   What am I doing?

7. Let's try and see if this potato stamp works. *What did we have to put on the other stamps to get them to mark the paper?*

8. *Do that with the potato.* Great—it worked!

Making a Potato Ink Stamp

Materials

Drawings made in different media (crayon and paint), several rubber stamps, birthday invitations, ink pads of a different color than the rubber stamps, potato, pen, knife

A. Recognizing Materials for Writing

1. Today, we are going to be talking about things we can write or draw with. *Can you name some different things you use to draw on a paper or write on a paper?*

2. Look at that paper over there. It has something on it that was made with something you can write or draw with.

   [Referring to paper with crayon or paint designs.]

   What do you think it was made with?

3. And now look at this design over here.

   [Referring to paper with design in alternative medium.]

   Was it made in the same way?

4. *What do you think was used to make it?*

5. We've been talking about different things for drawing and writing and today we are going to use something that is less common. It's an ink stamp (rubber stamp). *Do you know what an ink stamp is?*

   [Provide definition if necessary.]

B. Understanding the Use of an Ink Stamp

1. Ink stamps are sort of funny. When you use the other means of writing or drawing like a pen or pencil, you can make any design you want. *Can you do that with an ink stamp?*

2. *Why not?*

3. So ink stamps don't allow you to change. Whatever the stamp is, that's the way it is going to stay. There are times when people need this. Sometimes you have to do the same thing over and over again. If you're sending out a lot of birthday invitations, you might use an ink stamp. *What would the ink stamp for a birthday invitation have on it? What kinds of information?*

   [Have birthday card invitations available to show.]

4. When you have an ink stamp, like this ink stamp, *what do you have to do so you can mark the page the way you want?*

5. *What things do we need?*

6. We need some ink. Here is some. *Why don't you try a couple of the stamps?*

7. *If you want to make the design in blue, what color ink would you have to use?*

8. *If you wanted to make the design in green, what color ink would you use?*

9. So the color of the ink matters because that's what is going to determine the color of the design. *Does the color of the material that the stamp is made out of matter? Will that affect the color that comes out on the paper?*

10. *Why not?*

11. OK, here's a stamp. *Why don't you try it, doing what you said you had to do to make a mark?*

C. Making a Stamp Pad Out of a Potato

1. The stamp pads we have been using are made out of rubber, but there are lots of other things they could be made out of. They could even be made out of certain kinds of vegetables. *Name some vegetables.*

2. [If the child names an appropriate vegetable like a carrot, say, "I don't have a carrot here but I do have a potato. Let's try that." If the child hasn't named something appropriate, say, "You've named all kinds of vegetables, but you haven't named the one I have here. What is this?"]

3. We need a fairly flat surface to make the design. This potato is round. *What could we do to get a flat surface on the potato?*

4. You have the flat surface, but *if you used it just as it is, what sort of design would appear?*

5. We could use a design like that, but it would be more interesting to have something that has a specific shape or pattern. How about using a design that represents the letter your name starts with. *What is the first letter of your name?*

6. *Draw it on here. Now let's cut it out.*

7. *Cut it out so the part around your letter is lower than the letter.*

8. *Why do we want the letter to be sticking up?*

9. Fine, *go ahead and cut it.*

10. *Let's try and see if it works.*

Comments in conversation are vital. Be sure to comment as frequently as you question.

Making a Drum

Materials

Pencil, spoon, a picture showing several musical instruments, various musical instruments, a large can with both ends removed, pieces of rubber or stretchy material, large rubber bands, stick(s) for playing drum

A. Recognizing the Presence of Sounds

1. There are lots of different sounds in our world. *Close your eyes and tell me when you hear me making a sound.*

   [Tap the table with a pencil.]

   Did you hear a sound?

2. *Open your eyes* and I'll make the same sound. *What am I using to make the sound?*

3. *Let's do that again.*

   [Repeat the sequence, tapping a spoon on a chair and then tapping a shoe on the floor.]

4. *Now you think of something that we could use to make a noise.*

B. Recognizing Musical Sound

1. Here are some pictures of things that not only make sounds, but they can make the sounds of music. *Find one thing that can be used to make music.*

2. *What is it called?*

3. [Repeat the sequence with two other instruments.]

4. [Put away the pictures.]

   Name the three things you just pointed out to me.

5. I don't have all the musical instruments here that were in the picture, but I do have some musical instruments here. This one is a harmonica. *Say "harmonica."*

6. You play it by blowing into it. *Try it.*

7. This one is called a xylophone. *Try saying that.*

8. You play this by tapping with a stick. *Try it.*

9. And here is a drum. You play it a little bit like the xylophone. *How did you play the xylophone?*

10. *Try playing the drum.*

C. Making the Drum

1. I thought you might like to make a drum that you could take home. There is something over there that is the shape of a drum. *Bring it here.*

    [The can and clearly inappropriate objects such as a ball and a stuffed toy should be evident].

2. This is a good shape for a drum, but there is something missing. *Can you show me where something is missing?*

3. We can put on some material to cover the missing part. The material is in the bag next to the sink. *Go get it.*

4. *Try putting the material on the drum.*

    [Pick up the drum so the material falls off.]

    Is the material staying on?

5. Here is something we can use to get it to stick on.

    [Holding up a rubber band.]

    What is this called?

6. *Try putting it on.*

7. *Does it work?*

8. Now we have to do the other side. *Show me the other side that needs to be done.*

9. [Repeat the sequence.]

10. *Let's try the drum and see if it works.*

Making a Drum

Materials

A musical instrument like a zither and pick, pictures of musical instruments including several stringed instruments, a large can with both ends removed, pieces of rubber or stretchy material, scissors, large rubber bands, stick(s) for playing the drum

A. Recognizing the Presence of Sounds

1. Something that is very common in our world is sounds. They're all around us. *Can you name three different things that make sounds?*

2. Sounds don't have to be made only by things. They can be made by people, or the parts of bodies of people. For example, look at your hands and think of what sounds you can make by using your hands. *Go ahead and do it.*

3. *Look at your feet and think of a sound you can make with your feet.*

4. *Go ahead and do it.*

5. *Do you know how sounds are basically made?* It's really when any two things hit against each other or rub against each other. *Watch my hands.*

   [Clapping.]

   Did you hear anything?

6. Now *watch my hands.*

   [Moving your hands in a clapping motion but not to the point of touching.]

   Did you hear anything?

7. *You try it. Move your hands but don't allow them to touch each other. Did you hear anything?*

8. *Why not?*

B. Recognizing Musical Sounds

1. The sounds we have been making are just noises. Noises are sounds, but not particularly pretty sounds. There are things that make really nice sounds that are different from noises. They're the sounds of music. Here is one musical instrument that makes some of those sounds

   [Holding up a zither.]

   It's a zither. *Say that, "zither."*

2. *What did I say has to happen for a sound to be made?*

3. So somehow two things have to rub together to get sound out of this zither. Here's a pick. *What do you think you can do with it to get sound?*

4. OK, *try doing that.*

5. *Is it making a sound?*

6. Depending on which strings you hit, you are going to get different sounds. Let me do a sequence of sounds. *Now you do the same one.*

7. *Now you do a different one.*

8. Some instruments have strings. Lots of instruments have strings. You make a sound by touching or moving a string. Here, look at this picture. *Find some other musical instruments with strings. Point to them.*

9. The instruments we've been looking at have strings to make music. There are lots of other kinds of musical instruments. For instance, look at this.

   [Showing picture of a drum.]

   What is it?

10. *Does that instrument have strings? Can it make its sound through string?*

11. *How does it make its sounds?*

12. *Do what you just said.*

C. Making the Drum

1. Most musical instruments are made in very fancy ways. But we can make a rough kind of musical instrument. And I thought we could do that here—we could make a drum. If we're going to make a drum, *what parts do we have to have?*

2. So we need a round shape for this part of the drum. *Go over to the shelf and find something we could use.*

3. *What two parts do we still need?*

4. If those parts are going to cover the ends of the drum, they have to be made of something we can stretch. *Can you find some material over there that can be stretched?*

5. *What did I say was important for this material to be able to do?*

6. *Show me that you can stretch this material.*

7. But a problem is that it's not the right shape now. *What shape do we need it to be in so it fits over the ends?*

8. *What can you do to the material to make it that shape?*

9. *Go ahead and do it.*

10. Let's do what I said before. Let's stretch it over. Oops, it's not staying. It's not remaining attached. *What do you think we could do so it would stay attached to the end of the drum?*

11. *Let's do the other side.*

12. That also needs to be attached. *What did we use before?*

13. OK, *let's do the same thing and attach this end.*

14. Remember, we said that the drum didn't make its sounds by strings, but instead by being hit. *What could we use for hitting the end of the drum to get the sounds we want?*

15. OK, *find some over there.*

Additional Lesson Suggestions

1. Making a Seesaw
2. Making a Puppet on a String
3. Making a Guitar
4. Making a Garage for a Car
5. Constructing a Box to Hold a Present

Frosting Cupcakes

Materials

Two pictures of frosted cakes, boxed frosting mix, other boxed mixes such as macaroni and cheese and pancakes, bowls, spoon, ingredients for the frosting, measuring cups and spoons, fork, food coloring, cupcakes, knife or small spatula for spreading frosting

A. Focusing on the Cake's Frosting

1. Today we're going to make something that's good to eat. I have a picture of it on the table. *Go get that picture.*

2. Good. That's the picture, *what is it a picture of?*

3. This cake has a lot of different parts. There's this part on the bottom

   [Pointing]

   that's resting on the plate and there's this part on the top. And the top has something special on it. *Do you know what this special something is called?*

   [Provide label if necessary.]

4. There's another picture over there of a cake with frosting. *Bring it to me.*

5. *Show me where the frosting is on this cake.*

6. *And on this cake*

   [Pointing]

   and this cake

   [Pointing]

   both have __________ .

B. Making Frosting

1. Today I thought we could make some frosting like the frosting in the pictures. To do that, we have to start with some material that's in a box. *Go over to that shelf and find me the box you think has stuff for frosting in it.*

   [The box should be with other kinds of boxed foods.]

2. You picked the right box, but we still haven't got the frosting itself. *What do we have to do to the box so we can get to the frosting?*

3. *Open the box and pour the stuff that's inside into this bowl.*

4. This is quite a lot of stuff for frosting. I don't want to use it all. *Let's take a couple of spoonfuls out and put them in this little bowl.* Here's a spoon for you to do that.

5. Now we'll work with what's left. First, we have to do something to it to make it into frosting. The directions are here on the box.

   [Pointing to the directions.]

   They say to put some butter into the mixture. *What does it say we have to do?*

6. Here's some butter. *Put it in the bowl.*

7. I'll mix it up with this fork and while I'm doing that, you get the next thing we need. And that next thing is some water. *Take this cup and fill it with water.*

8. That's perfect. But we have to get some of the water into the bowl. I only want a little bit. *So take this spoon and fill it with water,* because that's all we'll need.

9. *Now put it in the bowl.*

10. *Stir it up.*

11. Now it really looks like frosting. *But did it look like that when we first opened the box or did it become different after we added the butter and water?*

12. [Regardless of the child's response, return to the portion of the mix that had previously been set aside.]

    Let's go look at some of the stuff we saved from the box and see.

    [To the child who was correct:]

    Look, you were right.

    [To the child who was wrong:]

    No, they aren't quite the same. The stuff in the box was soft and powdery. *Touch the powdery stuff. Now brush it off your finger.* The stuff we mixed up was sort of wet and sticky. *Touch the wet and sticky stuff. Now try brushing it off your finger.* See, you can't do it. It's different from the stuff that came out of the box.

The above is an example of a simplification sequence discussed in Treatment of the Wrong Response, page 17. Sequences of this kind can be pursued when a child is experiencing difficulty. But they should occupy only a small percentage of the discourse. Frequent need for simplification means that the child is experiencing too great a rate of failure.

C. Changing the Color of the Frosting

1. The frosting that we made is white like the frosting on the box.

   [Pointing.]

   I thought it would be interesting to separate it and make some of it a different color.

   [Offering bottles of food coloring.]

   These are food colors. They can change the color of foods. We can use them for our frosting. *Which of these would you like to use to change the color of the frosting?*

2. Remember, I said we are only going to change part of the frosting, so let's divide the frosting into two bowls. *Leave some in this bowl and put some in this bowl.*

3. *Which of these*

   [Pointing to bowls]

   this one or this one, would you like to change the color of?

4. OK, *put the other bowl over here.*

5. *And put some coloring in this one.*

6. *What did you just do to this frosting?*

7. *Now mix it up.*

8. *What are you doing now?*

D. Putting Frosting on Cupcakes

1. *The frosting in the picture we looked at was on a* __________.

   [Show the picture if the child cannot answer.]

2. I don't have a big cake like that here to frost. I have what you could say are small cakes, but they're not called "small cakes."

   [Bring out the cupcakes.]

   Do you know what these are called?

   [Provide label if necessary.]

3. Let's divide them into two groups. *Put the ones over here that you want to put the white frosting on.*

   [Pointing.]

4. *And put over here*

   [Pointing.]

   the ones you'd like to put yellow (or whatever color) *frosting on.*

5. *Which do you want to do first, the white or the yellow?*

6. Do that. *Take this knife and put the yellow frosting on these.*

7. [Help child frost the cupcakes.]

Restating information in a slightly varying form gives the child more opportunity to understand the language demand and more time to process language.

Frosting Cupcakes

Materials
Pictures of plain items, picture of a frosted cake, boxed frosting mix, necessary ingredients, bowls, measuring spoons, mixing fork or spoon, food coloring, cupcakes, knife or small spatula for spreading frosting

A. Focusing on the Cake's Frosting

1. Today, we're going to talk about decorating something. Decorating means that you take something that's sort of plain and fix it up so it looks pretty. For example, you might have a plain box and you want to use it to hold a present. *What could you put on it that would decorate the box?*

2. And there's something that a lot of people decorate each year at Christmas. They take trees that are just plain and put some things on them. *What sort of things do they put on Christmas trees*?

3. *When the tree is all fixed up we can say it is __________ (use the child's word).*

4. There are other things we can decorate. *Look at these pictures and find something that has been decorated.*

   [The only pictured item decorated should be a cake.

5. You're right. This cake is decorated. But it's not decorated with bows like a box or bells or stars like a Christmas tree. *Instead, it's decorated with __________ .*

B. Making Frosting

1. I thought we could make some frosting today. I have some in that box on the shelf. *Please, go get it.*

2. *How can you tell there might be frosting in this box?*

3. *If we open the box do you think the stuff inside will look like this picture or not?*

   [If the child says "No," ask "Why?"]

4. *Let's open the box and see if you are right.*

5. It *is* different. *In what way is the stuff inside the box different from the picture?*

6. We can do some things to make the contents of the box look like the picture, but we have to follow a set of directions. *Can you find a set of directions on the box?*

7. I'm going to read these directions to you. Try to remember them because I'm going to ask you to tell me what they are.

   [Reads directions.]

   OK, *what are the directions telling us to do?*

8. *Let's do the first thing the directions said which is to* __________.

9. *Go ahead and do that.*

10. The next thing is to add three tablespoons of butter. *Let's see you do that.*

11. [After the child has added two tablespoons of butter:]

    How many tablespoons have you put in so far?

12. *How many do you still have to put in?*

13. Now we have to add some tablespoons of water, but the directions call for fewer tablespoons of water than butter. *Does that mean we are going to have more than three tablespoons of water or fewer than that?*

14. Right. In fact, it says just one tablespoon. *Add it in.*

15. There's one more thing. To get this frosting smooth like it looks in the pictures, *what do we have to do?*

16. *Go ahead and do it.*

C. Changing the Color of the Frosting

1. The color of the frosting we've ended up with is the same as the color of the frosting on the box. But it doesn't have to stay this way. We can change the color. *Do you have any idea how we could do that?* (If the child mentions food coloring, accept the response. If the child has used an alternative such as chocolate, say, "That's a good idea. But I don't have chocolate. All I have is this," and show the food coloring.)

2. If we make some of the frosting into every one of these colors, how many parts do we have to divide the frosting into?

3. OK, let's do that. *How many bowls are you going to need?*

4. *Go get them.*

5. *Now divide the frosting the way you said you would.*

6. *Let's add three drops of coloring into each one of these bowls.*

7. Again, you have to mix it up. You mixed something before. *What was it?*

8. OK, *now mix these.*

D. Putting Frosting on Some Cupcakes

1. *The frosting you saw in the picture was on a* __________.

2. I don't have a cake like that here. I mean I don't have a big cake. I do have what could be considered some small cakes—some very small cakes. Except they're usually not called "small cakes." *Do you know what I'm talking about?*

   [Bring out the cupcakes.]

3. Here they are. As I said, they're not called "small cakes," although they could be. Instead they are called "cupcakes." *Why do you think they are called "cupcakes?"*

4. *How many cupcakes are there here?*

5. OK, there are eight cupcakes. If we divide them into four groups, so there is the same number of cupcakes for each type of frosting, *how many will be in each group?*

6. *Go ahead and do it.*

7. *Were you right?*

8. *Go ahead and frost the cupcakes.*

9. At the start we said there was a word for describing when something is all fixed up. *Do you remember what that word is?*

10. [If time permits, ask the child to review the lesson sequence.]

Making Orange Juice

Materials

Pictures of fruit juice (orange, tomato, prune), oranges in a paper bag, knife, juicer, cups

A. Focusing on Orange Juice

1. One of the things people do everyday is eat. *What are some things to eat?*

2. There is something people do with food that's like eating, but it's not quite the same. It's drinking. *What are some things you can drink?*

3. [Show a picture of oranges.]

   Here's something else to drink.

   [If the child has mentioned it, say "Here's what you just said."]

   This is ___________ .

4. This is tomato juice.

   [Showing picture.]

   And this is prune juice.

   [Showing picture.]

   Prune juice comes from prunes. Tomato juice comes from tomatoes and *what do you think orange juice comes from?*

B. Making Orange Juice

1. I thought we would make some orange juice. *What will we need?*

2. There are oranges in the paper bag under the desk. *Please get them.*

3. *Take out two oranges, one in each hand.*

4. *Now put them on the table.*

5. There's juice inside this orange and we have to figure out how to get it out. We can't just squeeze it.

   [Demonstrating.]

   See, I'm squeezing it and *what's happening? Is there any orange juice coming out?*

6. [Repeat the step using the action of rolling the oranges.]

7. We have to do something else. We somehow have to get the orange open. Look what I have here. *What can I use the knife for?*

8. OK, watch me do it. *What's happening to the orange?*

9. *What's this?*

   [Pointing to drops of juice.]

10. We need to get lots more juice than this. To do that, we have to squeeze the orange. Watch me. *What am I doing?*

11. *Now you do it.*

12. *What are you doing?*

13. *When you squeeze the orange, what comes out?*

14. *So what two things did we have to do to get the juice out of the orange?*

15. [This sequence can be repeated for a second orange with appropriate modification in the language.]

C. Drinking the Juice

1. Now that the juice is all made, I thought we could drink it. *What do we usually drink from?*

2. We have some over there. *Go get them.*

3. For one person, we need one cup. But there are two people here (or whatever number is appropriate). *Point to the two people who are here.*

4. *So how many cups will we need?*

5. *Give out a cup to each person.*

6. *How are you going to get the juice from this container into the cups?*

7. *Go ahead and do that.*

8. *Now let's drink the juice.*

Making Orange Juice

Materials

Oranges, frozen orange juice concentrate with self-open top, pitchers, picture of whole orange and one cut in half, knife, juice squeezer, grapefruit, spoon, strainer, glasses

A. Focusing on Orange Juice

1. There are lots of things people can eat. *Name some of them.*

2. There are lots of things people can drink. *Name some of them.*

3. Eating and drinking are alike in certain ways. *Name a way that eating and drinking are alike.*

4. Eating and drinking are also different. For example, you could have an apple and you could have apple juice. *What would be a major difference between taking in an apple and taking in apple juice?*

5. Not all things you drink are juices. Milk is not a juice. There's water, that's not a juice. But we are going to be talking about a juice today. It's a juice that comes from this fruit.

   [Showing an orange.]

   What juice am I talking about?

B. Making Orange Juice

1. I actually have something here that could be made into orange juice.

   [Take out container of frozen orange juice concentrate.]

   Do you know what this is?

2. You see this kind of can in stores. *What kind of stores would you find it in?*

3. There's juice inside this can, but first we have to open it. *Do you see the place on here that we have to pull to open the can?*

4. *Go ahead and do it.*

5. *Take the contents of the can and put it in the pitcher. What do I mean when I say the contents of the can?*

6. *Take the stuff that's inside the can and put it in this pitcher.*

7. The stuff you put in the pitcher has the color of orange juice, but it needs something done to it so it will be more like orange juice. Look on the can. *Find some pictures on the back that will help you figure out what has to be done to make it more like orange juice.*

8. *What do you think has to be done?*

9. *What things—what information—told you to do that?*

10. OK, *go ahead and do what you said needed to be done to the juice.*

11. *Now stir it up.*

12. You know, the juice you made is the way most people now have orange juice. *Have you heard of fresh orange juice? Do you know what that means?*

    [Provide the definition if necessary.]

13. What I thought we could do today is to make some fresh orange juice. If we're going to do that, we can't just get a can. *What do we have to get?*

14. OK, *bring over the oranges that are over there.*

15. There is juice in these oranges, but something is preventing it from coming out of the orange. *What is the thing that the orange has that prevents the juice from coming out?*

16. Right—if we want the juice, we have to get through the peel. One way is to open an orange like that.

    [Showing a picture of an orange cut in half.]

    How do you think we can get the orange to look like this?

17. OK, *go ahead and do it.*

18. This is a squeezer that you can put the orange on to get the juice out. *Do you know why it's called a squeezer?*

19. *Go ahead and squeeze the oranges now so you can get the juice out.*

20. The pulp is the thing that's left inside the orange after you squeeze the juice out. *Can you show me the pulp in your orange?*

21. Remember, I said we were making fresh orange juice. *In what way is the fresh orange juice different from the can of juice we used before?*

22. Over here is a grapefruit. It's a little bit like an orange. It's round, you can cut it open, and it has juice inside.

    [Demonstrating.]

    Do you think the juice we get out of a grapefruit is called orange juice?

23. *Why not?*

24. The juice you've gotten so far fills only a little bit of a glass. *If we wanted to get more juice what do we have to do?*

25. *Go ahead and do it.*

C. Drinking the Juice

1. You've done a good job making the juice but it has some little things floating it it. *Do you know what they are called?*

   [Provide label if necessary.]

2. I think it would be a good idea if we took the seeds out of the juice. *What's one way we could take the seeds out?*

3. *Go ahead and do it. Take some of them out.*

4. There's another way. *What do you think will happen if we pour the juice through the strainer? What will happen to the seeds?*

5. *Try doing it.*

6. *What did the strainer do to the seeds? Where did the juice go? Where did the seeds go?*

7. Now the juice is ready to drink. Let's divide it up among all of us. *How many glasses will we need if we each get a serving of the juice?*

8. *Why did you say we need (however many) glasses?*

9. OK, *go ahead and get them and let's drink the juice.*

Mixing Colors

Materials
Coloring-book pictures of trees with leaves, paints and crayons without green, blue and yellow food coloring

A. Making a Painting

1. We haven't made a painting in a long time. Let's make one of these.
   [Referring to coloring-book pictures.]
   Which would you like?

2. You have the picture, now you need the paints. *Go get them.*
   [Green should not be one of the paints.]

3. Which would you like to do first,
   [Pointing to two objects on drawing.]
   This or this?

4. *What is that?*

5. *What color would you like to use for it?*

6. [Repeat steps 2-5 for the other object in the picture using crayons.]

B. Mixing Colors to Make Green

1. We haven't done this yet.
   [Pointing to tree leaves.]
   This is usually done in green. That's this color.
   [Holding up or pointing to any item that's green.]
   Look at your paints and see if you have anything that's green like this color.

2. I have an idea. Let's try mixing colors. Maybe we could get green. Let's mix this (red) and this (yellow). *Put some here and put some here.*

3. *Did it make green?*

4. We'll have to try again.
   [Repeat procedure with red and blue.]

5. [Then repeat procedure with blue and yellow.]

6. Great, we got green. *What two colors did we use to get green?* [If the child can't label, permit pointing.]

7. OK, *now color the leaves of the tree.*

C. Creating Green with Other Materials

1. We were able to get green by using blue and yellow paint. Do you think it might work if we mixed blue and yellow in some other material than paint? Let's try crayons. *What two crayons do you need?*

2. *Now try coloring one on top of the other.*

3. *Did it turn to green?*

4. [Repeat procedure with food coloring in water.]

5. [If time allows, have the child review the sequence with guided questions such as "What did we need?" "What did we do?"]

When a child working at the complex level gives a high percentage of inappropriate responses, continue the topic by moving the lesson to the simple level.

Mixing Colors

Materials

Completed multi-colored design (handmade, simple abstract pattern), an identical but only partially colored design (blue, yellow, and red only), paints, color-code chart indicating results of color combinations (blue + yellow = green, red + yellow = orange, blue + red = purple), transparent plastic sheets of various colors, food coloring, small glasses or bowls

A. Focusing on a Design

1. Here's an interesting pattern someone made. I thought I would reproduce it here. *What do you think I mean by* "reproduce it?"

2. So far I've only put in a certain number of colors. *Which colors have I put in?*

3. Look over here at the one that's completed. *Does it have more colors than the one I've done?*

4. *Name some colors it has that are not yet in the design that I'm making.* Yes, the colors I need are orange, green, and purple.

5. Look over here at the set of paints I have. *Do you see the colors that I've just named?*

6. If the design we're going to make is like this model, then we have to get some more colors. *What colors do we have to get?*

B. Mixing Colors to Make Other Colors

1. The problem is that I don't have orange, green, or purple. But I think there's a way we could make them with the colors we have. Over here I have a color-code chart. It tells how to mix colors. Look at the first line and try to interpret what it says. *What do you think it means?*

2. If we mix blue with ____________, *we'll get what color?*

3. *What is the next line? What do you think that means?*

4. *And what does the bottom line say we should do?*

5. OK, *which set of colors do you want to mix first?*

6. *Pour some (color) and (color) in here. What's happening?*

7. *Did the thing happen that the card said would happen?*

8. You try the next set. *What are you going to mix? OK, go ahead and do it.*

9. *Did it work?*

10. [Repeat with the third pair of colors.]

11. I'm going to ask you something very hard. So far, you've been looking at the cards and the colors and telling me what's happening. Look carefully at the card—I'm going to take it away. Then I'm going to ask you some questions about it.

    [Taking card away.]

    If we mix red and yellow, what color should we get?

12. *To get purple, what colors do we mix together?*

13. *And if you mix green and yellow what color do you get?*

14. Let's use the colors we've made to finish the design.

15. *First, fill in the greens, the purple.*

16. *What color still has to be filled in?*

17. *Go ahead and do it.*

C. Creating Color Mixtures with Other Materials

1. To get those colors, we were mixing paints together. *Do you think it might work if we used things other than paint?*

2. For example, here are some plastic sheets. *Let's go back to the color card.*

3. *Find two sheets that are this color.*

    [Pointing to blue and yellow.]

4. *Overlap them. Do you know what I mean by "overlap?"*

    [Demonstrating.]

    Hold them up to the light. What color do you see?

5. *Is it the same color that resulted when we mixed the paints?*

6. Try it with one other set. *Which one would you like to use?*

7. *Did it work?*

8. So far, we've gotten the same colors to come out when we've used paints *and when we've used* ___________.

9. Let's think of one other thing we could try. Look at this.

   [Pointing at food coloring.]

10. [Repeat the above sequence with food coloring.]

11. [Ask the child to summarize what happened.]

Cleaning a Fish Bowl

Materials

Fish bowl with fish, bowls, picture of a boy using a fish net, fish net, felt-tip marker, water, sponge

A. Preparing a Place to Transfer the Fish

1. The water in this fish bowl is dirty and I want to throw it out. But if I throw the dirty water out, the fish will have no water to stay in. First, we have to find someplace else to put the fish. *Find something to put the fish in.*

2. Good, but that bowl has no water for the fish to swim in. *What do we have to put in so the fish can swim?*

3. *Put some water in.*

4. *Can we put the fish in now?*

B. Catching the Fish

1. Now we have to get the fish over into this other water. Let's see what we can use. Look at this picture. *What is the boy doing to get the fish?*

2. *Do you know what that thing in his hand is called?*

   [Provide label if necessary.]

3. *Do you see something on the shelf that is like that fish net?*

4. *Go get it.*

5. *Try catching the fish.*

   [Help child if necessary.]

C. Putting Clear Water in the Bowl

1. Now the fish is out and we can do to the dirty water what I said at the start. *What did I say I wanted to do with this dirty water?*

2. OK, *throw it out. But where are you going to throw it?*

3. OK, *do it.*

4. [If there is time and the children have the necessary attention span, have them clean the bowl thoroughly with a sponge.]

5. *What do we have to put in the bowl to replace the dirty water?*

6. There is some clean water over in that bucket. *Where did I say the water was?*

7. *Go get it.*

8. I'm going to make a line on the bowl. *Pour the water in so that it reaches this line.*

   [Make a line on the bowl with the felt-tip pen.]

D. Returning the Fish to the Bowl

1. Last time when we moved the fish, *what did we use?*

2. This time, we can do it differently. If we just pour the water in this can into the bowl, *where do you think the fish will end up?*

3. Let's try it.

4. *Where is the fish?*

5. We moved the fish in two ways. *What were they?*

Cleaning a Fish Bowl

Materials

Fish bowl with fish, temporary bowl for fish, picture of person catching fish (fish should have hook in mouth), fish net, water, sponge

A. Preparing a Place to Transfer the Fish

1. I think we ought to clean this fish bowl. *Take a look at it and tell me why it ought to be cleaned.*

2. Before we do it, I think we had better transfer the fish. *What do you think I mean by transferring the fish?*

3. There are lots of times when you have to transfer things or want to transfer things. Imagine you have a big bowl that has only a little food left in it. But you don't have room in the refrigerator for the big bowl. *What could you transfer the food into?*

4. Right, you could transfer it into a little bowl. But let's get back to the fish. *Why do you think we should transfer the fish to another place while we're cleaning the bowl?*

5. *Get the container that we could transfer the fish into, and let's do it.*

B. Catching the Fish

1. Before we transfer the fish, of course, we have to catch it. Now there are a lot of ways to catch fish. When people go fishing, they certainly catch fish, but that isn't the way we want to catch this fish. Here, look at this picture of someone catching a fish. If we were to catch our fish this way, I think it would be a very bad idea. *Why do you think I think that?*

2. *Why doesn't it matter to the fisherman in the picture that the fish has been caught by a hook?*

3. We want to keep our fish and have him in a healthy state, so let's think of an alternative.

4. Look over here.

   [Give the child a choice of objects including a fish net.]

   One of these things would be useful to catch a fish. *Which one am I thinking about?*

5. *Where are you going to have to put the net in order to catch the fish?*

6. *Go ahead and catch the fish.*

C. Putting Clean Water in the Bowl

1. Now the fish is out. *What do you think we could do with the water that's in the bowl?*

2. OK, *go ahead and do it.*

3. A lot of the dirt went out with the water, but there is still quite a bit of dirt left. We could get rid of the dirt by doing the same thing to the bowl that people do to dirty dishes when they have to clean them up. *What are some of the things you do with dirty dishes?*

4. Let's get the things we need. *Go get them.*

5. *Now let's clean the bowl that way.*

6. We say that the sides of the fish bowl were dirty. *How do they look to you now?*

7. *What helped to get rid of the dirt on the sides of the fishbowl?*

8. OK, the bowl is clean, but it still isn't in a state to return the fish to. *What would happen if we put the fish in the bowl the way it is now?*

9. OK, so we have to get some water. *Will it be enough if we put in this much water?*

   [Indicating a small cup of water.]

10. *Why wouldn't this be a sufficient amount of water?*

11. *What do we have to do instead?*

12. OK, *do it.*

D. Returning the Fish to the Bowl

1. We have to get back to the way things were originally before we started cleaning the bowl. *Describe how things were at the start. In other words, where was the fish, the water, and so on. Tell me how it looked.*

2. Let's reverse the operation. We started out by taking the fish *out* of the bowl. *If we are going to reverse the operation, where are we going to put the fish?*

3. OK, *let's do it.*

4. Now things are exactly like they were at the start except for one thing. *What is the difference between the bowl now and the bowl at the start of this operation?*

5. Remember what I said we were going to do when we began this? *What did I say we were going to do?* (Clean the fish bowl.)

6. *Did we achieve that?*

The most demanding part of the lesson should occur during the first half of the therapy session. If the child tires during the last half of the session, the demands may be simplified and reduced.

Making Gelatin Dessert

Materials
Bowl with ready-to-eat flavored gelatin, spoons, box of flavored gelatin powder, box of pudding mix, bowls, water, equipment for heating water, measuring cup, mixing spoon, refrigerator

A. Focusing on Gelatin

1. Look at this bowl. *Tell me what's in it.*

2. *Would you like to taste it?*

   [Accept any answer and let child taste it.]

3. We can make another one like this, but we need to get the materials. *Bring those two boxes over there.*

4. *Which one has gelatin in it?*

5. *What do you have to do to get the stuff out of the box?*

6. *Do it.*

B. Making the Gelatin

1. We said this could be gelatin

   [Pointing to box.]

   But is it like this gelatin that is already made?

2. Right, it isn't. We have to do something. What we have to do is put the mix in the bowl and add hot water. *What do we have to do?*

3. We said we needed a bowl. *Go get one.*

4. *Where are you going to put the gelatin powder?*

5. *Put it there.*

6. *What are you going to do with the paper?*

7. *Is all the mix out of the paper bag?*

8. Now we have to add some hot water. Here is one cup. *Pour it very slowly.*

9. It's beginning to mix, but the water is mainly on top. *What's staying at the bottom?*

10. *What could we use to stir it up so it will get all mixed up?*

11. *So let's add another cup of hot water.*

C. Comparing the Two Gelatins

1. The gelatin is almost finished, but *is it like the gelatin we first looked at?*

2. [Referring to original gelatin.]
   Try tilting the bowl. Does the gelatin move?

3. *Let's try doing it with the gelatin we just made. Does it move?*

4. One of the gelatins is firm and doesn't move. *Which one is that?*

5. One of the gelatins is not firm and does move. *Which one is that?*

6. There's something we could do to fix this situation. If we put the gelatin that moves into a very cold place, it will get hard. *Look around the room and find a place where the inside is cold.*

7. *What is that called?*

8. *Let's put the gelatin in the refrigerator* (or whatever word the child has used).

9. *Let's leave it there for a while and check it later to see what happens.*

Making Gelatin Dessert

Materials

Two boxes of flavored gelatin mix, unflavored gelatin powder, bowls, measuring cups, mixing spoon, water, equipment for heating water, refrigerator, timer, paper, pencil

A. Focusing on Gelatin

1. We're going to be working with what most people consider a dessert. *Do you know what a dessert is?*

   [Provide definition if necessary.]

2. So desserts are usually sweet things that are eaten at the end of a meal. *Name some desserts that you know.*

3. Here's one other dessert.

   [Showing a box of flavored gelatin mix.]

   I'm pretty sure you know what it is. *Tell me it's name.*

4. This gelatin powder is a little different from this gelatin mix to make a dessert. Here's some plain gelatin powder and here's some gelatin dessert mix.

   [Pour some of each into separate bowls and hold out bowls so the child can see the difference.]

   Put your finger in and taste the gelatin powder. Now put your finger in and taste the dessert mix. Tell me the difference in taste between the plain gelatin and the gelatin for dessert.

5. If we wanted to use the plain gelatin powder instead of the dessert mix and we wanted it to be sweet like a dessert, *what could we add to the plain powder to get it that way?*

B. Making the Gelatin

1. Making gelatin is pretty easy, but it still takes a few steps. The steps that we have to follow are on the box. *Do you know the name that is used to describe the steps in making food?*

   [Accept any appropriate answer such as recipe, directions, or instructions.]

   Look at the back of the box and tell me what the steps are in this recipe (or whatever word the child used).

2. One of the steps you said was adding water. But there's something special about the water. *Do you see the little marks above the cup?* They are suppose to represent steam. *What do you have to do to the water so steam will come off it?*

3. So we don't just need plain regular cold water. *What kind of water do we need?*

4. Let's get some water heated while we start doing the other steps. *What was the first step in the recipe (or whatever word the child used)?*

5. *OK, let's follow it through.*

6. *How many steps do we still need to carry out?*

7. The step involving the water told us not only does the water have to be hot, but it told us the amount of water that has to be added. *What amount of water needs to be added?*

8. *What if we added only a tiny bit of water instead of the amount they said? What do you think will happen if we add this?*

   [Referring to less than a quarter cup of water.]

9. Go ahead and do it.

10. *What happened?*

11. *Why do we need to have more water?*

12. *Fine, go ahead and add the amount they said.*

13. Remember, they told us to add hot water. *What do you think would happen if we had added cold water instead of hot water?*

14. Let's try it. Here's another box of the same flavored gelatin mix. Let's go through all the steps but instead of adding hot water, we're going to add cold water. *Go ahead and do it.*

15. [Help child through sequence.]

    What happened?

16. *Why do you think it told us to use hot water instead of cold water?*

C. Completing the Gelatin

1. The gelatin is almost finished, but it isn't quite like the gelatin we're used to. *In what way is it different?*

2. If we're going to get it to be like that, we have to do something to it. We have to put it in a cold place so it can get firm. *Can you think of a place that's cold where we could put it?*

3. *Go ahead and put it there.*

4. [Ask this question immediately after the child places the gelatin in refrigerator.]

   If we took it out right now, *do you think it would be firm the way we want it?*

5. *Why won't it be firm?*

6. *What do we have to do in order for it to be firm?*

7. I have an idea. Let's clock the amount of time needed for the gelatin to get firm. Let's put on this timer and check the gelatin every 20 minutes. We'll make a chart here and make a mark for every 20 minutes that we are going to check it. If the gelatin is firm, we'll put a check mark. If the gelatin is not firm, we'll put a dash. *Let's do it.*

8. [Help the child keep a record of the observations.]

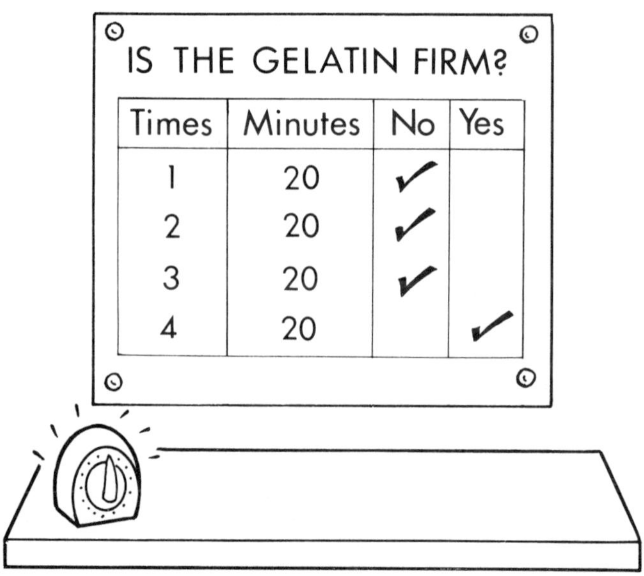

Making Fruit Salad

Materials

Picture of various fruits, picture of non-fruit, 4 or 5 kinds of washed fruit for a salad (only two with edible skins), potato, knife, pictures of people eating fruit, picture of a fruit salad, pictures of other foods, pencil, paper, knife, bowl, sugar or dressing for salad, paper plates, forks

A. Focusing on Fruits

1. There are some foods in this picture. *Tell me what some of them are?*

2. *Name some foods that are not on this page.*

   [Show non-fruit picture if necessary.]

3. You've mentioned a lot of different foods. *What is the thing we do with food—all food?*

4. [Returning to fruit picture.]

   All the foods on this page are one kind of food. They're fruits. Fruits are foods that have seeds in them. Here is an apple. Do you see any seeds?

5. *Right now you can't see any seeds, but if we cut open the apple, you will be able to. You will see the seeds. I'll do that. What am I doing?*

6. *Do you see the thing I said you would see?*

7. *What do you see?*

8. *Take some of them out.*

9. *Try to squeeze them.*

10. You can't because they are very hard. *Say that.*

11. Here's a potato. It is not fruit. So if we cut it open, *do you think we will see seeds inside?*

12. Let's cut it.

    [Cut the potato yourself or closely supervise cutting.]

13. *Are there any seeds?*

14. *Why aren't there?;*

B. Focusing on a Fruit Salad

1. We can eat fruit just as it is—without doing anything special to it. See, here is a boy (picture of a boy eating a fruit). *What is he eating?*

2. And here is a woman. *What is she eating?*

3. *Were the boy and the woman eating the fruit whole or was the fruit cut up?*

4. We could also eat it cut up. And we could do something even more than that. We can cut up lots of different fruit together. That is called a "*fruit salad.*" *Tell me what I said a fruit salad is.*

5. Look over here at these pictures. One of them is a fruit salad. *Which one is it?*

C. Making the Fruit Salad

1. Here is a bunch of fruits and I thought we could make them into salad. Remember, I said a salad needs different fruits. *So pick out three different fruits.*

   [If the child has trouble counting, draw three circles on paper and tell the child to put a fruit in each circle.]

2. Let's start with this.

   [Show a fruit with edible skin.]

   What is it?

3. Let's cut it up. But first, we have to decide what size pieces to make.

   [Draw two circles of different sizes appropriate for fruit in a fruit salad.]

   Do you want the pieces to be this size or this size?

4. OK, I'll make a whole bunch of circles this size, and *on each circle you put a piece of fruit we've cut.*

5. *Let's put them in the bowl.*

6. Let's cut this fruit.

   [Holding up fruit with edible skin.]

   You did so well cutting, I don't think I have to make circles. *Just cut up the fruit.*

7. *Now put it in the bowl.*

8. Here's a fruit we have to do something different to. You were able to cut up the other fruit without taking anything off the fruit. But this fruit has a part that I think we should take off. Here, *try biting into the fruit.*

9. It's awfully tough. I think we ought to get rid of it. Look what I'm doing to get rid of it. *What am I doing?*

10. *Do you know what this part that I'm getting rid of is called?*

    [Provide label if necessary.]

11. *Find some peel on this other fruit.*

12. *And find some peel on this fruit.*

    [Referring to a third fruit.]

13. Let's get back to the fruit I peeled. *What do you have to do to it before you put it in the fruit salad?*

14. OK, *let's do it.*

15. [Complete the fruit salad. Sugar or dressing may be added before eating the salad.]

Making Fruit Salad

Materials
Various fruits, knife, bowl, sugar or dressing for salad, paper plates, forks

A. Focusing on Fruit

1. We're going to be focusing on some fruits today. *Can you name some fruit for me?*

2. I'm going to offer you some choices and *you tell me if the thing I mention is a fruit or not: banana—is that a fruit?*

3. *Egg, is that a fruit?*

   [Continue with an orange and a peach.]

4. So fruits are a kind of food but not all foods are fruit. *Name a food I mentioned that is not a fruit.*

5. Do you know what makes something a fruit? It's a food that has seeds in it. Here's an apple. It's a fruit. I just said a fruit is something that has seeds in it. *Do you think this apple has seeds?*

6. But I can't see any seeds. *Why do you think I can't see any seeds?*

7. *How can we get to the inside of the apple to see if there are seeds?*

8. *Go ahead and do it.*

9. Let's try doing the same thing with a pear. *What do we have to do to get to the seeds?*

10. I'm going to ask you a tricky question. I have a banana here. It has seeds, but the seeds are not as easy to see as the seeds in an apple, or a pear, or an orange. *Let's cut a banana and let's see if you can see anything that looks like seeds.*

    [Carefully supervise child's use of knife.]

11. So seeds are in all fruits, but they're not on the outside of a fruit. *Where are seeds found?*

B. Focusing on Fruit Salad

1. We can eat them whole. What do I mean by "eat them whole?"

2. We can also eat them cut up. *Take this apple and cut it up.* You can eat it if you like. Now there is something further we can do with cut up fruit. Not only can we cut a single fruit, we can cut up a whole bunch of fruit and mix it together. And then we have something that's called a "fruit salad." *So is this cut-up apple a fruit salad?*

3. *Why not?*

4. *What could I do so it would become part of a fruit salad?*

5. Salad doesn't apply just to fruit. It can apply to other things. You can make a vegetable salad. *What would be the difference between a fruit salad and a vegetable salad?*

6. *What would be the same between a fruit salad and a vegetable salad?*

C. Making the Fruit Salad

1. I thought it would be a nice idea if we actually made a fruit salad. Remember we have to have more than one fruit. *How many fruits would you like to include?*

2. *Go ahead and pick them out.*

3. Over here we have a pear. We can cut up the pear just the way it is or we can take the skin off. *Do you know what I mean by the skin? Point to the skin.*

4. You know there is also skin on our bodies. *Do you know where the skin is on our bodies?*

5. *What is the same about the skin on our bodies and the skin on the fruit?*

6. I said before that we can keep the skin on the pear or we can take it off. *What would you like to do?*

7. OK, *go ahead and cut up the pear.*

8. Here's a fruit you picked and we don't have much choice about the skin.

   [Holding up an orange or a grapefruit.]

   Can we keep the skin on this and still just cut it up into the salad?

9. *Why not?*

10. *What do we have to do with this skin?*

11. *Did we have to do that with the skin on the pear?*

12. *Why not?*

13. *Find another fruit over there that we have to remove the skin from—that we don't have a choice about leaving the skin on.*

14. *And go over and find a fruit that we do have a choice about leaving the skin on or taking it off.*

15. *Let's finish cutting up the fruit and put it in the salad.*

16. The fruit in the salad sure looks different from the way it started. *Tell me the steps that we went through, from start to finish, to get to the point where the fruit looks like this.*

17. [Sugar or dressing may be added to the salad before eating.]

Any play activity that lends itself to sequenced development can form the basis of a lesson. The lesson plans in this book can be used as models to frame the new lesson.

Making Popcorn

Materials

One closed paper bag with a handful of popped popcorn, one closed empty paper bag, unpopped popcorn, popcorn maker, picture of popcorn maker, bowls, butter (pan for melting if needed), salt if desired

A. Focusing on Popcorn

1. I made something most of us like, but there is only a little left. It's in one of the two (identical closed brown) bags. *Shake this one.*

   [Pointing to the bag containing the popped corn.]

2. *Did you hear anything?*

3. *Now shake this one.*

   [Pointing to the empty bag.]

4. *Did you hear anything?*

5. *Which of these two bags do you think has something in it? The one that made a noise or the one that did not make a noise?*

6. *Take that bag.*

   [Pointing to the bag containing popcorn.]

7. *Open it.*

8. *What's inside?*

B. Focusing on the Popcorn Maker

1. It's popcorn, but it's only a little bit. I thought we could make more. We can do that with a popcorn maker. *What did I say we need?*

2. Here's a picture of a popcorn maker. And there's a real popcorn maker on the shelf over there.

   [Popcorn maker should be with other unrelated items.]

   Go get it.

3. If it's a popcorn maker, it should make popcorn. These are the kernels that become popcorn. *Let's put them in the popcorn maker and see what happens.*

   [Popcorn maker should **not** be plugged in.]

4. [Ask over the next few minutes,]

Is anything happening to the kernels?

C. Making the Popcorn

1. Nothing has happened. I think there's something else we have to do. Let's look at the popcorn maker. Here's a part of it.

[Holding up the plug.]

What do you think it's called?

[Provide label if necessary.]

2. I think we forgot to do something with this plug. *Where do you usually put a plug when you want something to work? Look at the plug on the lamp. Where is it?*

3. Look at the plug on the clock. *Where is that plug?*

[Other appliances may be used as examples.]

4. *Where do you think we have to put the plug on the popcorn maker?*

5. OK, let's watch. *You tell me if the popcorn starts changing.*

6. [After child reports change,]

What's happened to the popcorn? Is it still in the form of kernels or is it different?

7. [Complete the lesson by adding butter and salt if desired and sharing the popcorn with the child.]

Making Popcorn

Materials

Uncooked rice, puffed rice, uncooked wheat, puffed wheat, unpopped popcorn, popped corn, popcorn maker, measuring cup, pencil, bowls, butter and salt if desired

A. Focusing on Popcorn

1. There are lots of foods you can eat without cooking. You can eat them just the way they are. You can eat a banana or a carrot. But some other foods have to be cooked and they change when they're cooked. Think about spaghetti or noodles before they're cooked. *How do they feel?*

2. Then after they're cooked, *how do they feel?*

3. So when you cook things, it changes them.

4. What we are going to be talking about today is an unusual form of change that happens when you cook certain kinds of foods. For example, look at this. *What is this?*

   [Holding up a grain of rice.]

5. Look at this. You may not know what this is.

   [Holding up some puffed rice.]

   This is puffed rice. It comes from rice but it goes through a special form of cooking where it sort of blows up and pops out. Look at this.

   [Holding up wheat and puffed wheat.]

   It's uncooked wheat and this is wheat that has been cooked in that special way and has puffed out. It's called puffed wheat. There's one other form of food that does this that you probably know very well. *Do you know what this is?*

   [Show popcorn kernels.]

6. We wouldn't want to eat them this way. In fact, *try it—taste it. How does it feel?*

7. But we can do something to this that makes it nice for eating. *Do you know what I'm talking about? Do you know what we can do to it?*

8. [Regardless of child's answer, show popcorn that has been popped.]

This is what happens when it's cooked. And it's similar to the rice when it got puffed out and to the wheat when that got puffed out. *What happened to the popcorn when it changed from corn to popcorn?*

B. Focusing on the Popcorn Maker

1. Remember, to make the popcorn you have to use a special form of cooking. Like other forms of cooking, you have to apply heat. *What thing do you use in most kitchens to apply heat to food?*

2. We could use the stove and put the popcorn in a pot on the stove, but there's another appliance we have that can do it just as well. It's this one. *Do you know what this is called?*

   [Provide label if necessary.]

3. For cooking we have to have heat, and I said we could cook the popcorn in this popcorn maker. *But feel the popcorn maker. Is it hot?*

4. So just having a popcorn maker won't make popcorn. We have to do something to make it hot. *Do you have any idea of what we could do to the popcorn maker to make it hot?*

5. OK, you plug in the popcorn maker. That's certainly not the only appliance we plug in. *Can you think of any other appliances that we plug in?*

C. Making the Popcorn

1. While the popcorn maker is heating up, we had better measure out the popcorn. If we put in this many kernels of corn,

   [Indicating about a quarter of cup]

   do you think that's all the popcorn we could get out? Or do you think the popcorn would be bigger than this?

2. *Why?*

3. Let's see if you are right. Let's mark the cup here to see how high the kernels go. *Now we put those kernels into the popcorn maker. Tell me when the popcorn gets done.*

4. Now let's measure the amount of popcorn that we had. *Let's fill up the cup to the line where we measured it before. Does the popcorn just reach to the line or is there much more popcorn than that?*

5. *What do you think happened to the kernels so that the popcorn was much larger than the kernels?*

6. We can eat it just this way, or we can add something to it. Some people like to add butter and salt. *Would you like to do that?*

7. [Follow the child's decision.]

Have nonrelevant materials available to help the child recognize the distinction between relevant and nonrelevant materials and ideas.

Cooking Eggs

Materials
Eggs, pictures of different kinds of cooked eggs, non-stick pan for cooking, stove or hot plate, spatula, saucepan, water for cooking eggs, paper plates, crayons, paper

A. Focusing on Eggs

1. Here is something you probably know. *What is it called?*

   [Hold up egg and provide label if necessary.]

2. This is something else you probably know. *What is it?*

   [Showing picture of a scrambled egg.]

3. And here is still one more thing you may know. *What is it?*

   [Showing a a hard-cooked egg cut open or a picture of one.]

4. You said all three of these things were eggs, but they look so different. We're going to find out what made them different. *Tell me what I said we are going to do.*

B. Cooking Eggs

1. If we're going to work with eggs, we have to first get some eggs. There's some in a box over there. *Go get them.*

2. *Take out one egg.*

3. Here is a pan.

   [The pan should be hot.]

   Crack open this egg and drop it in the pan.

   [Carefully supervise the child when using hot utensils.]

4. It's beginning to look like one of the eggs we saw before. *Which one is it beginning to look like?*

5. *What did we do to the egg to get it to look this way?*

6. When you put the egg in the pan, there was a part you didn't use. *Find it.*

7. *What is it called?*

8. *So what is the part of the egg called that you don't use?*

9. *Which of these two eggs would you like to make next?*

   [Pointing to scrambled and hard-cooked eggs.]

10. [Follow the child's choice and cook it.]

11. You made these two eggs look very different. *What did you do to get the egg this way?*

    [Pointing to the fried egg.]

12. *What did you do to get the egg this way?*

    [Referring to either the scrambled or hard-cooked egg.]

C. Making a Two-Dimensional Representation of Eggs

1. You can't take the eggs home, but you can make a picture of what we have done and take that home. If you are going to make a picture, *what things do you need?*

2. *Go get them.*

3. Here, I'll draw a picture of one of the eggs you made.

   [Draw the hard-cooked egg.]

   Look at this white part I drew. Show me where it is on the real egg.

4. And here is the yellow part I drew. *Show it to me on the real egg.*

5. [Repeat the procedure with the scrambled egg.]

6. We still haven't drawn this egg.

   [Referring to fried egg.]

   Go ahead and draw it.

Cooking Eggs

Materials

Uncooked and cooked rice, raw and cooked carrot, raw and cooked celery, raw potato and mashed cooked potato, potato chips, pictures of different kinds of cooked eggs, eggs, various pans for cooking, water for cooking eggs, cooking utensils (fork, bowl, spatula), paper, pencil

A. Focusing on Eggs

1. We're going to do some cooking today. Things happen when you cook foods. Here's uncooked rice and here's cooked rice. *Tell me the difference between cooked and uncooked rice.*

2. Here's a carrot that's been cooked and one that has not been cooked. *Feel them. Tell me the difference again between the uncooked carrot and the cooked one.*

3. Here is some celery that has been cooked and some that has not been cooked. *How do you think the cooked celery will compare with the uncooked celery?*

4. *So what can cooking do to foods?*

5. Cooking can soften some foods but the food often stays looking like it did before. Here's the cooked rice and the uncooked rice and it still looks like rice.

   [Compare cooked and uncooked carrot and celery.]

   Some foods you can cook in different ways and it totally changes how they look.

   [Show the uncooked potato]

   What is this?

6. Now look at this.

   [Showing mashed potato.]

   What is this?

7. [Show the potato chips.]

   These three foods look different, but they all come from the same vegetable. *Where do they come from?*

8. I'm going to show some pictures of something else. When this is cooked, it ends up totally different.

   [Show pictures of scrambled egg, sliced hard-cooked egg, and fried egg.]

9. This is all the same kind of food. *Do you know what kind of food it is?*

B. Cooking Eggs

1. We can make each of the different kinds of eggs that we just saw. To end up with different looking eggs, we have to cook them differently. Look at this.

   [Pointing to picture of hard-cooked egg.]

   Do you know how you have to cook these to get the egg to look this way?

   [Provide answer if necessary.]

2. *Let's try it and see if it works.*

3. While that egg is cooking in water, let's see about the other eggs. *Do you have any idea how to cook this egg?*

   [Pointing to picture of the fried egg.]

4. Let's go ahead and do it.

   [Carefully supervise the child while working with hot utensils.]

5. Now let's look at this last egg.

   [Pointing to the picture of the scrambled egg.]

   We're going to cook it in a way that's similar to the way we cooked the fried egg. But before you cook it, you have to do something so that it gets all mixed up. If you don't mix it up, *how is it going to look when you cook it?*

6. That's right. It will look just like the fried egg. *What can you do to mix the egg up?*

7. When you do that, it's called scrambling the egg, so this is called a scrambled egg. Let's try making an egg that way.

C. Making Two-Dimensional Representation of the Eggs

1. I'm going to ask you to do something very hard. I want to see if you can make up a diagram or chart of the things we did. *If you draw the steps we took in making the hard-cooked egg, what would you put here?*

   [Guide the child to diagram the pot of water and the egg.]

2. *If you make a diagram of how we made the fried egg, how would you draw it?*

3. *Go ahead and do it.*

4. *If you make a diagram of the scrambled egg, how would you do that?*

5. OK, *do it.*

6. This diagram shows that we did very different things to the eggs. *When you do different things in cooking the same kind of food, what happens to the food you cook?*

Comments in conversation are vital. Be sure to comment as frequently as you question.

Additional Lesson Suggestions

1. Baking a Cake
2. Making Tuna Fish Salad
3. Changing Snow (Ice) to Water and Water to Ice
4. Making Playdough
5. Making Soup

Constructing a Jigsaw Puzzle

To expand this lesson, ask the child to paste the pictures on oak tag before cutting them up. The puzzle pieces will be firmer and easier to handle.

Materials
Large box containing a variety of toys including some that can be separated into parts, plastic or wood construction set, 12-16 piece puzzle, pictures in duplicate, felt-tip pen or marker, scissors

A. Focusing on Toys

1. There is a big box on the table that has some things it it. *Please go get it.*

2. We need to have that box close to us, *so put it over here.*

3. I'd like to see what's in the box. I'll bet you would too. But in order to do that, we have to open it. *What do we have to do?*

4. OK, *do that.*

5. There sure are a lot of things in that box. *Do you know what all these are called?*

   [All are toys.]

B. Recognizing That Some Toys Have Component Parts

1. Let's start by taking out some of the toys. *First take out a ball.*

2. *Next take out a dog.*

3. *And take out a block.*

   [The toys named so far should have no separable parts.]

4. *Put all the toys you've taken out in one pile here.*

5. *Now take out* ___________.

   [Name a toy that can be separated into parts.]

6. *And take out the construction pieces.*

7. *And take out the train.*

   [These last three toys named must have removable parts.]

8. *Put the three you've just taken out on the table.*

   [Indicate a place separate from the other group of toys.]

9. All the things you've taken out are toys, but they're different from one another. One group has parts you can put on and take off. And one group does not. *Point to the group that has parts you can put on and take off.*

10. *What did I say was special about that group?*

11. One group does not have parts you can put on or take off. *Which group is that?*

12. *What did I just say was the same about all the ones in that group?* That's right.

C. Recognizing That Puzzles Are a Special Form of Toy With Parts

1. Before, you showed me the toys that had parts or pieces. I have another toy on the shelf over there that has a lot of pieces, but it's a little different from these.

   [Pointing.]

   Please go get it for me.
2. *Do you know what this is called?*

   [Provide the label if necessary.]

3. *Do you remember what I said this would have? Tell me what I said it would have.*

4. And it does! It really does have a lot of pieces! *Show some of them to me.*

5. So if we were going to put the puzzle with one of the groups of toys,

   [Pointing]

   which one would it go with, *this one with no parts or this one with parts?*

D. Constructing a Puzzle

1. The puzzle we've been looking at was made by someone else. I thought we could make our own puzzle just like the person who made this puzzle. This puzzle has a picture. In fact, it's a picture of __________ .

   [Have the child finish the sentence.]

2. *Would you like our puzzle to be the same sort of picture or a different one?*

3. *Go over to the table and bring a picture that is similar* (different).

   [The choice for the child should include pictures that are similar to puzzle pictures and some that are different. All pictures should be in duplicate.]

4. We have the picture you wanted, but it's still one whole piece, and remember we said that puzzles are not one whole piece. Instead, they're __________.

   [Have the child complete the sentence.]

5. See, we have a problem. We have to somehow get them into pieces. *Watch me.* I'm going to show you something we can do.

   [Take another picture and draw lines with a pen or marker to designate puzzle pieces.]

6. *What did I do?*

7. *Now you do the same thing with the picture.*

8. *What did you just do?*

9. Right, you made marks on it (the child's words) so that it looks like the pieces of a puzzle. But it still doesn't come apart the way this puzzle does. You could make it come apart by cutting it on the lines you drew. *Go ahead and do that.*

   [Help the child cut if necessary.]

Concluding Comments to the Child

You've done a great job. Why don't you put the puzzle together? Here, you can use this picture as a guide to see where the parts go.

[Offering duplicate pictures.]

Constructing a Jigsaw Puzzle

Materials

Ball, picture showing a variety of toys, large box of toys including some that can be separated into parts, plastic or wood construction set, 12-16 piece puzzle, pictures in duplicate, felt-tip pen or marker, scissors

A. Focusing on Toys

1. You know this room and practically any room that people use has things in it that are useful. That is, they help people do things. For instance, there are things in here to sit on. *What are they called?*

2. And there are things to give us light. *What are they called?*

3. There are things to let air come in and out. *What are they called?*

4. We could go on and on talking about all the different things in the room like the doors, and the chairs, and the sink.

   [Mention several other items in the room.]

   Those are all things that are put in rooms because they are useful. They help you do certain things. There's another group of objects that are not really useful but they're nice to have around because they're fun to play with. *Do you know what these kinds of objects are called?*

   [Provide label if necessary.]

   That's what we are going to be talking about today. We're going to be talking about certain kinds of toys.

B. Recognizing That Some Toys Have Component Parts

1. Certain toys are just in one piece, all by themselves. Like a ball. *Is that in one piece or in many pieces?*

2. *Look at this picture.*

   [Show a picture or page from a book
   that depicts a variety of toys.]

   Here is a picture of a ball. *Find two other toys that are all in one piece and don't have any parts.*

3. Many toys have parts. A lot of times, they're construction toys with different parts so you can change their shape. For example, here is a robot.

   [Referring to a toy.]

   What are some of the things you can change on him?

4. You can change the parts of construction toys. In fact, you can change even more parts than with the robot. *Name some of the different things that you can make from the same construction set.*

5. With games that have parts, the parts allow you to do something. *What do they allow you to do?*

C. Recognizing That Puzzles Are a Special Form of Toy With Parts

1. So far, we've been talking about toys with different parts and, each time the parts are put together, different shapes can be made. But there are also a group of toys that are almost the opposite, that is, they have different parts but it always leads to the same shape. *Do you know what they are called?*

   [If child does not know, show the jigsaw puzzle, saying,]

   This is what I meant. *What is it called?*

2. If you take out all the pieces of the puzzle and then try to put them together again, *what design* (picture) *will it make?*

3. If I did it again and again, *what design would it always make?*

4. *Would this puzzle make any other design?*

5. So a puzzle is somewhat unusual. *It is like construction toys and some other toys in that it* __________.

   [Let the child complete your sentence.]

6. *But it's different from these toys with pieces in that it* __________.

   [Let the child complete your sentence.]

D. Constructing a Puzzle

1. The puzzle(s) we've been looking at had to have been made by somebody. I thought it would be fun to make up one of our own. Puzzles always have some design or picture. *This one is a picture of* __________ *?*

   [Let the child complete your sentence.]

2. *This one is a picture of* __________.

3. *And this one is a picture of* __________.

4. *If we are going to make a puzzle, what do we need?*

5. I have some pictures over there. *Go over and find one you would like to make into a puzzle.*

6. It's a good picture, but something has to be done to it for it to become a puzzle. *What has to be done?*

7. Before cutting it up, I think you should plan the way you want the parts to be cut up. That means you have to mark the picture to indicate where the cutting lines will be. *What could we use to mark it?*

8. *Go ahead and do it.*

9. Now you're ready to cut it out. *Go ahead.*

10. You've worked very long and hard on this. I wonder if you can *tell me all the steps you went through in constructing this puzzle.*

Concluding Comment to Child
You worked very hard today and you made a beautiful puzzle. You can take it home.

Making a Playdough Doll

Materials
Playdough doll with different colors for different parts of the body, cans of colored playdough

A. Focusing on a Playdough Doll

1. Someone made this. *What do you think it is?*

2. *What's this part?*

   [Pointing to head.]

3. *And what's this part?*

   [Pointing to the legs.]

4. You also have legs. *Show me your legs.*

5. Legs are useful and can do things for us. *What can you do with your legs?*

6. *Show me the arms of the playdough doll.*

7. You have those too. *Name some of the same things that you have, and I have, and the playdough doll has.*

B. Getting the Materials for the Playdough Doll

1. We can make a doll like this, but we need some playdough. *Do you see any playdough over there?*

2. *Bring it here.*

3. *Find the colors that were used in making this playdough doll.*

4. This color is yellow.

   [Pointing to playdough doll.]

   Show me the can that has yellow in it.

5. [Repeat for two other colors.]

C. Making the Playdough Doll

1. Now we'll start the doll. Let's start with the head. The head on this doll is red. *Do you want the same color or a different color?*

2. *Go ahead and do it.*

3. [Repeat for the body.]

4. So far, we've made the head and body. *What does it still need?*

5. *Go ahead and make the arms (or legs), but this time I think you should make them the same color as the model.*

6. [Repeat for the legs (or arms).]

The lesson may be extended by making parts of the face or changing the leg shapes so they are in a running position, etc.

Restating information in a slightly varying form gives the child more opportunity to understand the language demand and more time to process language.

Making a Playdough Doll

Materials

Playdough doll, towel or cloth, playdough in various colors, cards or pieces of paper, crayons

A. Focusing on a Playdough Doll

1. [Have the playdough doll covered with a towel or cloth.]

   I have something here that has arms and legs and a head. *What do you think it is?*

2. I think you may be right, but let me ask you something first. A person has arms, legs, and a head. *Why didn't you say it was a person?*

3. Let me show it to you. Here it is. It is a doll, but it's a doll made out of a special material. *Do you know what kind of material it is?*

4. Here's some other playdough. This playdough is very soft. *Feel the doll. Feel the regular playdough. How are they different?*

5. *Why do you think this playdough and the doll feel so different?*

B. Getting Materials for the Playdough Doll

1. We can make a playdough doll, but I thought it would be good if we used totally different colors from the ones we have here. What I'd like you to do first is *make a mark on this card representing each color in this doll.*

2. *Go over to the shelf and get any cans of playdough that are not the colors you have marked.* That way we'll have different colors for this new doll.

3. *How many colors are left that we have not used already?*

4. *Tell me what they are?*

5. Remember, I made up a difficult rule. I want to use totally different colors. But let's be systematic about it. I'll show you what I mean. *This doll has what color head?*

6. *What color are you going to replace it with?*

7. *Let's put that on a card so you can remember it.*

   [Across the child's red mark make a green mark so the child has a card with a color code for both the old head and the new head. Repeat this procedure for each color used in the playdough doll.]

8. Let's see if you can use the code you have set up. It's really hard so be careful. Can you draw what the playdough doll is going to look like when you convert the colors? Go ahead and do it.

9. OK, *go ahead and make the playdough doll.*

10.

   [Take away the dolls, the playdough, and the coded cards.]

   Let's see if you can remember some of the things you did. *Do you remember what color you substituted for the red? For the blue,* etc.?

11. Let's see if you are right.

12. [Proceed with each color used for the original playdough doll.]

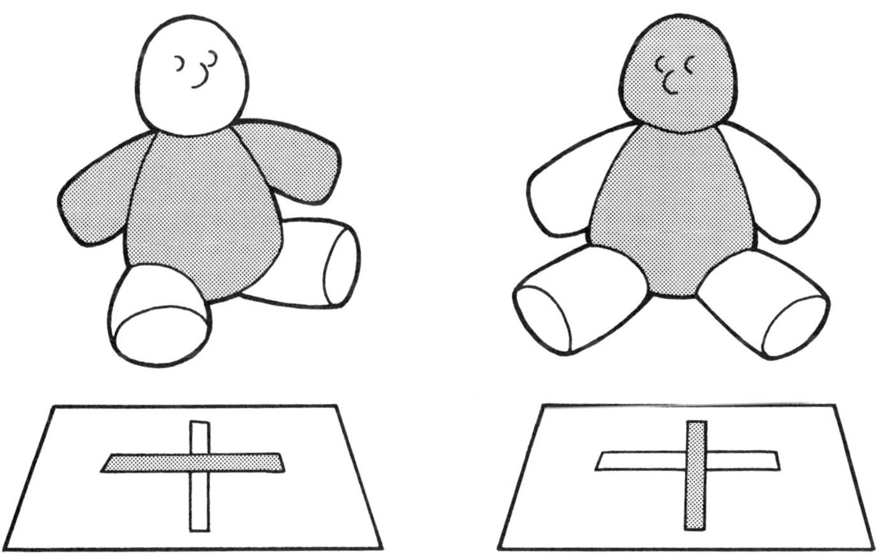

Making a Playdough Pie

Materials

Pictures of food and non-food items including a pie, completed pie made of playdough (white dough and red "cherries"), knife, red and white playdough, rolling pin, metal trays or cookie sheets, pie pans

A. Focusing on a Pie

1. We've made lots of different foods here. Some of them are in these pictures.

   [Show pictures of food and non-food items.]

   Tell me what some of them are.

2. Here is a food we have never made.

   [Show a picture of a cross sectional cut of a pie.]

   Do you know what it's called?

   [Provide the answer if necessary.]

3. A pie has some dough on the top over here and it also has dough on the bottom. *Show me the dough on the bottom.*

4. It also has something sweet in the inside like apples or peaches. Now I'll name some other things. You tell me which ones might be inside a pie. *Could it have marbles, or pears, or paper clips?*

5. This pie has cherries in the middle. *Point to the cherries.*

B. Focusing on a Playdough Pie

1. So far we've looked only at pictures of pies. Now, I'm going to show you another kind of pie. It's not a picture, but it's also not a real pie. It's a make-believe pie made of playdough. *What did I say it was made of?*

2. Now, here it is. You can't see the sweet part inside, but you can see the dough. *Show me the dough.*

3. Inside the pie, there are playdough cherries that are red. *If we cut open the pie, what color will you see?*

4. *Go ahead and cut a slice. Look inside.*

5. *What color do you see?*

6. *Were you right when you said you would see __________?*

C. Making a Playdough Pie

1. I made this pie. I thought you could make one just like it. *Go get the can of playdough with the colors we'll need.* You'll need this color.

   [Pointing to white.]

   And you'll need this color.

   [Pointing to red.]

2. Now, to make the dough the right shape, you have to roll it like this with the rolling pin.

   [Model the action.]

   What did I say this was called?

   [Holding up rolling pin.]

3. *Go ahead and roll the dough.*

4. Look, my dough is resting in a metal tray.

   [Placing dough on tray.]

   I think you should get the same thing. *What will you get for your dough?*

5. *Go get it.*

6. We have the bottom part of the pie, but we have to put in the cherries. *Get the can we need to make the cherries.*

7. *Roll out the cherries so they look about like this.*

   [Holding up a model.]

8. *Put the cherries in.*

9. *What does the pie need on the top?*

10. *Go ahead and make it.*

11. *Now put the top on.*

12. Let's cut away the extra dough now. *If we slice this pie the way we sliced mine, what colors will you see?*

13. *Go ahead and do it and let's see if you are right.*

Making a Playdough Pie

Materials

Picture of pie and cake, complete pie made of playdough (white dough and red "cherries"), knife, paper, crayons, red and white playdough, rolling pin, small and large pie pans

A. Focusing on Pie

1. One of the things most people like is food, particularly food that is sweet and that you can eat for dessert. *Name some of those.*

2. [Show a picture of a cake and a pie.]

   Here are two foods that are sweet. *Do you know what they are?*

3. They're both sweet. But they're also different. *Can you tell me what is different about a cake and a pie?*

4. Now, pies and cakes can be made out of a lot of different materials. *What are some of the things that you could put inside a pie?*

5. Here's a pie.

   [Show a playdough pie.]

   Of course, it's not a real pie because *it's made of* __________.

6. You can see only the top of the pie, but imagine that you cut a slice. *What would you see?* First, let me tell you what's inside. It has cherries inside. *Draw me what the side of a piece of pie would look like if you cut a slice.*

7. *Now cut a slice.*

8. Compare your drawing to the slice. *Were you right?*

9. *If the pie had been made of blueberries instead of cherries, what color would you have put in your drawing?*

B. Making a Playdough Pie

1. The pie we've been working with is one I've made. I thought now you could make one. Tell me the sequence you would have to follow to make a pie. *What would you have to do first?* I'll draw a symbol for that.

2. *What would you do second?* I'll draw a symbol for that.

   [Continue in this manner until all the steps have been noted by symbols on separate pieces of paper.]

3. *What symbol is that?*

   [Pointing to one of the steps of the sequence.]

   And that?

   [Continue pointing to the steps until all steps have been named.]

4. [Cut the symbols apart.]

   Here are all the steps you said you had to go through, but they are out of order. *Put them in the right order so they are the way you said they should be.*

5. Now you have them in the right order. *What are you going to do first?*

6. *Go ahead and do it.*

7. [Let the child roll out the first layer of dough.]

   It has to go in a pan. Here are two pans.

   [Offer one small pan and one large pan.]

   Do you want the pie to be the same size as the one I made or do you want it to be a different size?

8. *Which pan are you going to use?*

9. Now you have to make the cherries. *Approximately how many cherries do you think you'll need to fill the pie?* I'll write that down.

10. *Go ahead and do it.*

11. *Is the number you said the amount you had to make?*

12. *Now roll out the top.*

13. You've been using a rolling pin for rolling out the dough. If we didn't have a rolling pin, *can you think of any other thing we could use to roll out the dough?*

14. *Why did you say we could use that? What does it have that makes it good to use?*

15. We have a (whatever child said). *Do you want to roll out the dough with that or with the rolling pin?*

16. You're rolling out the dough for a purpose. We're making something out of it. *Do you know what it is?*

17. If we didn't roll out the dough and just put it on top of the pie, there would be a problem. *What would it be?*

18. This isn't a real pie, so we aren't going to treat it like a real pie. But if it were real, there would be one more step we would have to go through before we could eat the pie. *What would that be?*

When a child working at the complex level gives a high percentage of inappropriate responses, continue the topic by moving the lesson to the simple level.

Making a Bracelet Out of Candy

Materials

Pictures of various pieces of clothing and jewelry, completed candy bracelet, round multicolored hard candies with holes in the centers, string, scissors

A. Focusing on Clothes

1. One of the things people usually have on is clothing. You are wearing clothing now. *Name some of the pieces of clothing that you are wearing.*

2. I'm wearing some clothing. *Name some of the pieces that I'm wearing.*

3. Here, look at this picture.

   [Show a picture of various articles of clothing.]

   It has some of the clothing you named. It has pants. *Show me the pants.*

4. And it has shirts. *Show me a shirt.*

5. It also has some things you did not name. For example, it shows a skirt. *Point to it.*

6. And it has this.

   [Pointing to another item not yet identified.]

   What is this?

B. Focusing on Jewelry

1. There are things we wear like we wear clothing, but they're not clothing. We wear them mainly to make us look pretty or nice. They're called jewelry. *What did I say they are called?*

2. Jewelry can be things like rings. *Show me a ring I'm wearing.*

3. Or earrings. *Show me my earrings (or whatever appropriate items are available).*

4. Here's a picture that shows some jewelry.

   [Showing picture of pieces of jewelry.]

   There is a woman in the picture with a necklace. *Show me her necklace.*

C. Making a Bracelet

1. Usually, jewelry is worn on parts of your body. A ring is worn on your finger. *And earrings on your ___________.*

2. *And a necklace is worn on your ___________.*

3. I thought today we would make a piece of jewelry that people wear on their wrists. It's called a bracelet. *Say bracelet.*

4. Here is the kind of bracelet I thought we could make.

   [Show candy bracelet.]

   It's a funny kind of bracelet because it's made out of candy instead of the things jewelry is usually made out of. The candy pieces are on a string. *Go get the string.*

5. Here is some candy you can use. I want you to make your bracelet in the same sequence of colors as this one. The first one is this color.

   [Pointing to one of the pieces of candy on the string.]

   Get a piece of candy that's this color.

6. [Continue the sequence following the model. Finish the bracelet by helping the child tie a knot in the string.]

Making a Bracelet Out of Candy

Materials
Pictures of clothes, bracelets, round multicolored hard candy with holes in the centers, candy, string, scissors, completed candy bracelet

A. Focusing on Clothes

1. We're going to be talking today about something that's a little like clothes, but it's different. First, let's see if you know what clothing is. *Tell me what you think clothing is.*

2. *Name four different items of clothing.*

3. Look at this picture.

   [Showing picture of clothes.]

   Find some of the items you just named.

4. *And now find some items of clothing that you didn't name.*

B. Focusing on Jewelry

1. I said before that the thing we are going to be talking about is like clothing, but it is different in a certain way. It's like clothing in that you put it on, and so you wear it. It's called jewelry. *Can you name some items of jewelry?*

2. *Look carefully at me.* Don't say anything. I'm wearing some jewelry. *Close your eyes and tell me some of the jewelry pieces that I'm wearing.*

3. *Are you wearing any jewelry?*

4. *The jewelry I'm wearing on my ears is called ___________.*

5. *And the jewelry I'm wearing on my finger is called ___________.*

6. I don't have any jewelry on my wrist, but if I did, *do you know what it would be called?*

   [Provide the label if necessary.]

C. Making a Bracelet

1. A bracelet is what I thought we would make today. I don't have the material that bracelets are usually made of. *Look at the bracelets inside this bag and tell me the material that they are made of. (Metal or plastic).*

2. I thought the bracelet we make today could be made out of these.

   [Holding up candy.]

   Do you know what these are?

3. Before we use them, we have to have something to put them on to hold them together. OK, *get that please.*

   [The child gets string or other appropriate material.]

4. *Who would you like the bracelet to be for, you or me?*

5. If it's for you (me), *what size should we cut the string to make sure it will fit? How could we measure that we're cutting the right amount?*

6. *Wrap the string around your arm and see the amount that you need.*

7. *If you were making the bracelet for me (you), would you have to use more string or less string?*

8. *Why?*

9. *And if you were making the bracelet for you (me), would you have to use more candy or less candy?*

10. *Why?*

11. Before you put the candy on the string, I want you to look at the pattern that the candy is in on this bracelet I've made.

    [Show completed bracelet made with a pattern of repeated colors such as red, yellow, red, yellow.]

    How would you describe the pattern of the candy?

12. *Would you like to use the same sort of pattern, or would you like to double the pattern?* If you double the pattern, that means every time there is a piece of candy in one color on mine, you have to put two pieces of that color on yours. Which would you like to do? *Do the same as I have or a double of what I have?*

13. [Let the child follow through with the decision.]

    Now you've gotten the candy on the string, but they're almost sure to slip off. *What could you do to the string so that doesn't happen?*

14. OK, *go ahead and do it.*

Creating a Set of Written Directions

This lesson should be done only after the child has experience in following a recipe on a box.

Materials
Box of crayons, shoe box, shoes, 2 boxes of instant pudding mix (1 with damaged box), 2 measuring cups, water, bowl, spoon, paper, scissors, glue, mixer or beater (optional)

A. Recognizing That Boxes Can Have Messages on Them

1. *Go over and bring me some of the boxes you see on the table.*

2. These boxes can be used to hold things and the pictures on them tell the kinds of things they can hold. This box has pictures of crayons. It can hold some crayons. *Put some crayons in it.*

3. This one has some pictures of shoes. It could hold some shoes. Here, *put these shoes in it.*

4. So these boxes have pictures of the sorts of things you can put in them. There are other kinds of boxes that have even more things written on them than that. *Go over and bring me that box.*

   [Pointing to a pudding box.]

5. Look, it has more than pictures. *Point to what it has on it.*

   [Referring to the directions.]

   These are called directions. *Say, There are directions.*

6. Directions tell how to use the material inside. They show that you should pour two cups of water. *Show me the cups.*

7. *Now fill them with water.* See, now they are more like the pictures on the box.

8. And it shows that you should pour the water into a bowl with the pudding. *Show me the bowl.*

9. *Now pour the water into the bowl.* We don't have the pudding in this bowl right now, but we were able to do all the other things the directions told us to do.

B. Recognizing That a Box Can Be Damaged and the Directions Ruined

1. I have another box of pudding on the counter that also has directions. *Go get it.*

2. *What did I say this box would have on it?*

3. *Find them—find the directions.*

4. You can sort of see the directions, but there's something wrong.

   [Pointing to the ripped paper.]

   What's wrong?

C. Preparing the Directions

1. Let's fix the directions. First we need some paper. *Get the paper.*

2. *Let's cut it so it fits the box.*

3. *Now you can put some glue on it.*

4. Well, now the paper isn't ripped, but there are no directions you can see. Let's copy the directions from the box that is *not* ripped. First it shows two cups. *Draw in two cups.*

5. Then it shows a bowl. *Draw in a bowl.* Now I'll write in the words that belong.

6. [If time allows, help the child follow the directions to make the pudding.]

Creating a Set of Written Directions

Materials

Various boxes of food mixes and commercial items such as shoes and toys (one of which has been damaged), paper, tape, pencil

A. Recognizing That Boxes Can Have Messages on Them

1. When we've worked together, we've often used boxes for various things. *What are boxes for?*

2. That's right, they can hold things, but they can do it in different sorts of ways. That is, there are different kinds of boxes. There are those boxes that when the box is closed, you don't know what's inside. *Find me a box like that over there.*

3. There are also boxes with pictures on them. *Go find one like it over there.*

4. *What do you think this picture tells you? If a box has a picture of crayons on it, what is it likely to hold?*

5. *If a box has a picture of shoes on it, what is it likely to hold?*

   [Ask about other objects such as toys.]

6. Now this is a very hard question. *Does the box* HAVE *to have in it the things that are like the picture on the box?*

7. *Why not?*

8. So far, we have discussed two kinds of boxes. One kind that has no pictures and one kind that has pictures. Look at this.

   [Showing the box with written directions on it.]

   It has more than just pictures. *What does this box have on it?*

9. *And what is that writing telling you to do?*

B. Recognizing That a Box Can be Damaged and the Directions Ruined

1. *What is a box usually made of?*

2. Paper (cardboard or whatever word child has used) can be very useful, but it can also be a problem. Paper (cardboard) isn't very strong and things can happen to it. *What would happen if someone ripped the box?*

3. *And what would happen if the box got soaking wet?*

4. Those are things that can ruin a box. If that happened, *what do you think might happen to the directions on the box?*

5. See what happened to one of the boxes that I have. *Go over there and find one of the boxes that something has happened to that's similar to what we talked about.*

C. Repairing the Directionsg

1. I think it would be a good idea to try to fix the box so a person who uses it could read the directions. *What would be some materials we would need to repair the box?*

2. Paper would be good. Here's some paper, but it's much too large for this box. *What could we do so it would fit better?*

3. Also we don't want it loose. We want it attached to the box. *What could we do so it would be attached?*

4. We have to get the directions written on the paper. *Shall we make up our own directions or would you like to copy the directions from the box we saw that wasn't ripped?*

   [Follow the child's directions.]

5. [Allow the child to write the directions (or draw if the child cannot write) as completely as possible. Or child could both write and draw the directions.]

6. These instructions you've written (or drawn) are for making pudding. Instructions for making food are often called recipes. If you were given a recipe not for making pudding, but for making sandwiches, *what are some of the things you would have to include in that recipe?*

   [Any familiar food such as fruit salad or chicken noodle soup could be discussed.]

Creating a Sand Painting

Materials
Several children's paintings, paintbrush, paint, paper, cotton, completed sand painting, sand, glue

A. Focusing on Paintings

1. On the wall are some paintings that children have done. *Point to one of them.*

2. *What is it a painting of?*

3. [Repeat the same questions with two other paintings.]

4. Those paintings were made in a certain way. The person took a paintbrush. *Would you please go get a paintbrush.*

5. And the person took some paint like this,

   [Offering some paint]

   and put the brush into the paint and put the paint onto the paper. Here, *you try doing that.*

B. Focusing on a Sand Painting

1. Look over there and *bring me that piece of paper.* That also has some things on it like the painting. But it wasn't made with paint. Here, *feel this.* This is cotton. *Say, Cotton.*

2. *Now feel this.*

3. This is sand. *Say, Sand.*

4. Now, *feel this.*

   [Referring to a sand painting.]

   Do you think it's made of cotton or sand?

5. That's right. It's made of sand, and it's called a sand painting. Instead of just painting with paints, we can paint with sand. *Say, This is a sand painting.*

C. Making a Sand Painting

1. I thought you could make a sand painting of your own. If we just put the sand down though, it will fall off the paper.

   [Demonstrating.]

   Here, *try it.*

2. *What's happening?*

3. We have to do something so it will stick. *Do you know what this is?*

   [Hold up glue and provide the label if necessary.]

4. *And what does glue (sticky stuff or whatever word child used) do?*

5. That's right. Because it sticks, it will help the sand stick. The sand will only stick where the glue is, so we have to decide where to put the glue. *Put the glue on the paper so it makes a design you like.*

6. The paper now has glue on it, but *does it have any sand?*

7. Well, let's get some sand on it. *Pour sand on the paper.*

   [Help the child if necessary.]

   Let's wait a few minutes until the glue dries.

8. [Returning to painting]

   There's lots of extra sand here. It's both where the glue is and where the glue isn't. *Let's shake the paper and see what happens.*

9. *What's happening?*

10. [If time allows, the child can add additional designs.]

Creating a Sand Painting

Materials

Two sand paintings (one abstract and one realistic), sand, paper, pencil, glue, funnel

A. Focusing on Paintings

1. There are lots of different things on the walls in this room. *Look around the walls. Don't say anything. Now close your eyes and name some of the things that you've seen.*

2. Some of the things you've named are put on walls because they're very useful. You mentioned a mirror. *What use is a mirror?*

   [Ask similar questions about clocks, hooks, etc.]

3. There are also things that people like to hang up on walls not because they're particularly useful, but because they make the walls look pretty or attractive. *Can you find something on the walls that was put up to make the room look pretty or attractive?*

4. A lot of rooms have paintings. This room has paintings. You've done some painting too. *Can you tell me how a painting is made?*

B. Focusing on a Sand Painting

1. The paintings you described were made from paints. But there are also some unusual forms of paintings. One is called "sand painting." *What do you think sand painting is made from?*

2. If I were to show you a sand painting and you were to touch it, *how do you think it would feel?*

3. *Why do you think it would feel that way?*

4. I happen to have a sand painting. *Go ahead and touch it and see if you were right.*

5. *Were you?*

6. Sand is usually this sort of color.

   [Pointing to an appropriate spot on the painting.]

   But this sand painting has lots of different colors. *How do you think the sand was made into these different colors?*

7. [The lesson may be expanded by coloring the sand before using it in a painting.]

C. Painting a Sand Painting

1. There are actually lots of different ways you can make a sand painting. I thought we'd try one today. One of the easiest is to put something on paper that would hold the sand. *What do you think we could put on paper that the sand would stick to?*

2. *If we didn't put down glue to help the sand stick, what would happen to the sand when we picked up the paper?*

3. *Let's try it and see if you are right.*

4. We are going to be using the glue before we use the sand. *Why?*

5. It would be good to have a plan of the design you want the glue to have so you know what your sand painting will look like. Think of some designs that you might make. Look at these two. This one is called an abstract design. That means it doesn't have any particular or clear shape. This one is not an abstract design. It's a realistic picture. *What is it a picture of?*

6. *What would you like to do, an abstract design or a realistic picture?*

   [Follow the child's choice.]

7. *Draw on this paper the kind of design you plan to use.*

8. Here is the paper you are going to use for the sand painting. *Why don't you put the design you have drawn on the paper, except do it with the glue.*

9. Now we have to get the sand on the painting. It's pretty hard to work with sand. Let me show you something we can use to help control the flow of sand as you put it on. Look at this.

   [Holding up the funnel.]

   Do you know what this is called?

   [Provide the label if necessary.]

10. *Let's slowly pour the sand through the funnel and then gradually spread it across the paper.*

11. Look, there is sand now all over the paper. You can barely see the design you made. Is it going to stay that way or is there something we can do to make the sand painting come out the way you want it. In other words, we want the sand to be just on the places where you put the glue. *What is it you could do?*

12. OK, *go ahead and do it.*

13. [The lesson may be expanded by painting the sand different colors after it has dried.]

The most demanding part of the lesson should occur during the first half of the therapy session. If the child tires during the last half of the session, the demands may be simplified and reduced.

Making a Room Plan

Materials
Box (the size of a dollhouse), pictures of rooms with furniture, toy furniture, paper, crayons

A. Focusing on the Idea That a House Has Rooms with Furniture

1. Here is a box we can use for a dollhouse. See, it already has a door. *Show me the door.*

2. And it has some windows. *Show me some windows.*

3. Right now, the room in the house is empty. It has no furniture in it. Look at this room.

   [Referring to the real room.]

   Is it empty or does it have furniture?

4. *Name some of the furniture it has.*

5. Let's look back at the dollhouse. I'd like to put some furniture in it. Right now, it's empty. *Say, The dollhouse is empty of furniture.*

B. Arranging the Furniture in a Room

1. We can make this room into any kind of room we like. It could be a bedroom. Look at this picture.

   [Holding up a picture of a bedroom.]

   If it were a bedroom, it would have this type of furniture. *What are these pieces of furniture called?*

   [Pointing to the bed, chest of drawers, chair, etc.]

2. [Repeat with pictures of a living room and kitchen.]

3. *Which room would you like this room to be: a bedroom, living room, or kitchen?*

4. Some living room (or bedroom or kitchen, depending on the child's choice) furniture is in that box. *Point to the box that I mean.*

5. *Now go get it.*

6. *Which piece do you want to take out?*

7. *Take it out.*

8. *Show me where you want to place it.*

9. *Put it there.*

10. [Repeat steps 6-9 for three or four pieces of furniture.]

C. Making a Plan of the Room

1. I think it would be interesting to make a drawing of the room you arranged. It's a nice room.

   [Draw a rectangle to represent the room and position it directly over box.]

   Look, what's in this corner?

2. *Draw a shape over here that's like the shape of the chair (table, bed, etc.).*

3. [Repeat the placing of the paper over the box and the drawing of the piece of furniture until each item in room is shown.]

4. [If the child is functioning well, move the diagram so it no longer corresponds with the room. Ask the child to identify what piece of furniture each drawing represents. You can also remove the pieces of furniture and ask the child to position them again based on the room plan.]

Making a Room Plan

Materials
Box for a dollhouse, toy furniture, diagram outlines as described below in C-1, crayons

A. Focusing on a Room

1. I have something here we may have seen before. It started out as a box, but it's been made into something more than just a box. *Do you know what that is?*

2. *What is there about it that made you say it was a house (or room)?*

3. It's designed to be a room, but most rooms are not empty like this one. *What are the things that rooms are usually filled with?*

4. You mentioned a chair and table and things like that. We have chairs and tables in this room. *Can we put them in the box?*

5. *Why not?*

6. *What kind of furniture would we need to go in this box?*

7. We have some furniture like that over there.

   [Referring to the doll furniture.]

   Go get it.

B. Creating the Identity of a Room

1. *Name some rooms in a house.*

2. *What kind of room do you want this one to be?*

3. If it's going to be a bedroom (or kitchen or whatever word the child used), *what would be the sort of furniture you would want to put in it?*

4. *Go pick out that kind of furniture.*

C. Making a Plan of the Room

1. You've got the furniture you want. But before you put it in, I'd like you to draw a diagram indicating how you are going to place the furniture in the room.

   [Offer the child two different diagrams: one that is an irregular shape and one that is the shape of the box.]

Which of these two drawings would be good to use if you're going to duplicate the box?

2. *Why did you pick that drawing?*

3. OK, one of the things you brought over is a table. *Where do you want it to go? Draw it on the diagram.*

[Repeat this with each piece of furniture the child has chosen.]

4. Basically, what you have just done is called a "floor plan" of the room. *Do you have an idea of why it is called a "floor plan?"*

D. Arranging the Furniture in the Room

1. Now we're going to use the floor plan for putting the furniture in the room. *Put in one of the pieces from your diagram.*

2. *What piece is next to that piece on the diagram?*

3. *Go ahead and put that in.*

4. *What piece does the diagram show is across the room from that piece?*

5. According to the floor plan, *how many pieces still have to be put in?*

6. *Can you find those pieces?*

7. *Which one do you want to put in next?*

8. *Go ahead and do it.*

9. *Now put in the remaining ones.*

10. *Close your eyes.* I'm going to play a kind of trick on you. I'm going to move a couple of pieces around. *Now open your eyes. Look at the floor plan and look at the pieces in the room. Which pieces did I move around?*

11. *Change them back so they'll fit your original plan.*

Making a Doll's Sofa with a Construction Set

Materials
Chair for child to sit on, picture of furniture that includes a sofa, doll's sofa made from construction set, construction set, small dolls

A. Focusing on a Sofa

1. There are some things in this room that we use all the time, but we don't talk about them much. We don't talk much about the things you're sitting on. *What are you sitting on?*

2. *Is that the only chair in the room, or are there other chairs in the room?*

3. *How many people can sit on each chair at one time?*

4. There are other kinds of things people sit on where more than one person can sit at the same time. *Look at this picture and find something several people can sit on at the same time.*

   [Holding up picture of furniture.]

5. *Do you know what that's called?*

   [Provide label if necessary.]

B. Focusing on a Toy Sofa

1. So far, we've looked only at sofas for real people. There could also be sofas for dolls. I made a sofa like that. It's on the shelf behind you. *Turn around.*

2. *Can you see it? Point to it.*

3. *Go get it.*

4. This sofa is made out of a special material. It's not like other sofas. *What is it made out of?*

5. *Who did I say it was for?*

6. If it's for dolls, some dolls could sit on it. *Go find some dolls to sit on it.*

7. [If time allows and the child is able, ask the child to draw a diagram of the original sofa. Use the diagram rather than the actual sofa as a guide for constructing it.]

C. Making the Sofa

1. I thought it would be interesting to make a sofa just like this one. If you're going to do that, *what are you going to need?*

2. *Go get them.*

3. I'd like the sofa to be the same colors as the one I made. Let's do the back of the sofa first. *Show me the back.*

4. *Get a color like the one you just touched.*

5. [Repeat steps 3 and 4 until the sofa is complete. Use color names if the child has no difficulty with them. If difficulty exists, avoid them by following the example above.]

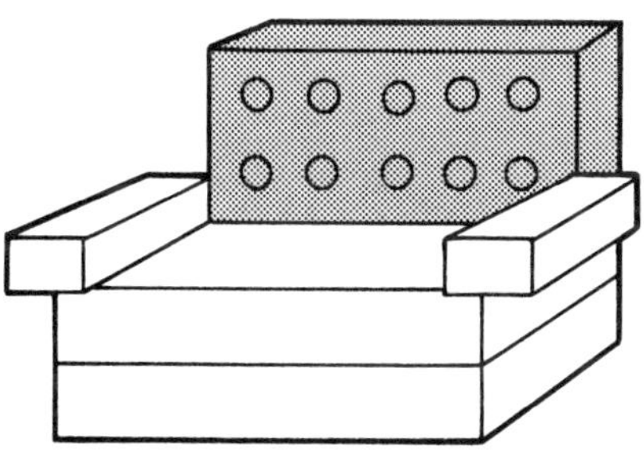

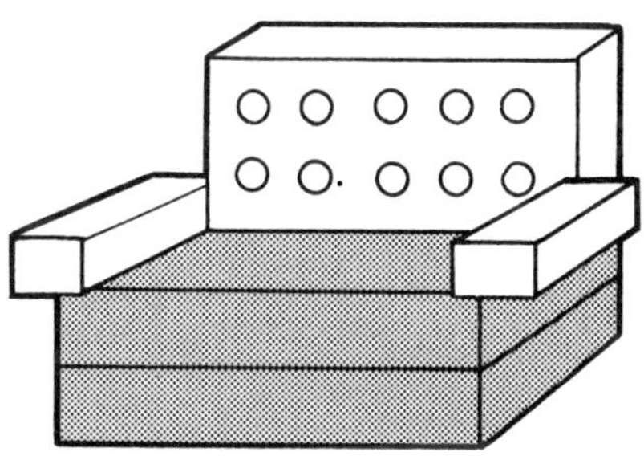

Making a Doll's Sofa with a Construction Set

Materials
Pictures of chairs and sofas, doll's sofa made from construction set, pieces of cloth, construction set, completed designs as described below, crayons

A. Focusing on a Sofa

1. Today I brought in a picture of some furniture.

   [Showing pictures of chairs only.]

   Look at the picture carefully because I'm going to ask you some questions about it.

   [Put the picture away.]

   There were pieces of furniture in the picture you could sit on. *Tell me what they are.*

2. Now look at this picture.

   [Show picture of sofas and put it away.]

   This picture I just showed also had things to sit on, but they weren't chairs. *What were they?*

3. They're similar to chairs in that you can sit on them. But they're also different. *How are they different?*

B. Focusing on a Toy Sofa

1. These sofas that you were talking about were for real people. *If you were making a sofa for a doll, how would it be different?*

2. Yes, a toy sofa is smaller. I made a toy sofa for a doll. It's on that table. *Go get it.*

3. It's not only smaller, it's made out of different material. *What material are real sofas often made out of?*

   [Show pieces of cloth if child needs assistance.]

4. *How is the material of this toy sofa different from the material of a real sofa?*

5. *Would that make it more comfortable (nicer) to sit on or less comfortable (harder) to sit on?*

C. Making the Sofa

1. I think it would be interesting if you made a sofa like this one, but that you did it by reversing the colors. "Reverse" means that you do it the opposite of the colors I've used. Two colors are in this sofa: red and white. If you reverse, that means where I have put red, you can put white. Where there is white, you can put red. *What does "reverse" mean?*

2. Before you do it, try reversing something else.

   [Show a design that has a sequence of alternating thick blue and thin red lines.]

   Here is a design like it.

   [Show another design.]

   But the colors have not been put on it. *Fill in the pattern, but put the colors in reverse order from this one.*

3. *Now you can go ahead and make the sofa with the construction set. But remember, you're going to reverse the colors for the sofa.*

4. You did very well in reversing the colors. I'm going to ask you something hard. *Can you tell me in words what "reversing" means?*

Additional Lesson Suggestions

1. Constructing the Missing Pieces of a Puzzle
2. Constructing Holiday Ornaments
3. Reproducing the Layout of a Board Game (To reconstruct the uncompleted game play for the next session)
4. Constructing a Roadway for Toy Cars
5. Creating a Duplicate of a Poster Collage

Playing a Bowling Game

Materials
Soft light ball, simple targets such as paper circles and strips, 1 picture of people bowling, 2 pictures of activities without a ball, toy bowling pins, large card with circles to indicate bowling pin positions, paper, pencil

A. Focusing on Hitting Targets

1. I've seen you playing with a ball and I know you like doing it, so I brought in a ball today for you to use. It's in the box next to the table. *Please go get it.*

2. One thing to do with a ball is to see if you can reach a target. See that circle on the wall? That can be the target. *Throw the ball and see if it hits the target. See if it hits the circle.*

3. *Did it hit the target?*

4. Targets don't have to be only on walls. They can be in lots of places. For example, they can be on the floor. *Put this strip of paper on the floor over there and it will be our target.*

5. Let's see if you can remember what I said. *What did I say the strip of paper was going to be?*

6. It's hard to throw at a target on the floor. It's generally easier if we roll the ball. This time, *let's try rolling it.*

7. *Did it reach the target this time?*

8. You don't have to just roll the ball. You can also bounce it. *Try bouncing it so it hits the target.*

9. *Did it hit the target that time?*

B. Focusing on Bowling

1. So far, we've just been trying different things with a ball, but we can use it to play an actual game. A game is what we play when we have to follow rules. One game is bowling.

   [Show pictures of three different activities: one bowling picture and two others that do not include a ball.]

   One of these shows people bowling. *Which one is it?*

2. That's the game I think we could play. Before, when we were playing around, we had a target. *Show me the target we had on the wall.*

3. We also had a target on the floor. *Show me that one.*

4. We also have a target in bowling, but it's more complicated. Here, see these pins.

   [Pointing to one.]

   They're the target. Here's one pin. *Show me another.*

5. *And another.*

6. *And what did I say these things were called?*

7. Now, we'll need pins for our game—*they're in this box, take them out.*

8. See that card over there?

   [Looking toward a card on the floor with circles indicating bowling pin positions.]

   Point to it.

9. *Take these pins and put one on each circle.*

10. Good. Those pins are the target. *Say that.*

C. Playing the Game

1. We need a ball to play the game. There's one in the box. *Take it out.*

2. Remember I said that this was a game with rules. Let me tell you what the rules are.

   [The rules may be altered and simplified according to child's level.]

   First, each person has a chance to roll the ball. So if you and I are playing, *who's going to be rolling the ball?*

3. The second rule is that you try to roll the ball to reach the target. *So what's the second rule?*

4. The third rule is that you count the number of pins that you knocked down. If I knocked down these pins,

   [Dropping two pins]

   how many pins did I knock down?

   [Help the child to count if necessary.]

5. OK, let's try it. You go first. *Stand here beside this line and roll the ball to the target.*

6. *How many pins did you knock down?*

D. Keeping Score

1. We're going to roll the ball a lot of times, and it's going to be hard to remember how many pins are knocked down. So let's keep score on this piece of paper.

   [Hang a large piece of paper on the wall.]

   I'll put a line down the paper and this side will be yours and this side will be mine. Since you're littler than I am, I'll make a little girl (boy) here to stand for your side.

   [Drawing a child stick figure.]

   What size figure should I make to stand for me?

   [Draw an adult stick figure.]

2. Now, on your turn, you knocked down three (or whatever number) pins, *so make three marks on your side.*

   [For each turn, draw a line under the marks the child makes to help the child keep track of the turns.]

3. Now it's my turn. *Where do I have to stand?*

4. *What do I have to do if I'm going to do all the things you did?*

5. OK, I'll roll the ball. *How many pins did I knock down?*

6. *So how many marks should I make on my side of the paper?*

7. [Game continues for several more turns.]

Concluding Comments to Child

You played a great game. Let's add up how many points you got and how many points I got. Wow, you have more points! You've won the game!

Playing a Bowling Game

Materials

Pictures of sports and games (baseball, tennis, bowling, basketball, darts, horseshoes), toy bowling pins, diagram showing positions of bowling pins, soft light ball, paper, pencil

A. Focusing on Hitting Targets

1. A lot of games need a large area for moving the thing you're playing with. Look at this picture of a baseball field. The ball can be hit all over the field and you can still make runs. *Show me some of the places where the ball might go to.*

2. And look at this picture of people playing tennis. You can hit the ball in a lot of places and still have it count. *Show me some of the places inside the lines where the ball could go.*

3. But some games are different from these. In the games I'm talking about, if you are going to score points, you have to hit a specific spot. The specific spot is called a target. *What did I just say a target was?*

4. Now, here's a game that has a target.

   [Holding up picture of a basketball game.]

   Do you know what this game is called?

5. In basketball, the target is the basket that is high up. *Find it.*

6. And here's one other game with a target.

   [Holding up a picture of darts or horseshoes.]

   Point to the place where the target is.

   [Provide information if necessary.]

B. Focusing on Bowling

1. Today I thought we'd play a game that has a target.

   [Holding up a picture of people bowling.]

   Do you know what the target is in bowling?

   [Provide information if necessary.]

2. Let's actually set up a game and see how we have to arrange things. I have a bowling game in a box over there. *You get it*

3. The target will be the pins. But it's not just one single pin. *Count how many pins form the target in bowling.*

4. Now set the pins up at the end of the room.

   [Pointing.]

   And set them up so they look like this diagram.

   [Offer the child the diagram.]

5. We need to set up a place where we have to stand when we throw the ball. That takes some thought. It wouldn't be much of a game to set it up here.

   [Indicating a point about two feet from the pins.]

   Why wouldn't it be good over here?

6. So we need to be further away. *How about counting out 15 paces (or whatever number is appropriate) and let me know what point that is.*

7. We ought to mark the point or we might forget it. *What can we use to mark the point so we won't have to keep marking it over and over again?*

   [Use any reasonable suggestions the child makes.]

8. *OK, please do it.*

9. Now, we need one more thing. We need the thing to use to hit the target. What do you think that is. *Go get it.*

C. Playing the Game

1. Bowling is a game not only with a target but with rules. *Do you know what the word* rule *means?*

   [Provide the answer if necessary.]

2. Now, the rules in bowling are . . .

   [Provide rules at a level the child can handle.]

   OK, let's see if you've learned what the rules are. *Tell me what the major rules are.*

3. Since one of the rules is that the players take turns, *who is going first?*

4. *What should I (you) do?* (Use *I* or *you* depending on the child's response.)

5. OK, I (you) rolled the ball. *How many pins were knocked down?*

D. Keeping Score

1. Oh, wait! I forgot one thing. We're going to be rolling the ball a lot and it's going to be hard to remember the number of pins that were knocked down each time. *Can you think of where we could write down the score so that we'll keep track of how we're doing?*

2. Here's a paper we could use as a score sheet (or whatever term child has used), but we have to somehow mark the two people who are playing. How about using our initials. An initial is the first letter of your name. *What is your initial?*

3. *Go ahead and mark it down.*

4. And my initial is this.

   [Showing it on paper.]

   What letter is that?

5. Now, on my (your) turn, four pins (or whatever number) were knocked down. *So where are you going to enter the number four?*

6. *Whose turn is it now?*

7. [Game continues for a reasonable number of turns. If time allows, review the major points and rules of the game.]

Concluding Comments to the Child

That was a good game. Let's add up the points for each of us. *Who got more points? So, who won the game?*

Playing a Game That Has a Path to Follow

Materials
Board game with path to follow and cards that can be grouped into 2 or 3 categories, box for game, boxes not containing games (tissue box and shoe box), game pieces, index cards, crayons

A. Attending to the Game

1. There are three boxes on the table. Two of them are *not* games. *What are they?*

2. And there's one box left. *Is that a game?*

3. *Do you know the name of that game?*

   [Provide the label if necessary.]

4. If we are going to play the game, we have to do something to the box so we can get to the parts of the game. *What do we have to do to the box?*

5. *Go ahead and do it.*

B. Putting Out the Game Parts

1. There's a large board in the box. *Point to it.*

2. OK, *please take it out.*

3. There are some pictures and colors on this board,

   [The board is still closed]

   but you can't see them the way the board is now. *What do you have to do to the board to see what's on it?*

4. Now, there's a long path on the board like this.

   [Moving your finger through the air in patterns resembling the game path.]

   Can you find that path?

5. That's the path the pieces have to move along. Let's find some of the pieces so we can have them to put on the path.

6. *Which one would you like to be?*

7. *What color (one) do you think I should be?*

8. Now, there's one part left and it's got a lot of pieces like this.

   [Holding up one of the game cards.]

   Take these out.

9. Now, we're going to be playing with these cards but we don't have time to use all of them today. Let's divide them up and then we'll keep only some of them. Let's divide them into two piles: those that are just colors and those that have pictures.

   [Divide cards any way that seems logical by colors, by pictures, etc.]

   To help you remember which card goes in which pile, let's make two signs—one for each pile.

   [Help the child create signs on index cards that are appropriate for the two piles such as color marks for the color cards and a symbol for picture cards, or a red mark for the red cards and a green mark for the green cards, etc.]

10. *OK, go ahead and divide the cards.*

C. Playing the Game

1. Remember, I said we had very little time and we couldn't use all the cards. So let's put one pile of cards away. *Where would you like to put them?*

2. *Go ahead and do that.*

3. *What cards are left?*

4. [Play the game in the usual way but frequently ask the child at appropriate times, "OK, where will you move now?" and "How many turns have we had? Count the cards," etc.]

Playing a Game That Has a Path to Follow

This lesson may require several sessions to complete. To speed the process, the instructor may continue reproducing the gameboard and cards between sessions, leaving the final steps for the child to complete.

Materials

Board game, game cards, game pieces, variety of pictures

A. Attending to the Game

1. I have a game here that I think we've played before. It's called ________ . *Why do you think it's called ________ ?* (The name of the game should have some relevance to the way the game is constructed or played.)

2. You really seem to know the game well. I'll bet you could tell me all the rules for playing it.

   [The game board is open and close to the child.]

   Look at this.

   [Pointing to the path on the board.]

   What is this part of the game for?

3. *Now, what role do these cards play in the game?*

   [Holding out the cards.]

4. *And here are some game pieces. What do you do with them?*

5. *How many people can play the game the way it's set up now?*

6. *Why can't more than that number play?*

B. Adapting the Game

1. You really seem to know the game well. In fact, so well that it's probably a little boring for you to play. Let's play it, but let's make it a bit more complicated. *Do you know what I mean by "complicated"?*

   [Provide the information if necessary.]

2. One of the ways to complicate things is by making a person think about more things or have a person do more things than she is used to. For example, you said you have to take the card and move to the place the card tells you. What if we complicate it by making

you do something before you can move. Let's say when you pick up a red card, you have to name something that is red before you can go to the red space. Let's try that. *What thing can you name that's red?*

[Other possible tasks are to name words beginning with a specific letter, or name objects in certain categories, or do something physical such as clap hands and walk around the chair, or to make an animal noise, etc., depending on the type of cards in the game and the picture(s) selected for Step 5. One rule could be that an object of a particular color can only be named once during the game. Keeping note of the objects will help maintain that rule.]

3. *If we continue that, what will happen if you pick up a blue card?*

4. *OK, pick up a card. What will you have to do now?*

5. *OK, name something that's green.*

6. Now, this can get really hard because each time you name something, it has to be different than the thing you named before. That might be hard to remember. Let's allow a certain amount of help. If you can't name something the color of the card you pick up, you can look at this picture

   [Referring to one with many objects]

   and find something that color. For example, if you pick up a purple card, but you can't name anything purple, you can look at this picture and find something in the picture that's purple. *What did you find that's purple?*

7. It would be too easy if you could look up everything in the picture. Let's limit the number of times you can use the picture during the game. Each player can look at the picture three times and no more than that. So if after the third time you have a card and you can't name something, then you lose your turn. Let's try that. Let's imagine that you picked up a yellow card, you can't think of anything yellow to name, and you have used up your three turns for the picture. *So what's going to happen?*

8. You are doing great. This is a really hard game now. I want to make sure you know the rules, so let's go through the new rules. *First, what do you have to do before you move to pick up a card?*

9. *If you can't think of something in that color, what can you do?*

10. *How often can you do it?*

11. *If you've used up all those turns and you come up with a card but can't think of a thing with that color, what happens?*

12. Now, there's one more thing before we start. The only time you don't have to name anything before you move is when you get a __________ card.

    [Name an appropriate card category.]

    So the __________ cards are exempt from the rule. *What do you think the word "exempt" means? What does it mean when I say that the __________ cards are exempt from the rule?*

    [Provide information if necessary.]

13. [Play the game with these new rules.]

Any play activity that lends itself to sequenced development can form the basis of a lesson. The lesson plans in this book can be used as models to frame the new lesson.

Creating a Board Game

This activity is only for children who have some experience with at least simplified versions of board games.

Materials
Board game with cards, game pieces, cardboard, tape, pencil or pen, small colored squares of paper

A. Focusing on a Board Game

1. On the table is something that we played with some time ago. *Please go get it.*

2. *Do you remember what it's called?*

3. *Open up the box and take out the gameboard.*

4. *Show me some of the places on the board that you can move to.*

5. *Now show me the cards that tell you where to move.*

6. *Show me the pieces that you move around the board.*

B. Constructing the Gameboard

1. I thought it would be nice to make a game like this. First, for the board, we need some cardboard. *Would you please go over and get it.*

2. If we use just this one piece, it's not enough. *So what do we need?*

3. These two pieces are fine, but the pieces don't stay together like the gameboard does. We could use some tape to hold them together. *Go get the tape. Let's put the tape over here.*

4. Now, there's a long winding path on the board. I'll draw it on here.

   [Referring to the cardboard.]

   But the path I've drawn has no colors. Do you see the colored squares over there? We could use those. *Would you go get them.*

5. The first one here on the board is yellow, so *what color are you going to get?*

6. You have to put it in the very first space. *Where are you going to put it?*

7. [Guide the child through the task of reproducing the rest of the gameboard.]

C. Making the Cards

1. We have the gameboard, but we haven't made the cards that tell us where to move on the board. This time, instead of using colored squares, *how about drawing in the designs?*

2. [Guide the child through the task of reproducing the cards.]

D. Playing the Game

1. *Let's borrow the playing pieces from the game and let's play with the game you've made.*

Have nonrelevant materials available to help the child recognize the distinction between relevant and nonrelevant materials and ideas.

Creating a Board Game

Materials

Board game with cards, cardboard, tape, paints, crayons, colored paper, blank cards

A. Focusing on the Board Game

1. Some time ago, we played this game. *Can you remember how it's played?* I'll write down what you say and then we'll check it out.

   [The child explains the rules.]

2. Let's open it. Now let's see. You said __________ (a step or rule of the game that the child recalled). *Show me what you mean.*

   [Repeat with all the rules the child explained.)

3. *Do you know any other board games like this? What are they called?*

4. [Name one of the games the child mentioned.]

   You said __________ was a game like this one. *In what way is it also different?*

B. Constructing the Gameboard

1. Let's get back to our game. *Where do you think I got the game?*

2. That's right, I bought it, but you can make a game just like it. You don't have to buy it. *If you're going to make it, what are some of the things you'll need?*

3. *What would you use __________ for?* (Use whatever word the child used.)

4. *What would you use __________ for?*

5. One of the things you mentioned was the board. (Adapt verbalization to the child's words.) *Would you please go get that material.*

6. Each of the cardboard pieces you brought is smaller than the board on this game. *What could we do to make our board bigger?*

7. Now, *what is the most important thing on this gameboard?* It's the thing that winds all over the board.

8. *Go ahead and draw it on your board.*

9. Now we have to put some colors on the path that you have drawn. *What materials could we use for the colors?*

10. I'd like you to follow the same sequence of colors that are on the board. *What do I mean by* "sequence?"

11. *Go ahead and do it.*

C. Making the Cards

1. You have a board and that's part of the game. *What important parts are still missing?*

2. *What do you need the cards for?*

3. Some of the game cards have single squares (or other relevant item or color) on them and some of the cards have double squares (or other relevant item or color) on them. *What's the difference in terms of what happens in the game between a card with single squares and a card with double squares?*

4. I think it would be good to do it in order. *Which would you like to do first? A set of the double squares or a set of the single squares?*

[Help the child create the cards.]

D. Playing the Game

1. Let's borrow the playing pieces from the game I bought and let's play with the game you've made.

Creating a Game

Materials

Games child has played, different colored paper shapes about the size of the child's foot, diagrams to show placement of a pathway of shapes

A. Focusing on the Game

1. We've played a lot of games at the table. We've played this game. *What is it?*

   [Indicating a game the child already knows.]

2. When we played this game, we were sitting on chairs and the game was on the table.

3. [Repeat steps 1 and 2 with another game that was played at a table.]

4. Now this time, we're going to play a game where we have to *step* on things. If we're going to step on things, we're not going to play on the table. Instead we'll play on the place where we usually put our feet. We'll be playing on the ___________ .

5. *Show me the floor.*

B. Creating the Game

1. The game we are going to play is one where we put a pattern on the floor and you have to step on only certain parts of the pattern.

   [Give the child a set of shapes.]

   Put these out so each one goes on the white marks that are on the floor.

   [Any appropriate cue on the floor is acceptable.]

2. Now, if we were playing the game, I might ask you to step on only the circles that are red. Like this one.

   [Holding up a red circle.]

   Go ahead and do that.

3. You did very well, so well that we can make the game more complicated. *This time I want you to lay out a pattern that's just like this diagram.*

   [Show the diagram.]

4. *Shall we make a rule that you step only on the circles or only on the things that are not circles?*

   [Accept the child's choice.]

5. OK, *you go first. Step only on the* __________ *(child's choice) because that's the rule that you made.*

6. OK, now it's my turn. Which rule should I follow? *Should I step only on the circles or on the ones that are not circles?*

7. [Repeat steps 3-6 with a different set of shapes so that another rule has to be established.]

C. Extending the Game

1. Let's set out one more pattern. *Here's the diagram to follow.*

   [Be sure that the similar shapes are placed far enough apart that the child has to step on the floor to go from one to the other.]

2. OK, I think the rule we should follow is that you step on anything that has a round shape. *Show me the ones you're going to step on.*

3. I noticed that sometimes you didn't step just on the pieces, you also stepped on the floor. This time, I don't want you to step on the floor at all. *So, which are the only things you'll be stepping on?*

4. *Will you be stepping on this?*

   [Pointing to the floor.]

5. *Do you remember which ones I said you'd be stepping on?*

6. *Go ahead and do that.*

7. Hey, there's a problem!

   [As child is stepping on the floor.]

   Where are you stepping?

8. You weren't supposed to step on the floor. Your next step was suppose to be here.

   [Pointing at a round shape.]

   But can you reach this without stepping on the floor?

9. So we have to do something. We can't have the pattern this way and still follow the rule. We have to move the pieces of the pattern so they're closer together. Like this.

   [Demonstrating.]

   Go ahead. You do that to all the pieces, but make sure you keep the pieces in the same pattern as the diagram.

10. [Continue the game for two or three more turns.]

Comments in conversation are vital. Be sure to comment as frequently as you question.

Creating a Game

Materials

Two to four board games, colored paper for cards, paper cut in shapes, crayons, pencils, paper, small colored stickers (for markers)

A. Focusing on Commercial Games

1. I have a whole bunch of games here. They're all different. Like this one and this one.

   [Pointing to two or three games.]

   All these games are different, but they're also alike in one way. They're alike in that they are games you can buy. Someone makes them—usually they make them in a factory. And then you buy them. *And when you buy them, where do you buy them?*

2. Today we're going to do something different. We are going to work with games, but they're not going to be games that you buy. We are not going to get a box that has a game that's already made. Instead, we are going to make it. We are going to make the game up all by ourselves. *What's going to be the difference between these games here and the games we are going to be working with today?*

B. Creating a Game

1. One reason we're making up a game is that it's a game I want to make for very little children to play. Most of these games I just showed you are too complicated for little children, and you can't find many games for young children. So I thought we could make one. But there's a problem. Little children don't always like to sit around a table and play games. They like to move around a lot. So I think we have to set up the game on the floor. *What things do we have to move around in this room so we all have floor space available to us?*

2. Let's set up a task where we ask the children to move across the floor in a certain way. But we have to give them some kind of markers as to where they should move. I thought we could either use markers that are different colors or markers that are different shapes. *Which do you think would be better?*

   [Follow the child's answer.]

3. *Place these cards with the markers on the floor in a way that a little child can walk from one to the other.*

4. Now we have to make up some kind of card that tells the children where to walk. It wouldn't be very much fun if they just walked from one to another. Let's set it up so they have to think. Let's decide which ones you want them to walk on. OK, *which ones do you think they should walk on?*

5. *And which ones do you think they should* not *walk on?*

6. OK, *so let's draw a diagram to show how you've laid out the cards on the floor.*

   [Give the child paper and pencil to draw the diagram.]

7. Now we have to indicate on this diagram which cards the children should walk on. You can do it in one of two ways: You can either put a line across the ones you *don't* want them to walk on,

   [Demonstrate on a piece of paper]

   or you can put these stickers next to the ones you *do* want them to walk on. *Which way would you like to do it?*

8. OK, *go ahead and do it.*

9. So far we have only one diagram. It's not much fun to have a game with only one pattern. Let's make up two more patterns. Let's rearrange the cards that you laid out. Now let's draw a diagram of it. *Again, mark on the diagram where the children should and should not walk. Do you remember how we did it last time?*

10. *Do it that way this time.*

11. [Repeat this procedure for a third diagram.]

C. Playing the Game

1. I think you've made a great game, but let's try it out to make sure there are no problems with it. *Get the diagrams and pick one out. Now arrange the cards on the floor to follow the diagram.*

2. *Now let's see if you can follow the instructions on the card.*

3. *Were there any problems?*

4. [If time allows, the procedure may be repeated.]

5. This is an interesting game, but it's missing one thing. All the other games we started out with today have names. *Can you remember some of them? What will we call this game?*

   [If the child cannot think of a name, provide multiple choice titles ("Should we call it the Stepping Game or the Writing Game?")]

This lesson may be expanded by boxing the game and decorating the box.

Restating information in a slightly varying form gives the child more opportunity to understand the language demand and more time to process language.

Creating a Go Fish Game

Materials
A Go Fish game, card pairs in a single category (animals, toys, food), small picture pairs in envelopes by categories, small blank cards, glue

A. Focusing on Go Fish

1. Here's a game you may have played. It's called Go Fish. *What is it's name?*

2. In this game, each person has to get five cards. *You hand them out.*

   [If the child cannot count, have five marks on a paper in front of each player as a guide.]

3. Now, I'll ask you if you have a certain kind of card. For example, Do you have a bear? If you have it, you have to give it to me. *Do you have it?*

4. No, OK, then you say, *'I don't have it. Go Fish.'*

5. *So what do you have to say?*

6. Now it's your turn. *What are you going to ask me?*

7. I don't (do) have the card, *so what should I say (and do)?*

8. [Continue with the game for three or four turns.]

B. Creating a Go Fish Game

1. The cards we've been playing with are all pictures of animals (or other category). There's a bear. *Show me a bear.*

2. There's a tiger. *Show me a tiger.*

3. There's an elephant. *Show me an elephant.*

4. *And the elephant, the bear, and the tiger are all* ___________

5. But Go Fish could be about lots of different sorts of things. It doesn't have to be just about animals. It could be about toys. *Name some toys.*

6. Right, those are toys. And it could also be about foods. *Name some foods.*

7. Right, those are foods. And it could also be about things like furniture. *Name some furniture.*

8. Let's make up our own Go Fish game about one of the groups I mentioned. *Do you want it to be about toys or foods or furniture?*

   [Follow the child's choice.]

9. I have some pictures of toys in this envelope. *Open it.*

10. You said you wanted toys. *Name some of the toys you see.*

11. If it's going to be a Go Fish game, these little pieces of paper by themselves are too hard to hold. Let's put them on cards like the other Go Fish game.

12. *Do you see any cards over there? Go get them.*

13. [Help the child glue the pictures on the cards.]

14. [Continue the lesson by playing the game.]

Creating a Go Fish Game

Materials

A Go Fish game, card pairs in 4 categories (animals, vehicles, food, buildings), small blank cards, glue

A. Focusing on Go Fish

1. Here's a game I think you know pretty well. *What is it called?*

   [Provide the Go Fish label if necessary.]

2. This game, like a lot of games, is played by rules. *What's a rule?*

3. *What are the rules of Go Fish?*

4. Those rules seem easy. What you have to do is ask for a card. If the player has it, you get the card. A player who doesn't have it says, "Go Fish," right?

B. Creating a Go Fish Game

1. In fact, Go Fish is so easy that even kids three or four years old can play it. I thought it would be fun to make a Go Fish game for older kids. The way this Go Fish is played is that you have to match the identical card.

   [Holding up the Go Fish cards.]

   If a player has a card with a bear on it, it has to be matched with a bear. *If a person has a card with a lion, it has to be matched with a* ___________.

2. *And if a person has an elephant, it has to be matched with another* ___________.

3. That's what I mean by matching. It has to be exactly the same. Why don't we complicate it by not matching the identical card, but by matching to a group. I'll show you what I mean by a "group." It could be a group of animals. It could be a group of foods. *You name some other groups.*

4. Why don't you set up the cards so they are in what I call groups and then I'll show you how I think we can play the game. Here are some pictures and they contain four groups. "You look through the pictures and sort them into groups."

   [There should be no more than four or five pictures in a group.]

   So if these are going to be the groups we have in our Go Fish Game, what groups will we have?

5. Before you play, let's get them on cards. *Go over there and get the cards.*

6. [Help the child glue the pictures on the blank cards.]

C. Playing the Game

1. Let's mix up the cards. You deal them.

2. Go over the rule I said. Remember, the easy game was matching to the identical card. I have an airplane so if I want the identical card, I say, "Do you have an airplane?" Only now we aren't going to use the name of the object. We're going to use the name of the group. *What group does airplane belong to?*

3. So I'm going to say, "Do you have anything for transportation?" Let's look at your hand. *Do you have anything for transportation?*

4. OK, *give it to me. If you didn't have anything for transportation, what would you have said to me?*

5. Now you try it. *Take one of the cards in your hand. If you were playing matching the identical card, the easy way of playing Go Fish, what would you ask for?*

6. But we aren't playing that way. *What rule are we playing by?*

7. *So what are you going to ask me?*

8. [Continue playing the game with the new rule. If time allows, ask the child to explain how this game differs from the original version.]

Playing Basketball

Materials
Pictures of games being played (bowling, baseball, football), picture of a basketball game, 1 large ball, 1 small ball, straw basket or other container with bottom removed, string for hanging basket, masking tape, scissors

A. Focusing on Basketball

1. There are lots of games you play with balls.

   [Showing picture of people bowling.]

   Here is a picture of a game played with a ball. *What is it?*

   [Provide information if necessary.]

2. *Where is the ball that's used?*

3. [Repeat steps 1 and 2 with other ball game pictures.]

4. Here's one more game that's played with a ball. It's called basketball. *Where's the ball in this game?*

5. And the way you play this game is to toss the ball in the basket. *Where is the basket?*

B. Setting up the Game

1. In a game like bowling, the ball goes along the floor.

   [Showing the bowling picture again.]

   Here, take this ball and move it along the floor like a bowling ball.

2. But in basketball, the ball doesn't go along the floor, it's thrown up in the air. *Throw this ball up in the air.*

3. Just throwing it up is not enough. The idea is to throw it up so it falls through the basket. *Where does it have to go?*

4. It would be nice to try doing that here, but first, we need something like a basket that we can hang up. *Do you see something over there we can use?*

5. I think we can hang it here.

   [Indicating the spot.]

   You hold it while I attach it.

6. *Is it attached now? Is it staying up, or do you still have to hold it?*

7. Now we need a ball to toss through the basket.

   [Offer two balls, one much too big for the basket.]

   Which one of these should we use?

8. *Try it—see if it fits.* You made the right choice. (It doesn't fit. We'd better use the other one.)

C. Playing the Game

1. You can play basketball by throwing the ball from almost any place in the room. *Try throwing it from here.*

   [Indicating a point at close range.]

2. *And from here.*

   [Indicating a point at distant range.]

3. *And from here.*

   [Indicating some other point.]

4. Although you can throw it from any point, some points are easier than others. *Put this tape down at two places that are near the basket.*

   [Give two pieces of tape about 4-5 inches long to the child. Assist the child if the word "near" isn't familiar.]

5. *Put these two at places far from the basket.*

   [Give two more pieces of tape to the child.]

   Any place past this point.

   [Indicate a point at the far end of the room.]

6. *Now try throwing the ball into the basket from one of these far points.*

   [If the child has poor motor control, you toss the ball and modify the verbalization appropriately.]

7. *Did it go in?*

8. [Repeat steps 6 and 7 for the other far point.]

9. *So were you able to get it in from the far points?*

10. Now let's try the near points. *Which one do you want to start with?*

11. *Try it.*

12. *Did it work?*

13. Now let's do the other near point. *Throw it from here.*

14. *Did it work?*

15. *Where was it easier to get the ball into the basket? From the near points or the far points?*

16. [Continue the activity trying to get the ball in the basket from various points in the room.]

Playing Basketball

Materials

Various pictures of games (soccer, tennis, football, baseball), picture of basketball court, two baskets with bottoms removed, ball, two baskets with bottoms intact, masking tape, string, scissors

A. Focusing on Basketball

1. There are lots of sports that you play with a ball. For example, *do you know what sport this is?*

   [Showing a picture of a ball game such as soccer.]

2. Here is another game with a ball.

   [Showing a picture of another game such as tennis.]

   What is it called?

   [Provide the label if necessary.]

3. Soccer and tennis are both games you play with balls, but the games don't have "ball" in their names. It's not called "soccerball." *It's just called* __________.

4. And it's not called "tennisball," *it's just called* __________.

5. But there are some games that do actually have the word "ball" in their names. Take football. *Do you know why football is called "football?"*

   [Hold up a picture of a football game that clearly shows someone kicking the ball.]

6. And there's another game with "ball" in the name.

   [Show a picture of a baseball game.]

   I'm thinking of baseball. You may not know why it's called "baseball," but look at these things here. They're called bases. OK, *why do you think this game is called "baseball?"*

7. Now, there's another game that has the word "ball" in it.

   [Show a picture of a basketball game.]

   It's basketball. *Why do you think basketball is called "basketball?"*

B. Setting Up the Game

1. I thought we would set up one of the games we've been talking about in this room. We really don't have room to set up a baseball field and we don't have room to set up a football field. But with a little imagination, we could set up a little basketball court. *So what game do you think we are going to be playing today?*

2. Look at this picture.

   [Holding up a picture that shows a basketball court and a game being played.]

   Tell me the major components we are going to need if we're going to set up a basketball game.

3. Those are the things we need. I called them "components." *What do you think the word "components" means?*

4. Some of the chief components are the baskets. *Where do you think we should put them?*

5. It's not enough to just put them at the ends of the room. There's something else we have to take into account. *If we leave them here on the floor at the end of the room, will it be much of a game?*

6. *Why not?*

7. *So what do we have to do to the baskets to make the game a little more interesting?*

8. [Bring out two baskets similar to those being used, but with intact bottoms.]

   Here are two baskets that look like the other baskets we just put up. *Look at them and tell me if we should have used these baskets?*

9. *Why not?*

C. Playing the Game

1. One of the main rules of basketball is that you have to shoot from within the lines. *Show me the lines on the basketball court that we were looking at before.*

2. *What do we have to set up here?*

3. OK, *do you see any material over there we could use?*

   [The items should include masking tape.]

4. *How many sides are there on the court?*

5. *How many pieces of tape will we need?*

6. Let's go ahead and cut them. But wait—first let's measure. *Let's take a string and measure how long we want the court to be on this side. Now let's cut the tape so it's as long as the string.*

7. *How many sides do we still have left to do?*

8. OK, *would you please tape it on the floor.*

9. Now I think we can use the same string for this side of the court.

   [Indicating the line opposite and parallel to the one just done.]

   Why do you think we could use the same length of string here as we did there?

10. OK, *go ahead and cut the tape again.*

11. Now we have two more sides. *Are they going to be shorter or longer than the ones we've just done?*

12. *Show me on the picture why you said one was shorter and one was longer.*

13. We have to cut some new string. *Cut a string that's equal to the line we want to make here.*

14. *Now cut the tape.*

15. There's one more side to do. *Go ahead and do it.*

16. You've completed the court. Before, I told you the rule about what the lines of the court tell us. *Do you remember what I said?*

    [Provide information if necessary.]

17. *So would it be fair to shoot the ball into the basket from here?*

    [Indicating a point within court.]

18. *Why?*

19. *Would it be fair to shoot it from here?*

[Indicating a spot outside the court.]

20. *Why not?*

21. [The lesson may be extended by asking the child to review the process of setting up the game and the rules involved with playing the game.]

22. [If time allows, continue the lesson by playing the game, keeping it as simple or elaborate as the child's interest or abilities permit. Keeping score may be a part of the lesson.]

When a child working at the complex level gives a high percentage of inappropriate responses, continue the topic by moving the lesson to the simple level.

Playing Croquet

This is a good outside activity.

Materials
Board games, pictures of bowling, croquet set (or metal for hoops, balls and mallets), card showing a hoop shape, diagram for placing the hoops, playdough for supporting hoops indoors, pencil, paper

If the hoops are painted in different colors and the hoop symbols on the diagram are in matching colors, following the diagram will be easier for the child.

A. Focusing on Croquet

1. Lots of games we play have a number of different parts. Here's __________ (name a board game). *Name some of the different parts of this game.*

2. And here's bowling.

   [Showing a picture of bowling.]

   What are the parts in bowling.

3. And here is another game with parts. You may not know it's name. It's croquet. *Say "croquet."*

4. Croquet has some balls. You know what balls are. *Draw something that's the shape of a ball.*

5. Now, *find the balls in the croquet game.*

6. There are some other parts that you probably don't know. Some are shaped like this.

   [Hold up the card showing a hoop.]

   And these are called "hoops." *What did I say they were called?*

7. *Find those in the box.*

8. The last things are called mallets. *Take them out.*

9. The mallet is used to hit the ball and move it like this.

   [Demonstrating.]

   Now you do that.

B. Setting Up the Game

1. Before, we were hitting the ball. *When we were hitting the ball, was it just on the ground or did it go through something?*

2. If we are really going to play croquet, we have to make the ball go through something. You took out some parts before that the ball could go through. *Find them for me.*

3. *Do you remember what they are called?*

   [Provide the label if necessary.]

4. We can't set the hoops up in just any old way. There is a plan that has to be followed. And this is it.

   [Holding up the diagram.]

   What is this?

5. [Help the child place the hoops in the earth or on playdough foundations.]

C. Playing the Game

1. Now we get to play the game. We need the balls and mallets. *Please bring them here.*

2. *Which mallet do you want?*

3. Do you remember which part of the mallet is the part that has to hit the ball? *Show it to me.*

4. OK, so *let's put the ball here.*

   [Indicating a spot.]

5. Remember, the ball has to go through something. What does it have to go through?

6. OK, *hit it and see if you can get it through.*

7. [Play the game for a number of turns. Depending on the child's level and abilities, incorporate techniques such as keeping score and mapping the path of the ball through the hoops.]

Playing Croquet

Materials

Card with the word "croquet" printed on it, 7 cards with single letters of the word (1 card with C, 1 card with R, etc.), croquet set (or metal for hoops, balls, and mallet) diagram of hoop positions, blank cards, crayons, numbered stickers

A. Focusing on Croquet

1. We're going to play a game today that you've probably never heard of. It's got a very unusual name. It's called "croquet." *Can you say that?*

2. You're beginning to read and spell now. I thought it would be interesting for you to spell out the word "croquet."

   [Show the word card, then give the shuffled letter cards to the child.]

   Here's the word "croquet" and here are some letters that spell "croquet." *Put them in order so they look just like this word.*

3. So far we've seen the word. *Take the card that says "croquet" and go over there and find the game that has the same word on the box.*

4. Inside the box you'll find three major parts of the game. One part is the mallet. It is used to hit the ball. *Go ahead and try to find one.*

5. *What did I say it was called?*

6. Now the second part are hoops that are set up on the ground and you knock the balls through them. *What are hoops used for?*

7. *Find the hoops.*

8. *Count how many hoops there are.*

9. Now there's one other part of the game we haven't found. *Go inside the box and find it.*

B. Setting Up the Game

1. Now if we're going to play the game we have to set up the hoops as they look on this diagram.

   [Show the diagram.]

   The problem is that you need a lot of space to set up all the hoops in the game. *Do you remember how many hoops there are in the game?*

2. If we had a big area outside we could set them up, but in here, it's very small. So I don't think we can use all the hoops. How about using only five hoops. *Count those out.*

3. *Why did we choose not to use all the hoops in the game this time?*

4. The hoops have to be set up in a pattern that looks something like this.

   [Pointing to the diagram.]

   But we have fewer hoops so we have to create our own pattern. Here is a card. why don't you draw dots that represent each of the five hoops and make them in a pattern that sort of looks like the picture. That's going to be the pattern that tells us how to lay out the hoops. *Go ahead and do it.*

5. *Now place the hoops according to the diagram.*

6. The hoops are on the ground. But there's one thing more. You have to play in a certain order. You have to go through 1, then 2, then 3, then 4, and then 5. The problem is that we haven't numbered our hoops yet. We can do it in any way you like. Here are some stickers with numbers. *Put them on the hoops to tell which one is which.*

7. We need a starting point. *Do you know what I mean by "starting point?"*

8. *Where do you want the starting point to be?*

C. Playing the Game

1. Now everything is set up to play the game. Let me give you the rules.

   [Try to use actual rules and explain them in steps that are appropriate to the child's level.]

   What did I say the main rules are?

2. OK, *you go first.* This first one is easy because the starting point is straight in front of the hoop that you have to go through. If you had to go through that hoop over there instead of here,

   [Pointing to a hoop at an angle to the starting point]

   it would be much harder. *Why would it be harder to hit the ball into that one (the angled one) than into this one (the straight one)?*

3. So if the ball is straight in line, directly in front of the hoop it has to go through, then it's very easy. It's very difficult when the hoop is off at an angle. *What did I say was more difficult?*

4. Let's try that again.

   [Place the ball in front of another hoop.]

   Is the ball in front of the hoop or is it off at an angle?

5. [Change the position of the ball so it is different from the position in step 4.]

   I've moved the ball. *Is it directly in front, or is it off at an angle?*

6. *Which way will be easier to get it through the hoop?*

7. [Play the game as long as time permits or the child's interest allows.]

Creating a Large-Scale Model of a Two-Dimensional Game

Materials

Various board games, masking tape, scissors, diagram of a winding path of squares, square cards with shapes drawn or stuck on them, cards that indicate number of spaces playing piece moves

Start with the cards in pairs and separated in two piles. One pile will be used for the gameboard path.

A. Focusing on Location

1. We're going to play with a board game today. Most of them are small and you can play them on a table or desk. Here is __________ (name a board game). *Can you play this on a table?*

2. That's right. *Take out the board.* You can play it on the table because it fits on the table. *Put it on the table and see if it fits.*

3. *Does it fit?*

4. [Repeat steps 2-4 with another board game.]

5. Today, I thought we would do something funny. I thought we would play a board game like these, but on a big board. In fact, the board will be so big that it won't fit on any table. The only thing big enough for it will be the floor. *So what did I say we were going to use for the board?*

B. Setting Up the Game

1. If we're going to use the floor as a board, we'd better make an outline on the floor to mark the part to serve as a board. We'll take these and use them as markers.

   [Indicating long pieces of masking tape.]

   Here, take this one and place it here.

2. [Continue having the child place the pieces on the floor until an area approximately 4′ x 8′ is marked.]

3. Now, this part in here will be our board.

   [Indicate the inside of the tape rectangle.]

   What will it be?

4. At this point, let's fill it in so it looks like a board. I thought a path like this would be a good one to make.

   [Holding up diagram of a winding path containing a sequence of squares with different shapes in them.]

   Now look at the first one.

5. *Go over to the table and find a piece of paper containing that shape.*

6. [Continue the path construction in this manner taking turns with the child until a path of 10-12 squares is completed. Tape down the squares so the path does not move.]

7. Now, it's beginning to look like a board game. *Show me the outline of the board.*

8. *Show me the path on the board.*

C. Playing the Game

1. In games with paths, you usually have cards that tell you where to go. I have some over there. *Please bring them here.*

2. Now, we have the cards, but usually you need something else. Usually you need playing pieces. Pieces that you move. But we don't have any, so I thought of something unusual. Let us be the playing pieces. For example, if you are the playing piece that moves and you pick up a card with this shape,

   [Holding up a card]

   what place on the path would you move to?

3. OK, *do it.*

4. [Play the game with the players as the playing pieces.]

Creating a Large-Scale Model of a Two-Dimensional Game

Materials

Various board games, small book, paper, pencil, checkerboard, scissors, 2 paper squares (see step B-2), enough 6-inch red and black squares to make a checkerboard, large red and black circles (made of thick cardboard or comparable material) for game pieces

If the child has difficulty understanding the concept of checkers, the game may be simplified.

A. Focusing on Location

1. Here are a bunch of board games—games with boards. *What are the names of these games?*

2. When we play games like this, we usually use some furniture to play them on. *What furniture in the room did we usually use?*

3. Let's imagine that we entered a world of magic and in that world of magic everything suddenly expanded. That means it got much, much larger. *What does "expanded" mean?*

4. [Holding up a small book]

   For example, *if this book expanded so that it was twice its size, how big would it be?*

5. *Draw it for me.*

   [Give a large sheet of paper and a pencil to the child.]

6. It would be fun if we did something like that today with one of the board games—that is, if we actually expanded it.

   [Holding up the checkerboard]

   If we expanded a game like this and it really became too large to fit on any furniture, like a table, what part of the room might we use to hold the board? *Would we use the floor or the wall?*

7. *Why did you pick the floor and not the wall?*

B. Setting Up the Game

1. We're going to set up a board game on the floor and I thought this one would be a good one to do.

   [Show the checkerboard.]

What two colors do we need if we are going to make the two parts of a checkerboard?

2. [Have the child trace a square from the board and cut it out.]

This is the size of a square on the checkerboard, and I said we would REALLY expand it. *Which of these sizes do you think REALLY expands it?*

[Holding up two squares: one slightly larger than the child's square and one much larger (approximately 6 inches each side).]

If we are going to make a checkerboard, we sure need a lot of squares. *Count how many red squares we are going to need.*

3. *Count how many black squares we are going to need.*

4. *Is that the same number or a different number?*

5. *So are the black squares and red squares equal in number or are they different in number?*

[Bring out a lot of red and black squares of the expanded size.]

It would have taken a long time for us to cut these now, so I prepared them in advance. Now we have to get the right number. *Do you remember how many red squares there were?*

6. OK, *count that many squares.*

7. *Do you remember how many black squares there were?*

8. OK, *count them out.*

9. *Now lay them out and make sure they follow the same pattern as on the smaller checkerboard.*

10. Now we're going to need something else to play. For checkers, we need pieces like this and a board.

[Holding up small regular-size checker pieces.]

What shape are these pieces?

11. Well, I have some material over there that is cut up like the shape of these pieces, but they are bigger. *Go over there and find the ones I mean.*

12. Before, we counted the squares. This time we'll have to count the pieces. *How many pieces are there for the person who has the red? OK, count these.*

13. *How many pieces will there be for the black pieces? OK, count them.*

14. [Play the game.]

Additional Lesson Suggestions

1. Creating a Bingo Game
2. Creating a Concentration (Memory) Game (like Simple Simon)
3. Playing Musical Chairs
4. Creating a Memory Game (simplified version of commercially available games)
5. Playing a Computer Game

Enacting the Humpty Dumpty Nursery Rhyme

Material

Illustrated nursery-rhyme book with a bookmark placed at the Humpty Dumpty rhyme, raw and hard-cooked eggs, straight-edge shapes such as a block, a box, and a book, paper pieces for facial features, glue, small blocks

To prevent confusion, mark the cooked eggs with an **X.**

A. Recounting Humpty Dumpty

1. I thought today we'd act out a nursery rhyme that's in that book. *Please bring the book over here.*

2. Do you see a piece of paper that's sticking out of the book? *Put your finger on it.*

3. *Now open the book to the place where the paper is that you are touching.*

4. *What do you see on the page that you opened to?*

   [Accept any reasonable description from child.]

5. That __________ (using the child's words) is about a character called Humpty Dumpty. I'm going to read you a little story about him. Here's how it starts. Humpty Dumpty sat on a wall. So Humpty Dumpty is the name of the doll (use child's word) you noticed. *Point to him again.*

6. OK, Humpty Dumpty sat on a wall.

   [Continue reading the entire rhyme.]

B. Creating Humpty Dumpty

1. I have an idea. I think it would be fun to do what this rhyme says. First we have to make the main character, and that's Humpty Dumpty. Look at Humpty Dumpty and look at these.

   [Indicating a choice of egg, block, book, and box.]

   Which one of these looks most like the shape of Humpty Dumpty?

2. *So what do you think Humpty Dumpty is made out of?*

3. So we are going to use an egg to make Humpty Dumpty.

   [Holding up a raw egg.]

But Humpty Dumpty in the book has some things on his face that our egg doesn't have. Like these. *What are these?*

[Pointing to Humpty Dumpty's eyes.]

4. *And what is this?*

   [Pointing to the nose.]

5. *And what is this?*

   [Pointing to the mouth.]

6. *So we have to make a mouth, a nose, and __________.*

7. Let's start with the eyes. First, there are some things over here that we could paste on Humpty Dumpty so he'll have eyes.

   [Indicating small paper pieces.]

   Which one of these could we use for eyes?

8. To get them to stick on, we'll need glue. *Go get the glue.*

9. *Now glue them on.*

10. *What are your doing?*

11. *Now which one do you want to do, his nose or his mouth?*

12. *OK, find one we can use for his nose* (or mouth depending on child's choice).

13. We're going to have to attach this like we attached the eyes. *What do we have to use?*

14. *OK, go ahead and put on the glue.*

15. And now, the last one. *What do we have left to put on?*

16. *OK, find something we can use for the nose.*

17. OK, you have to glue it. *Go ahead and do it.*

18. Wow! Look at this.

    [Pointing to cgg.]

    This started out as an egg and you've made it into __________ (accept any reasonable label).

C. Creating the Scene

1. Now that we have Humpty Dumpty, we can begin to do what the poem says. First, it says that Humpty Dumpty sat on a wall. Well, we have Humpty Dumpty, but we don't have a wall. *So what do we still need?*

2. OK, let's make a wall.

   [Showing illustrations of the wall.]

   This wall looks like it's made of something in the shape of blocks. So we could use blocks. *Go get them.*

3. *Arrange the blocks so they look like a wall.*

   [The wall should be high enough to be a significant drop.]

4. Now we can go back and do the first thing I read. We can make Humpty Dumpty sit on the wall. *You put Humpty Dumpty so he is sitting on the wall.*

5. Now it says Humpty Dumpty had a great fall. *You say that.*

6. If you let him go, he'll fall just like the poem says. *So go ahead and let him go.*

7. Oh my goodness! *What happened?*

8. That's right. And now you know why it says what it says in the rest of the poem. It says all the king's horses and all the king's men couldn't put Humpty Dumpty together again. Why couldn't they fix Humpty Dumpty? *What was Humpty Dumpty made of that breaks when it falls?*

D. Remaking Humpty Dumpty

1. Poor Humpty Dumpty. Maybe if we hadn't made him out of a plain uncooked egg, things might have been different. Here is another uncooked egg. *Drop it and see what happens.*

2. Now here are some eggs I've cooked.

   [Pointing to the cooked eggs.]

   Drop one on the floor.

3. Look, the shell cracked, *but did all the stuff inside come pouring out?*

4. So maybe if we make Humpty Dumpty out of this kind of egg, a cooked egg, he'll end up in better shape. Let's make another Humpty Dumpty with this new cooked egg.

   [Repeat steps B-3 through C-7, keeping in mind that the child now knows the sequence and can progress more rapidly. For example, you can give the child all the parts of the face and say "Put these on."]

5. *Now, we have another Humpty Dumpty, but this time he's not made out of an uncooked egg, but a ________.*

6. Let's try sitting him on the wall. *Now let's try having him fall.*

7. *What happened this time?*

Concluding Comment to the Child

He did crack a little because you can get hurt when you fall. But he's in much better shape than the first Humpty Dumpty. You did a great job in making this one. Would you like to take him home or leave him here?

The most demanding part of the lesson should occur during the first half of the therapy session. If the child tires during the last half of the session, the demands may be simplified and reduced.

Enacting the Humpty Dumpty Nursery Rhyme

Materials
Illustrated nursery-rhyme book, raw and hard-cooked eggs, paper pieces for facial features, glue, small blocks

To prevent confusion, mark the cooked eggs with an **X.**

A. Recounting Humpty Dumpty
Given the lack of familiarity that many children now display with nursery rhymes, this part of the lesson will acquaint them with some key components of the genre.

1. There's a kind of story you may know about. These stories are nursery rhymes. They usually are about girls or boys or animals where something funny or special happens. Let me read you one.

   [Read Mary had a Little Lamb.]

   What was funny or special in that rhyme?

2. Now here's another.

   [Read Little Miss Muffet.]

   What happened to Little Miss Muffet in the nursery rhyme?

3. Here's another nursery rhyme. *When I read each line, I would like you to repeat it after me.*

   [Read Humpty Dumpty with the students repeating each line.]

B. Creating Humpty Dumpty

1. I have an idea. I think it would be fun to do what this nursery rhyme says. First we have to make the main character. *Who is that?*

2. And what do you think he is made of? *Look at this picture and tell me what we might use to make Humpty Dumpty.*

3. The egg is a good shape for Humpty Dumpty.

   [Using a raw egg.]

   But it doesn't have the features of the face. *What are the features, the things on everyone's face?*

4. OK, so we have to put those on Humpty Dumpty. *Look over there and find some things that would be good for that.*

   [Pointing to small pieces of paper.]

5. *Tell me the order you're going to use for putting on the features.*

6. That's fine. But remember, you can't just put them on. They've got to stick. *What do you need for that?*

7. *OK. Why don't you go ahead and get it.*

8. *What did you say you would put on first?*

9. *Go ahead and do that.*

10. *What did you say you'd put on second?*

11. *Go ahead and do it.*

12. You have only one thing left to put on. *What is that?*

13. *Go ahead and do that.*

C. Creating the Scene

1. Let's go back to the nursery rhyme. It says Humpty Dumpty sat on a wall. There were two things mentioned in that line. We have one of the two things. *What is it that we have?*

2. We are missing one of the things. *What is it that we still don't have?*

3. *Find something over there we can use to make a wall.*

4. *Go ahead and make the wall so that it sort of looks like this.*

   [Showing the illustration.]

5. *Let's arrange it so that Humpty Dumpty is on the wall.*

6. It says Humpty Dumpty had a great fall. *Where's he going to be when he falls?*

7. *Ok, let him go.*

8. *What happened to him?*

9. *Why did it happen?*

D. Remaking Humpty Dumpty

1. Poor Humpty Dumpty. But remember, not only was he an egg, he was an uncooked egg. *What does it mean when an egg is uncooked?*

2. Now, let's suppose we had cooked an egg so it was hard. *What would the inside of the egg be like then?*

3. Here, I have a hard-cooked egg. We can use it to make another Humpty Dumpty. *What are the things you have to put on first so it looks like Humpty Dumpty?*

4. *Go ahead and do it.*

5. Now lets *re-enact* the scene. *What do I mean when I say "re-enact?"*

   [Provide the answer if necessary.]

6. *Go ahead and re-enact the scene and say what's happening as you do each thing.*

7. *What happened this time?*

Concluding Comment to the Child

He did crack a little because you can get hurt when you fall. But he's in much better shape than the first Humpty Dumpty. You did a great job. Would you like to take him home or leave him here?

Pretend Visit to a Gas Station

Materials
Picture of a city street showing a gas station and other buildings, toy gas station with removable parts, toy cars, small dolls

A. Focusing on a Store

1. Streets can have lots of different buildings. *Point to some of the buildings here.*

   [Showing the picture.]

2. There are lots of buildings on this page.

   [Pointing to a house.]

   This building is a __________.

3. *And it's used for __________.*

4. *And this building is a __________.*

   [Pointing to a store.]

5. *What do people do in stores?*

6. Here's another building.

   [Pointing to a gas station.]

   What is this called?

7. *And what do people do there?*

B. Creating a Gas Station

1. We've just been looking at a picture of a gas station. We can do more than that. We can make something almost like a real gas station. But we'll need some objects. First, we'll need the building. *Go over there and find something that looks like a gas station.*

2. Sometimes cars are in this part of the gas station.

3. *Go get them.*

4. Outside the station we need some gas pumps. *Show me some gas pumps in this picture.*

5. *Go over there and get some we can use for our gas station.*

6. We've put down quite a few things. *What do we have so far in our gas station?*

7. Let's have a person in the station. *Let's put one person in the garage working on a car.*

8. Gas stations are designed so you can get gas, but the gas doesn't come out all by itself. *Who is needed to get the gas out?*

   [Accept any appropriate response.]

9. *Who else do we need in our station?*

10. *Get a doll over there that could be a mommy (man, driver, etc.).*

11. The mommy gets the gas out but *what does the gas go into?*

12. *So what do we need?*

13. *Go get it.*

14. *Show me where you are going to put the car so it's near the gas.*

15. *Put it there.*

16. And let's have one other person near the gas pumps. We have the person who gets the gas out so let's have an attendant (the person who helps get the gas out, cashier—the variability depends on the choice in step 10). *Put an attendant there.*

    [Indicate an appropriate location.]

C. Role Playing

1. Let's act this out. Let's pretend we're the people in the station. You can be the driver driving into the station. *So place your car outside the station.*

2. Now, you're thinking, "Oh oh, I don't have much gas. I'd better get some gas. That's where I can get some gas." *Say that.*

3. *Where do you drive your car up to?*

4. I'll be the person at the pumps and I'll say, "OK, what would you like?" and *you'll say* __________.

5. Now I'll say, "Boy, your car is really taking a lot of gas. The gas tank must have been nearly empty. Now it's filled up and you owe me ten dollars. Do you have ten dollars?" *Now what do you say?*

6. [Continue the dialogue for another three or four exchanges depending on the child's interest and skill.]

D. Reversing the Roles

1. *So far, you've been playing which part?*

2. *And I've been playing which part?*

3. I have an idea. Let's change. You can be the person who gives the gas. *That means I'll be* ___________.

4. [Repeat the role-playing sequence with reversed roles.]

Any play activity that lends itself to sequenced development can form the basis of a lesson. The lesson plans in this book can be used as models to frame the new lesson.

Pretend Visit to a Gas Station

Materials
Picture of a city street showing a gas station and other buildings, diagram of a gas station layout, toy gas station, small dolls.

A. Focusing on a Store

1. Here is a picture of a street in a city or town. Like most streets, it has lots of buildings. *Point to the buildings.*

2. A lot of buildings in the town are for people to live in. They're houses. Sometimes the houses can be low. *Find a low house.*

3. Sometimes they can be very tall. *Find a tall house.*

4. A tall house is often called an "apartment building." Like this one.

   [Pointing to an apartment building in the picture.]

   What is it called?

5. There are a lot of buildings in town that are not to live in.

   [Putting the picture away.]

   Think of some buildings. *Think of three kinds of buildings that people use, but they don't use them to live in.*

   [Provide help with the picture if necessary.]

B. Creating a Gas Station

To incorporate more children into the lesson, increase the number of characters that are present at the gas station.

1. One of the buildings you did (or didn't) mention was a gas station. I thought we could play around and actually make a gas station today. But before that, *why don't you tell me what a gas station is.*

2. Of course, the gas station we are going to construct will not be a real one. It will only be a play one. *What kinds of things do you need to construct a play gas station?*

3. I have some things like that in a box over there. *Bring them here.*

4. Here's a diagram of a gas station. *What things can you recognize on this diagram?*

   [Have the child read the labels or read the labels for the child.]

5. I thought we could lay out our gas station so it's like this diagram. It says we have the pumps over here. *Show me where you are going to put the pumps?*

6. Over here is the ________.

   [Referring to the garage.
   Let the child read the label if possible.]

7. *So where are we going to put the garage relative to the pumps?*

8. [Proceed until the gas station is
   laid out according to the diagram.]

9. Now we have all the parts of a gas station but we don't have the people to go in with it. First, there are the people who work in the gas station. *Would you like there to be one or two?*

10. OK, *go get one (two).*

11. Besides workers in gas stations, there are also customers. *What does "customers" mean?*

12. So we had better put a couple of customers in the gas station as well. *Go ahead and do that.*

C. Role Playing

1. Now I think it would be fun to make up a kind of script of what happens between the people in the gas station. *Do you know what a script is?*

   [Provide the definition if necessary.]

2. Let's pretend that the customer here is very angry. She is angry because the car was fixed at this station but the mechanic did a terrible job. So the customer is bringing back the car to complain. *What are some things a person who is very angry might say?*

3. *And what is that person's tone of voice?*

4. Now let's pretend that the mechanic is a very shy, quiet person and he doesn't know how to argue or fight back. *So how might that person look and act?*

5. *What would the tone of his voice be?*

6. We'll divide up the parts. *Which part would you like to play, the shy mechanic or the angry customer?*

7. OK, I'll play the other part.

   [Continue the role playing.]

D. Reversing Roles

1. That went pretty well. I wonder how it would feel if we each played the other person. *Which role did you just play?*

2. *And which role did I play?*

3. So if we reverse the roles, that means we are going to switch. *What role will you play?*

4. *What role will I play?*

5. Great. Let's try it that way.

   [Continue the role playing with the roles reversed.]

Creating a Story from Pretend Play

This lesson is based on *One Frog Too Many,* but any well-depicted story would be appropriate.

Materials

One Frog Too Many (Mayer 1975), small dolls and animals relevant to the story, small box, relevant illustrated pages cut from the storybook, several blank pieces of paper stapled together, crayons

A. Setting the Scene

1. I have some dolls and little toys over there in a bag that I thought we could play with. *Please go and get them.*

2. *What toys and dolls do you see in the bag?*

3. I thought we could make up a story about these toys and dolls. Let's set it up so that the little boy gets a present. So you need the boy and the box. *Put them here.*

4. The turtle and the dog can be standing next to the boy. *Would you go ahead and put them there.*

5. Then the boy opens the box. *What did I say he was going to do?*

6. *Let him do that.*

7. *What does he see inside the box?*

8. He takes the little frog out of the box and puts him on the ground next to the other frog. *Where are you going to put him?*

9. Now the other frog is very angry. *Make an angry face to show how the big frog feels.*

10. The big frog is so angry that he bites the little frog. *What part of his face would he use to bite him with?*

11. *Fix the frogs so it looks as though the big frog is biting the little frog.*

12. The boy wants to help the little frog so he picks him up. *Have him do that.*

13. And then he yells at the big frog for being such a bad frog. *Now you do that.*

B. Creating the Book

1. It would be interesting to make a storybook of what we've just done.

   [Referring to pages cut from the book and arranged out of sequence.]

   I have some pictures here that show scenes like the one we just did. And here is a book we could put them into.

   [Referring to the stapled blank pages.]

   Let's start again. *Set it up with the dog and the frog.*

2. And he's just gotten a present, so the little frog should be in the box. *Put him there.*

3. And the box should be closed. *Do that.*

4. *Which picture over here*

   [Pointing to the mixed-up pictures]

   looks like this scene?

5. *Paste it here in the book.*

6. Next, the boy opens the box. *Do that.*

7. Then he picks up the frog. *Have him do that.*

8. *Which picture over here looks like this scene?*

9. [Continue setting up scenes and matching them to the pictures in the story until three or four pictures are pasted in the book.]

10. You've done a great job. Let's go through the book you've made and, this time, *you tell me the story.*

Depending on the child's skill, more of the story may be incorporated into the lesson or the story may be continued in separate lessons.

Creating a Story from Pretend Play

Materials
Small dolls and toys relevant to the story, small box, *One Frog Too Many* (Mayer 1975), pictures depicting the story, additional storybook to demonstrate the purpose of titles, crayons, paper

A. Setting the Scene
The dolls and toys should be moved appropriately as the story proceeds.

1. I have some dolls and toys in that bag over there. *Would you bring it here?*

2. I thought we would play an unusual game today. Something that we haven't done before. I'm going to play with these characters and use them to tell a story. I want you to watch very carefully because then you will do the same thing I've done. The first thing we'll need is a boy, a dog, a frog, and a box with a bow on it. *Take those out.*

3. The story starts like this: The little boy gets a present and he's really excited. He thinks it's great. Since he's got a present, he does what most people do with a present. *What do you do with a present?*

4. That's right. He opens it up and he looks inside. *And what does he see?*

5. Yes, he sees another frog. This frog is a lot like the frog that's on the floor here, but he's different in a certain way. *How is he different?*

   [If necessary, help the child understand that the difference in size is relevant.]

6. The boy thinks it would be great if the little frog would join the other animals. The big frog doesn't feel that way at all. The big frog feels very mad at the little frog. *Why do you think he's mad about another frog in the boy's life?*

7. Anyway, even though the boy puts the frog down and hopes everything will work out, it doesn't. Instead the big frog reaches over and bites the little frog. The little frog, of course, yells "Ow!" as anyone who is bitten might do. The boy feels he should protect the little frog because now it belongs to him. Now I'd like you to take a turn at this and go through the scene I just went through. *Go ahead.*

8. Let's do it like we did it originally. The little frog has to go back in the box. *Is the box going to stay open?*

9. So the box is closed. Let's put the boy standing near the box and the big frog next to him. OK, *now go through the scene I just went through.*

   [Help child with details of the story if necessary.]

B. Creating the Book

1. We've told the story through dolls, almost like a play. We can also tell it through pictures. Then it would be a story in a book. I have some pictures here that tell the story of the one we've just done, but the pictures aren't in order. Why don't you put them in order so they tell the story as we just told it. *Which is the picture you're going to take first?*

2. *Why did you pick that one?*

3. OK, *what happens next?*

4. *Which picture are you going to put down.*

5. [Go through the picture sequence with the child.]

6. Fine, but you want to make sure the pictures stay in the right order. They are loose right now and could fall apart. *What can we do so the pictures stay together?*

7. OK, *go ahead and do that.*

8. Now let's think of a title we could put on the book you just made. Remember, a title usually picks up on an important part of the book like __________ (title of another book the child knows). *In your story, what do you think was the most important part?*

9. OK, *what would you like to make the title?*

Depending on the child's skill and interest, additional scenes from the book may be incorporated into the lesson.

Constructing a Scene from a Book

Materials

Are You My Mother? (Eastman 1960), relevant illustrated pages cut from the storybook, branches from a bush, playdough

If time allows, go outside with the child to collect the branches rather than having them available when the child enters the room.

A. Establishing the Characters in the Story

1. This is a book about a bird who's sitting on an egg.

   [Show the book and some pages from it.]

   Show me the bird.

2. *Show me the egg.*

3. There's a baby bird inside the egg. *Say that.*

4. The mother bird knows that the baby bird will be coming out of the egg soon, and she needs to get food for it. On the next page, she is flying away to get food. *Find that picture.*

5. Sure enough, just as she thought, the baby bird does come out. Look, he's scared because he's all alone. He wants his mother. He decides to go find her, but when he goes out of the nest, he can't fly, and he falls down. *Show me the pictures of him on the ground.*

B. Establishing the Necessary Components

1. I have an idea. Let's make this scene of the baby bird falling out of the tree. We'll need the things in this picture. *What is this that we'll need?*

   [Pointing to the tree in the picture.]

2. *And what is this?*

   [Pointing to the nest in the picture.]

3. *And what is this?*

   [Pointing to the baby bird.]

4. *What are the three things you said we needed?*

C. Creating the Scene

1. First, you said we need a tree. Look over on the table. I have something there that looks like a tree. *Go over there and find it.*

2. I'll use this playdough for the ground to put the tree in. *You stand the tree up in the ground.*

3. Now look in the book. *What's in the tree that we have to put in our tree?*

4. That's right, a nest. Let's make the nest out of playdough. *Here, you do it* and while you're doing it, I'll make the bird.

5. Great. You finished the nest. *Where are you going to put it so that it looks just like the picture in the book?*

6. *Now where are you going to put the bird?*

7. [If time allows, help the child to act out more scenes in the book.]

Constructing a Scene from a Book

Materials

Are You My Mother? (Eastman 1960), branch from a bush or tree, playdough

A. Establishing the Characters in the Story

1. This is a book that you may or may not have seen before. *Why don't you look through the first few pages and tell me what you think the story is about.*

2. You've mentioned two major characters in the story. *Who were the two major characters in the story?*

3. You know, the two major characters each have different roles. That is, they have different things that they have to do or different things happen to them in the story. *Tell me the major thing the mother bird has to do.*

4. *Up to this point, what has happened to the baby bird?*

   [Pointing to the page where the baby bird has fallen out of the nest.]

B. Establishing the Necessary Components

1. I thought it would be interesting to enact part of the story, that is, to make part of the story come to life. We can do it by making a scene of a few pages from the book. Like this scene.

   [Pointing to the picture.]

   If we were to make this scene, what are some of the things we would need?

2. *What material do you think we could use that would look like a real tree?*

3. We're not going to be able to get a real nest. We've used playdough before when we've needed things. Playdough is pretty versatile. I think it could even be used for the bird. Let's do it that way. *Do you think it would be OK to use playdough for the nest?*

C. Creating the Scene

1. We have a branch here that can serve as a tree, but there is a problem. It won't stay steady by itself.

   [Demonstrate how it falls down.]

What can we use so the branch will stay steady and look like the tree in the book?

2. Now we have to use the playdough for the other parts. *What did I say we would make out of playdough?*

3. OK, *do that.*

4. Now I'm going to ask you to do something very hard. I want you to look at the book because I'm going to take the picture away and ask you to reproduce the rest of the scene without looking at the picture. *Look at the picture.*

   [Put the picture away.]

5. *Go ahead and put all the things into place.*

6. Compare what you've done with the picture. *Is it the same?*

7. You've put the nest high in the tree and that's right. *Why do you think birds build their nests so high up in trees?*

8. Although it provides some safety, it does present problems. Some baby birds can fall out of the nest, like that one did, and hurt themselves. So there are advantages and disadvantages in placing the nest high up. *What are the advantages?*

9. *What are the disadvantages?*

10. [The lesson can be extended by creating other scenes from the book and discussing them in a similar manner.]

Enacting a Story

This lesson has different titles at the Simple and Complex Levels to represent the different focus at each level. It would be inappropriate to have a child at the Complex Level simply enact the story as the child does at the Simple Level.

Materials

A Boy, a Dog, a Frog, and a Friend (Mayer and Mayer 1971), tray to hold water, playdough, small dolls and animals, stick with string and small paper clip for fishing pole

A. Focusing on the Characters

1. This is a book called *A Boy, a Dog, a Frog, and a Friend.* Most of the things just mentioned are on the cover. First, there is a boy. *Show me the boy.*

2. Then it says a dog. *Show me the dog.*

3. Then it says a frog. *Show me the frog.*

B. Initiating the Story

1. *Now open to the page with the first picture.*

2. *The boy has a line and he is* __________. His friends, the dog and the frog, are just sitting near him.

3. [Point to the second picture.]

   Look what's happening here.

   [Point to the first picture.]

   Here, the boy was just sitting.

   [Return to the second picture.]

   But here, he's not. He's pulling and leaning back. *You lean back that way.*

4. *Now turn the page.*

5. Here he's not sitting and he's not leaning back.

   [The picture shows the boy being pulled into the water.]

   What's happening?

6. *Who's going in the water after him?*

7. *Now turn the page.*

8. There's a new character other than the boy, the dog, and the frog. *What is this?*

   [Pointing.]

9. *What does he have in his mouth?*

10. I think he's the one that pulled the boy into the water. Anyway, the boy thinks that and he's really angry. See, he's raising his hand like this.

    [Modeling the action.]

    You do that.

11. And he's shouting at the turtle, "You pulled me in. I'm so mad at you!" *You say that.*

C. Enacting the Segment

1. Let's see how all that happened. Let's set up things just the way they are in the book. First, we'll need some water because the boy was fishing in the water. *Take this tray and fill it with water.*

2. We also need something for the ground. Because look here, *what is the boy sitting on?*

   [Pointing to the appropriate picture.]

3. How about using this playdough and *putting it over there so it will be like the ground.*

4. Let's position these figures (boy, dog, frog) on the ground the way they are in the book. *You do it.*

5. Now let's look back at the pictures. The boy has something he's fishing with. It's a pole (rod). *Put this in the boy's hand for his fishing pole.*

   [Give the child the stick with the string and paper clip.]

6. There's one other animal we need. *Do you remember who was in the water and pulled the boy in?*

7. *Let's put him in the water.*

8. Now let's act out the scene. The boy puts his fishing line in the water. *Go ahead and do that.*

9. The turtle swims over and takes the hook into his mouth. *Do that.*

10. The boy starts pulling. *Help him pull back.*

11. But the turtle is also pulling and he's pulling even harder. *So start making the turtle pull.*

12. *What happened that's just like what happened in the book?*

Depending on the child's attention span and ability level, key segments of the remainder of the story may be recounted with minimum questioning. Use questions only to highlight or reinforce key points.

Have nonrelevant materials available to help the child recognize the distinction between relevant and nonrelevant materials and ideas.

Examining a Title

Materials

A Boy, a Dog, a Frog, and a Friend (Mayer and Mayer 1971)

A. Focusing on the Characters

1. This is a book and, like most books, it has a title. *Point to the title.*
2. That's right. I'll read the title to you. It says, *A Boy, a Dog, a Frog, and a Friend. Say that back to me.*
3. Now there are four characters mentioned in the title. *What are they?*
4. Three of the four characters are on the cover of the book. *Tell me which ones they are.*
5. One of the characters mentioned in the title is not on the cover of the book. *What is the name of that character?*
6. Let's read the book and figure out who that other character might be.

B. Telling the Story

1. *The story is about a boy who's doing what?*
   [The child is looking at the illustrations as you tell the story.]
2. He thinks he's caught a fish because he's pulling on the line, but instead of pulling out a fish, *what happens to him?*
3. *Turn the page* and we'll find out why he fell in the water.
4. Look at this page. *What do you think happened that caused him to fall in the water?*
5. He's really furious about it. But not only is he furious, his friend the dog is furious. He's furious at the turtle who pulled the boy in. *So what does the dog do to the turtle?*
6. *And what does the turtle do back to the dog?*

7. The turtle keeps biting and biting the dog. Before, the dog tried to rescue his friend, the boy. *What is the boy trying to do now for his friend, the dog?*

8. He gets the dog out and things seem to be all right when suddenly the dog is in trouble. He's being pulled in the water. The boy is going to the rescue again. *What is he doing this time to help the dog?*

9. The boy has taken all his clothes off. He's ready to go in, *but who's coming back to the land?*

10. The dog comes back, and right after him, another animal comes back. *Which animal is coming towards the land now?*

11. This time the turtle is in a very different position than he was before. Then he was standing on his legs and jumping on them. *Right now, what position is he in?*

12. The boy thinks the turtle is dead. Usually when turtles are on their backs they're dead. So the boy is very upset with the dog because he thinks the dog has killed the turtle. Then the boy gets very busy trying to bury the turtle. *Go on—turn the page.*

13. Oh my goodness! What happened? Look at this page.

    [Turning back a page.]

    The turtle is on his back and *what's happened on the page?*

14. So the turtle wasn't dead after all. The boy looks and he sees that and he's delighted now. And they all go home together.

C. Analyzing the Title

1. Remember, there was a problem at the beginning. There was a character in the title who was called a friend. *Who do you think that friend was?*

2. The turtle did end up being the boy's friend, the dog's friend, and even the frog's friend. *But did he start out that way?*

3. Remember when he pulled the boy in? Look at this page. *Do you think the boy thought he was an enemy or a friend?*

    [Provide the answer if necessary.]

4. So he started out as an enemy. *What made him an enemy?*

5. After that he did a number of things that made the boy and the dog still think he was their enemy. Then something happened that changed all that. *What happened that made the boy feel differently about the turtle?*

6. *When that happened the turtle changed from being the boy's enemy to being his ___________.*

   For a sophisticated child, expand the lesson to help the child realize that while the boy thought of the turtle as an enemy, the turtle also thought of the boy as an enemy. The turtle was in the lake first. It was his territory. Therefore, the boy was the enemy.

Comments in conversation are vital. Be sure to comment as frequently as you question.

Creating a Book That Tells a Story

Materials

Papers for making a book, aluminum foil, thin piece of wood, staples, several storybooks, 2 sets of picture sequences depicting simple but different themes—4 pictures per set (A boy waking up and eating breakfast could make up one set and an animal being given a bath would be another), glue

A. Focusing on the Components of a Book

1. We've read a lot of books here and we've looked at the pictures and words in them. But we've never looked at the material that the pictures and words are on. Look at this book and look at these materials. *Which one of these things is like the pages of a book?*

   [The choices should include paper, foil, and wood.]

2. *What is this?*

   [Referring to the paper.]

3. *So what do you think the pages of a book are made of?*

B. Putting the Components Together

1. We know that a book is made up of paper, but a book has more than one sheet of paper. Let's make a book. If we're going to do that, we need at least a few sheets of paper. *Go over there and get me a few sheets of paper.*

2. This paper is loose. See.

   [Demonstrating.]

   But the pages in a book stay together. See.

   [Demonstrating.]

   We have to get our pages to stick together. And to do that, we can use this.

   [Show a staple.]

   What is this?

   [Provide the label if necessary.]

3. Now, let's staple the pages here and here.

   [Indicating two appropriate points.]

4. *Is the book holding together now?*

5. *What did we do so that it did hold together?*

C. Constructing the Story

1. Now we have the pages of the book, but something is missing. Look at this book

   [Indicate an open book with illustrations.]

   What does it have in it that ours doesn't have?

2. *And what does this book have?*

   [Showing another illustrated book.]

3. *And what does this book have?*

   [Showing a third illustrated book.]

4. So I think our book should have some pictures.

   [Offer the child the two sets of sequenced pictures.]

   I have two stories here. *Which one would you like to use?*

5. *So your story is going to be about a* ________.

6. *Put the pictures in the right order to tell a story.*

7. *Now let's glue the pictures in so they're on pages.*

   [Guide child so that each picture is placed on a separate page.]

8. Before we finish, *tell me the story that you've made.*

If time allows, the lesson can include making a cover, writing the child's name as the author, and drawing pictures to supplement the story.

Creating a Book That Tells a Story

Materials

Several storybooks, papers for making a book, oak tag for a book cover, staples or glue, crayons, pencil

A. Focusing on the Components of a Book

1. We've used a lot of books in here, but we've never made a book. Today, I thought we could make a book. If we are going to do that, we have to know the materials that a book is made of. *Look at some of these books and tell me what you think the pages in the book are made of.*

2. The cover of the book is somewhat different from the pages. Feel this cover and feel the pages. *In what way is the cover different from the pages?*

3. We know we need paper for the pages. *What material do you think we could use for a cover?*

B. Putting the Components Together

1. If we're going to make a book, we are going to need paper. *Go get a bunch of paper over there.*

2. *Why do we need a bunch of paper?*

3. *If we're going to make a book, why didn't we need just a single sheet of paper?*

4. These papers are loose, but if they are going to be put into a book, something has to be done to them. *What has to be done to them?*

5. *Let's put them together.* (Use whatever words the child has used.)

   [Help the child staple or glue the pages together.]

6. *Where does the cover go?*

7. *Are you going to need a cover for the front and back of the book? Is that how most books are made?*

8. *Go ahead and attach the cover.*

C. Constructing the Story

1. We've got the parts of the book. The big problem is deciding on the content. *Do you know what I mean by "content?"*

   [Provide a definition if necessary.]

2. Let's get an idea from some other books.

   [Bring out three books that are familiar to the child.]

   Let's look at this book. *What's the content of this one?*

3. [Discuss the content of the remaining two books.]

4. *What would you like the content of the story in your book to be?*

   [If the child has trouble with this idea, encourage making a book about one of the three just discussed.]

5. [Help the child draw in the basic components of the chosen story for four or five pages.]

6. Now we've gotten the story, but we need a title. *Look at these books and show me where the titles are.*

7. The title tells you something about what's in the book. For example, this book is about a boy and its called *A Boy, A Dog, A Frog, and a Friend*. That's the title. *What would you like your title to be?*

8. *Write it in.*

   [If necessary, write the title for the child.]

9. In addition to the title on the cover, you have the person who wrote the book. That's the author. The person who wrote this book is Mercer Mayer. *Who is the person who wrote this book?*

   [Pointing to the book done by the child.]

10. *If you wrote it, whose name goes on it?*

11. OK, *write your name on the cover of the book.*

12. This is your name, and *your name is on the book because you are the ___________.*

Making an Advertising Poster

This lesson is based on a trip to the zoo. If the child has not been to the zoo, use any other meaningful trip.

Materials

Pictures and posters of places children might go (movie theater, fire station, museum), poster board, picture of animals and objects commonly seen in a zoo (the number of zoo pictures should be more than will fit on the poster board), pictures of objects not found in a zoo, glue

A. Focusing on Advertising Posters

1. Children are usually in school or at home. But sometimes they go to different places. For instance, they can go to a place like this.

   [Show a picture of a movie theater.]

   What is this?

2. That's one place kids can go. *What is this?*

   [Showing a picture of a fire station.]

3. Sometimes teachers and kids could go to interesting places but they don't know about the places. So people make up posters to tell them. This is a poster of a movie.

   [Showing a poster of a movie popular with children. Any other poster may be used as long as the content is appropriate.]

   What movie is this poster about?

   [Provide information if necessary.]

4. And this is about a museum we went to.

   [Showing a second poster about a museum or other suitable place.]

   Do you know which museum it is?

   [Provide information if necessary.]

B. Assembling the Components for a Zoo Poster

1. We've also been to a zoo, but some children can't go to the zoo. I thought it would be helpful to make a poster showing a zoo for those children. First, we'll need paper, a sheet of paper like this poster is on. *Go over there and find a sheet of paper we can use.*

2. *What things are on these posters that I showed you?*

   [Pointing to items on the posters.]

3. So our poster will need pictures too, but it will need pictures of things in a zoo. *What are some things in a zoo?* (Acceptable responses include trees, buildings, cages.)

4. Over here I have a bunch of pictures showing some of the things you said. I'd like you to sort them into two piles. One pile will be things in a zoo. *What will this pile be?*

5. And this other pile will be things that are not in a zoo. *What will this pile be?*

6. *Go ahead and sort them into two piles.*

C. Putting the Poster Together

1. Let's put the pictures on the poster the way you want them. *Go ahead.*

2. *Do the pictures fit, or are there too many pictures?*

3. Then we have to get rid of some of the pictures. *Which pictures do you want to get rid of?*

4. *Put them here.*

5. *Which pictures are you keeping?*

6. *Go ahead and glue them so they stick onto the paper.*

7. OK, you've made a great poster. *What is it a poster of?*

8. *Where would you like to hang it so the other children can learn about a zoo?*

9. *Let's do that.*

Making an Advertising Poster

Materials

Several community service posters, pictures related to a zoo, pictures unrelated to zoo, 2 signs as described in B-7, glue

A. Focusing on Advertising Posters

1. There are situations when people have to do things and they need help from someone else. For example, a very little kid might need a drink from a water fountain that she can't reach. *Who might she ask for help?*

2. The person she would ask would be someone she could see who was near her. But there are times when people need help and no one is around. They can't talk to anyone. And then no one knows what they need. The people who need help have to find other ways to ask for help. Look at these.

   [Showing some posters.]

   Do you know what these are?

   [Provide the label if necessary.]

3. This is what I meant when I said there were other ways of asking for help without speaking to people. Look at this first poster (a poster asking people not to litter). The people who made this poster want you to do something. *What do they want you to do?*

4. Here's another poster (a Smokey the Bear poster). In this poster, the people also want you to do something. *What do they want you to do?*

5. And here's one more poster where people are asking you to do something (a poster requesting water conservation). *What are they asking you to do?*

6. If you want help, if you want people to do something and you aren't able to talk to them, *what might you do to get your message across? What could you make?*

B. Assembling the Poster for the Zoo

1. I recently heard of a project where they need people's help just like some of the projects we saw on the posters. The project I'm talking about is about needing money for the zoo to improve things for the animals. I thought we could make a poster about that. *If we're going to make it, what materials do we need?*

2. *Please go over there and get them.*

3. *Do you remember what I said our poster is going to be about?*

4. *What things should we put on our poster?* Here are some pictures.

   [Show zoo-related pictures and non-zoo pictures.]

   Which of these pictures do you think we should use on our poster?

5. *Why did you pick those?*

6. So far we have the animals for the zoo, but *what did I say the zoo needed? Why are we making this particular poster?*

7. So we need some way to ask people for money. Here are two signs. The sign on this side of the table says, "Please give money to help the animals." The sign on the other side of the table says, "Be careful when you are driving." *Which one of these two signs is the right one to use with this poster?*

8. *Why did you pick that one?*

9. Sometimes when people talk about money, they don't use the word for it. Instead, there's a sign they use.

   [Draw a dollar sign ($) and show it to the child.]

   This is a dollar sign and it represents money. *Why don't you draw it and include it on your poster.*

10. *Why should we include a sign for money on our poster?*

11. Now I think you have all the parts for your poster. *Why don't you go ahead and glue them on in a way that makes a nice looking poster.*

Designing a Book That Does Not Tell a Story

Materials
Three storybooks familiar to the child, 3 category books (vehicles, animals, plants), 6-8 pictures from each of 3 category groups (food, clothes, furniture), paper, glue

A. Focusing on the Content of Books

1. There are lots of books that tell stories.

   [Hold up a storybook the child knows.]

   This one is about ___________ ?

2. *And what happens to the boy?* (Use whatever word the child used.)

3. So that's a story of a boy.

4. [Repeat the questions with the other two books.]

5. This is also a book.

   [Holding up a non-story book showing categories such as toys or vehicles.]

   But it doesn't have a story. If it had a story, it would have a person or animal doing something or something happening to the person or animal. Look at this page.

   [Show a picture of an inanimate object.]

   Is there a story about something happening to a person here?

6. *Or here?*

   [Showing another page.]

7. *Or here?*

   [Showing another page.]

8. That's right. This is not a storybook, but it is a book. This is one of the kinds of books about objects or groups of things. *What set of objects is this book about?*

9. And here's another book that's not a storybook.

   [Show a category that is clearly not a storybook.]

   What is it about?

10. And this one—*what is it about?*

B. Creating a Book That Is Not a Story

1. I thought it would be fun to make one of these books. If it's about groups of things, we need a group to use. It could be about food, or clothes, or furniture. *Which one would you like our book to be about: food, clothes, or furniture?*

2. I have some pictures about foods (or whatever choice child has made). They're over there. *Would you please bring them here.*

3. You wanted foods and there are a lot of foods here, but there are also lots of other pictures that are not foods. *Put all the foods here.*

   [Indicating a spot.]

4. *And all the ones that are not food, here. Go ahead.*

   [Help the child if necessary.]

5. I have some pages here we can use for the book. Let's put the pictures on these pages. But let's not put the pictures in any old order. Let's decide how to do it. Some of the foods are ones you can drink. *Put those in first. Go ahead.*

6. The foods that are left are things you don't drink. They are things you eat. *What do you do with these foods?*

7. *Go ahead and paste them in.*

8. *Do you remember what kind of book we said we were making, a book with a story or a book without a story?*

Designing a Book That Does Not Tell a Story

Materials
Reference books (telephone directory, catalog, book on magic tricks), liquid soap, jar of water, wire for blowing bubbles, 5 or 6 sheets of paper stapled together, crayons, pencils

A. Focusing on the Content of Books

1. Lots of books you know are storybooks. That means they tell a story. Think of three different storybooks you know. *What are they?*

2. In storybooks, something usually happens to the person or the animal that's in the book. For example, *what happened to the person in ___________ ?* (Name a book mentioned by the child.)

3. [Ask the same question about another book the child mentioned.]

4. Here are a group of books. Look them over and see if any of them tell a story. *Tell me if they do or if they don't.*

5. That's right. None of them tell a story. *This one is a ___________*

   [Holding up the telephone book.]

6. *And do you know what a telephone book does?*

7. This book also doesn't tell a story.

   [Holding up a catalog.]

   Instead it has what things in it?

8. *Why do you think people made a book like this?*

   [Provide information if necessary.]

9. *Look this book over and tell me what you think it is designed to do.*

   [Giving the magic book to the child.]

10. *Why did people put this book together?*

11. Yes, this book tells people how to do magic. In fact, this kind of book is a how-to book. *Can you say that?*

B. Creating a Book That Is Not a Story

1. I thought it would be fun to make one of these how-to books. We can make one about making soap bubbles—showing little children how to make soap bubbles. To make a book, we need paper. I have some papers stapled together over on the desk. *Please go get them.*

2. OK, now let's make some soap bubbles and then we'll know what to put in the book. But we won't have the liquid you buy in stores. We're going to make it up ourselves. We'll start with some water and some soap. *How about drawing a sketch of the water and the liquid soap on the first page.*

3. Look what I'm doing.

   [Pouring soap into the water.]

   Draw a picture of the position the soap container is in when I'm pouring the soap into the jar of water.

4. The next thing we need is this.

   [Holding up the wire for making bubbles.]

   What is this?

5. OK, *make a sketch over here showing the wire being put into the jar of liquid.*

6. *Have we made any bubbles so far?*

7. *What do I have to do to make bubbles?*

8. OK, *go ahead and try it.*

9. We need one final picture in our how-to book. *What do we have to show in this last picture?*

10. *Go ahead and do it.*

11. You've made a great how-to book but we have to put a title on it. *What do you want to make as the title?*

12. [If the child has trouble, say]

    Perhaps it should have the words *how to* in it, *like How to . . .*

Additional Lesson Suggestions

1. Creating a Pretend Shopping Trip
2. Enacting *Rosie's Walk* (Hutchins 1971)
3. Recreating a Scene from *Where the Wild Things Are* (Sendak 1963)
4. Creating a Poster Advertising a Cookie Sale or Other School Activity
5. Putting on a Puppet Show

HOW TO USE THE *DIRECTING DISCOURSE* CHECKLIST OF LINGUISTIC PROCESSES

The list on pages 228-229 may be used in the following ways:

1. As an informal assessment of the child's abilities.

   Give the assessment as you would a pre-test and a post-test. Additional columns are provided to administer mid-year probes.

2. To determine the appropriate lesson level (Simple or Complex) for the child.

   The processes are loosely arranged in developmental sequence, beginning with simple processes and ending with more complex ones. Difficulty with, or absence of, 40% (8 processes) or more of the linguistic processes indicates that the child should be in the Simple Level.

3. As part of the Individualized Education Plan (IEP).

   Attach a copy of the checklist to the IEP form and mark the target processes as indicated in section I.

This checklist identifies the major linguistic/cognitive processes encountered by the child in the lessons. Each process is followed by an example of how the child encounters the process in school and home situations as well as in these lessons. These examples are only suggestions to the instructor. However, any alterations in wording should not change the demand itself.

The linguistic processes should be approached as individual demands rather than as information derived from a particular lesson. No one lesson includes all the demands.

When using the entire checklist as an assessment instrument, allow 15-20 minutes to complete the processes.

To determine materials needed for the assessment, read through the checklist and gather the materials mentioned. Allow time before giving the assessment to arrange the materials as dictated by the demands.

DIRECTING DISCOURSE CHECKLIST OF LINGUISTIC PROCESSES

Student/Client: ______________________________ Date: ____________

Gather and arrange the required materials. Present the child with each demand ("Find one just like this.") Use a check mark (X) to indicate a linguistic process present in the child's language repertoire.

		Pre-Discourse Measure			**Post-Discourse Measure**
Demand on the Child	**Expressed by the Adult**	**Date:**	**Date:**	**Date:**	**Date:**
1. Scans for a matching object.	Find one just like this.				
2. Follows simple directions.	Bring me the box.				
3. Names objects.	Do you know what we call this?				
4. Imitates a simple sentence.	Say, ____________ .				
5. Remembers what was seen.	What did you just see in the box?				
6. Identifies an object by function.	Give me something to stir with.				
7. Describes a scene.	What's happening in this picture?				

10. Identifies differences.	How are a chair and a sofa different?				
11. Follows a set of directions.	Look in the box and bring me an apple.				
12. Arranges pictures into a sequence.	Put these pictures in order so they make a story.				
13. Generalizes about happenings.	What happened to all the toys?				
14. Selects an object by exclusion.	Put the fruit we don't have to peel over here.				
15. Defines words.	What does *reverse* mean?				
16. Predicts changes.	What will happen if we put only a little water in the gelatin?				
17. Justifies.	Why did we need to peel the fruit?				
18. Formulates a solution.	What could we do to fix the leg on the chair?				
19. Explains the construction of objects.	Why is a dress made of cloth and not sandpaper?				
20. Explain inferences.	How can we tell if the gelatin is ready?				

For an expanded list of linguistic processes, see Blank, Rose, and Berlin (1978a).

A NOTE ON THE INDIVIDUALIZED EDUCATION PLAN (IEP)

In assessing a child's skill in discourse, the school and test situation are typically designed to determine how effectively the child *responds* to the *questions* put to him by others ("What color is this?" "What will happen when . . .?" etc.) However, skill in discourse requires greater skill than responding to questions. It includes such abilities as responding effectively to comments as well as to questions, initiating relevant ideas without being asked, and a variety of other conversational behaviors. The seven steps presented in Goal II of the IEP form are designed to offer insignt into the child's ability to handle sustained verbal exchange in both responding and initiating.

INDIVIDUALIZED EDUCATION PLAN (IEP)

Choose one or more goals:

I. **Goal:** The student/client will demonstrate success with a range of linguistic processes.

(Attach a copy of the *Direct Discourse* Checklist of Linguistic Processes.)

Pre-Discourse Measure: _____ number of linguistic processes present.

Post-Discourse Measure: _____ number of linguistic processes present.

Short-Term Objectives: (Circle four or five):

During extended discourse the student/client will increase the number of linguistic processes present from _____ to _____.

II. **Goal:** The student/client will be able to offer relevant, spontaneous verbalization during discourse.

Pre-Discourse/Post Discourse Measure: Behaviors observed during a spontaneous language sample.

Short-Term Objective: During a 15-30 minute discourse interaction, the student/client will:

1. Respond to initiations of others that are in question form.
2. Respond to initiations of others that are in command form.
3. Offer comments relevant to material.
4. Offer comments (not in response to questions) relevant to what partner has said.
5. Offer comments (not in response to questions) relevant to both material and to what partner has said.
6. Ask questions requesting information about material.
7. Ask questions requesting clarification about what partner has said.

III. **Goal:** The student/client will be able to sustain an age-appropriate conversation.

Pre-Discourse/Post Discourse Measure: Amount of time student/client participates in conversation during a spontaneous language sample.

Short-Term Objective: The student/client will increase length of time from _____ minutes to _____ minutes.

REFERENCES

Bates, E. 1976. *Language and context.* New York: Academic Press.

Blank, M. 1983. *Teaching learning in the preschool: a dialogue approach.* Cambridge, MA: Brookline Books.

Blank, M. In press. Classroom text: The next stage of intervention. In *Language Perspectives* II, edited by R. Schiefelbusch, Austin, TX: Pro-Ed.

Blank, M., S. Rose, and L. Berlin. 1978a. *The Language of learning: The preschool years.* Orlando, FL: Grune and Stratton.

Blank, M., S. Rose, and L. Berlin. 1978b. *The preschool language assessment instrument.* Orlando, FL: Grune and Stratton.

Damico, J. 1985. Clinical discourse analysis: A functional approach to language assessment. In *Communication skills and classroom success,* edited by C. Simon, 165-203. San Diego, CA: College-Hill Press, Inc.

DiSimoni, F. 1978. *The token test for children.* Hingham, MA: Teaching Resources Corporation.

Dorval, B., and C. Eckerman. 1984. Developmental trends in the quality of conversation achieved by small groups of acquainted peers. *Monographs of the Society for Research in Child Development,* 49 (Serial No. 206).

Eastman, P. 1960. *Are you my mother?* New York: Beginner Books.

Friel-Patti, S., and G. Conti-Ramsden. 1984. Discourse development in atypical language learners. In *Discourse development: Progress in cognitive developmental research,* edited by S. Kuczaj, 167-194. New York: Springer-Verlag.

Halliday, M., and P. Hasan. 1976. *Cohesion in English.* London: Longman.

Hutchins, P. 1971. *Rosie's walk.* New York: Macmillan.

Mayer, M., and M. Mayer. 1971. *A boy, a dog, a frog, and a friend.* New York: The Dial Press.

Mayer, M. 1975. *One frog too many.* New York: The Dial Press.

Porch, B. 1979 *Porch index of communicative ability in children.* Palo Alto, CA: Consulting Psychologists Press.

Preschool Language assessment instrument (PLAI) 1978 Orlando, FL: Grune and Stratton.

Prutting, C. 1982. Pragmatics as social competence. *Journal of Speech and Hearing Disorders,* 47:123-133.

Rees, N. 1978. Pragmatics of language: Applications to normal and disordered language development. In *Bases of language intervention,* edited by R. Schiefelbusch, (269-318). Baltimore, MD: University Park Press.

Roth, F., and N. Spekman. 1984. Assessing the pragmatic abilities of children: Part I. *Journal of Speech and Hearing Disorders,* 49, 2-11.

Semel, E. and E. Wiig. 1980. *Clinical evaluation of language functions.* Columbus, OH: Charles E. Merrill Publishing Co.

Sendak, M. 1963. *Where the wild things are.* New York: Harper Row Junior Books.

Spekman, N. 1983. Discourse and pragmatics. In *Language learning disabilities,* edited by C. Wren, 157-215. Rockville, MD: Aspen Corporation.

Uttley, A. 1980. *Squirrel goes skating.* Great Britain: Collins Colour Cubs.

Weschlser, D. 1974. *Weschlser intelligence test for children—revised.* New York: Psychological Corporation.

Weschlser, D. 1967. *Weschsler preschool and primary scale of intelligence.* New York: Psychological Corporation.

Westby, C. 1984. Development of narrative language abilities in *Language learning disabilities in school-age children,* edited by G. Wallach and K. Butler, 103-127. Baltimore, MD: Williams and Wilkins.